Reading Philippians after Supersessionism

Series Preface

The **New Testament after Supersessionism** (NTAS) is a series that presents post-supersessionist interpretations of the New Testament. By post-supersessionism, we mean "a family of theological perspectives that *affirms God's irrevocable covenant with the Jewish people as a central and coherent part of ecclesial teaching*. It rejects understandings of the new covenant that entail the abrogation or obsolescence of God's covenant with the Jewish people, of the Torah as a demarcator of Jewish communal identity, or of the Jewish people themselves" (spostst.org). Although the field of New Testament studies has made significant strides in this direction in recent years, the volumes in this series, written by Jewish and gentile believers in Jesus, seek to advance the conversation by offering post-supersessionist readings of the New Testament that address the question of ongoing Jewish particularity, and the relationship of interdependence and mutual blessing between Jew and gentile in Messiah.

SERIES EDITORS

J. Brian Tucker
Moody Theological Seminary, Plymouth, MI

David Rudolph
The King's University, Southlake, TX

Justin Hardin
Palm Beach Atlantic University, West Palm Beach, FL

PROJECTED VOLUMES

New Testament After Supersessionism, Introductory Volume
—Justin K. Hardin, David J. Rudolph, and J. Brian Tucker

Reading Matthew After Supersessionism
—Anders Runesson

Reading Philippians after Supersessionism

JEWS, GENTILES, AND COVENANT IDENTITY

Christopher Zoccali

CASCADE *Books* · Eugene, Oregon

READING PHILIPPIANS AFTER SUPERSESSIONISM
Jews, Gentiles, and Covenant Identity
New Testament after Supersessionism

Cascade Books
An Imprint of Wipf and Stock Publishers
199 W. 8th Ave., Suite 3
Eugene, OR 97401

www.wipfandstock.com

PAPERBACK ISBN: 978-1-62032-958-0
HARDCOVER ISBN: 978-1-4982-8859-0
EBOOK ISBN: 978-1-5326-3988-3

Cataloguing-in-Publication data:

Names: Zoccali, Christopher

Title: Reading Philippians after supersessionism : Jews, gentiles, and covenant identity / Christopher Zoccali.

Description: Eugene, OR: Cascade Books, 2017 | Series: New Testament After Supersessionism | Includes bibliographical references and index.

Identifiers: ISBN 978-1-62032-958-0 (paperback) | ISBN 978-1-4982-8859-0 (hardcover) | ISBN 978-1-5326-3988-3 (ebook)

Subjects: LCSH: Bible. Philippians—Criticism, interpretation, etc. | Jews in the New Testament | Gentiles in the New Testament | Jews—Election, Doctrine of | Bible. Epistle of Paul—Theology

Classification: BS2705.52 Z63 2017 (print) | BS2705.52 (ebook)

Manufactured in the U.S.A.   OCTOBER 18, 2017

Permission was granted for significant portions of the following articles to appear in this volume:
Zoccali, Christopher. "'Rejoice, O Gentiles, with His People': Paul's Intra-Jewish Rhetoric in Philippians 3:1–9." *Criswell Theological Review* 9.1 (2011) 17–31. (Author's revised version on ATLA database).
Zoccali, Christopher. "What's the Problem with the Law? Jews, Gentiles, and Covenant Identity in Galatians 3:10–12." *Neotestamentica* 49.2 (2015) 377–415.

Dedicated to Joe, Nick, and Tina

Contents

Acknowledgements

I WOULD LIKE TO thank the general editors of the *The New Testament After Supersessionism* series for inviting me to write this volume. The subject matter has been of interest to me for a number of years now, and I thoroughly enjoyed the opportunity to further explore the important issues revolving around the question of "supersessionism" in Paul's letter to the Philippians.

As a *post*-supersessionist reading of Philippians, this book will be centered upon four key premises: (1) the irrevocable character of God's covenant relationship with the Jewish people; (2) the Jewish people's unique role and priority in God's redemption program; (3) the continuing distinction between Jew and gentile within the Christ community; and (4) the continuing function of full Torah observance as an appropriate expression of covenant faithfulness to God for Jews in Christ. Of course, each of these premises possess a fair amount of complexity and nuance, and it is my aim to provide a careful articulation of how, exactly, all four find resonance with Paul's teaching to the Philippians. I will also be concerned to explore important relatable issues that bear on the question of ethnic difference vis-à-vis Christ community identity, and how this, in turn, properly relates to the salvific hope contained in Paul's gospel.

I would like to offer a special thanks to one of the series' editors, Dr. J. Brian Tucker. Brian and I both did our doctoral work under the supervision of Drs. William S. Campbell and Kathy Ehrensperger at the University of Wales, Trinity Saint David. I have learned much from his work, and have greatly appreciated his generous collegiality and friendship over the years. His careful reading of earlier drafts of this book was enormously helpful in shaping my argument. Of course, any errors that remain are strictly my own doing.

I would also like to extent my appreciation to the B. Thomas Golisano Library at Roberts Wesleyan College in Rochester, NY for the resources they made available to me in my research.

Lastly, I would very much like to thank my family for their support in all of my endeavors, academic or otherwise. My parents, Guy and Mary, have been an ever-present fountain of encouragement in my life. My siblings, Joe, Tina, and Nick, to whom I have dedicated this book, have likewise made themselves readily available to me whenever their help was needed. Having such a close, supportive family is a treasured possession that God has graciously given me, and for which I am abundantly grateful.

List of Abbreviations

AAJ	Approaches to Ancient Judaism
AB	Anchor Bible
ABD	*Anchor Bible Dictionary*. Edited by D. N. Freedman. 6 vols. New York, 1992
ABR	*Anglican Biblical Review*
ANTC	American New Testament Commentary
ASE	*Annali di Storia dell'Esegesi*
Bib	*Biblica*
BibInt	*Biblical Interpretation*
BNTC	Black's New Testament Commentaries
BR	*Biblical Review*
BZNW	Beihefte zur Zeitschrift für die neutestamentliche Wissenschaft
CBNTS	Coniectanea Biblica, New Testament Series
CBQ	*Catholic Biblical Quarterly*
CCWJCW	Cambridge Commentaries on Writings of the Jewish and Christian World, 200 BC to AD 200
CPIR	*Group Processes & Intergroup Relations*
CTJ	*Catholic Theological Journal*
CTR	*Criswell Theological Review*
EC	Epworth Commentary Series
EJSP	*European Journal of Social Psychology*

EuroJTh	*European Journal of Theology*
EvT	*Evangelical Theology*
ExAud	*Ex auditu*
ExpTim	*Expository Times*
FRLANT	Forschungen zur Religion und Literatur des Alten und Neuen Testaments
HeyJ	*Heythrop Journal*
HTKNT	Herders theologischer Kommentar zum Neuen Testament
HTR	*Harvard Theological Review*
IBC	Interpretation: A Biblical Commentary for Teaching and Preaching
ICC	International Critical Commentary
Int	*Interpretation*
JBL	*Journal of Biblical Literature*
JETS	*Journal of the Evangelical Theological Society*
JJMJS	*Journal of the Jesus Movement in its Jewish Setting*
JJS	*Journal of Jewish Studies*
JR	*Journal of Religion*
JRS	*Journal of Religious Studies*
JSJ	*Journal for the Study of Judaism*
JSNT	*Journal for the Study of the New Testament*
JSNTSup	Journal for the Study of the New Testament: Supplement Series
JSPL	Journal for the study of Paul and His Letters
JTS	*Journal of Theological Studies*
KEK	Kritisch-exegetischer Kommentar über das Neue Testament (Meyer-Kommentar)
LCBI	Literary Currents in Biblical Interpretation
LD	Lectio divina

LNTS	Library of New Testament Studies
LTQ	*Lexington Theological Quarterly*
MNTC	Moffatt New Testament Commentary
NAC	New American Commentary Series
NCB	New Century Bible Commentary
Neot	*Neotestamentica*
NIB	The New Interpreter's Bible
NICNT	New International Commentary on the New Testament
NIGTC	New International Greek Testament Commentary
NovT	*Novum Testamentum*
NovTSup	Novum Testamentum Supplements
NTM	New Testament Monographs
NTC	New Testament in Context Series
NTS	*New Testament Studies*
OTL	Old Testament Library
PS	*Psychological Science*
PSPR	*Personality and Social Psychology Review*
PRS	*Perspectives in Religious Studies*
PSBSup	*Princeton Seminary Bulletin Supplements*
PSPB	*Personality and Social Psychology Bulletin*
RB	*Revue Biblique*
RevQ	*Revue de Qumran*
RQ	*Römische Quartalschrift für christliche Altertumskunde Kirchengeschichte*
SBL	Society of Biblical Literature
SBLDS	Society of Biblical Literature Dissertation Series
SBLSP	*Society of Biblical Literature Seminar Papers*
SCJR	*Studies in Christian-Jewish Relations*

SGR	*Small Group Research*
SNT	Studien zum Neuen Testament
SNTSMS	Society of New Testament Studies Monograph Series
SP	Sacra pagina
SPQ	*Social Psychology Quarterly*
Them	*Themelios*
TynBul	*Tyndale Bulletin*
TNTC	Tyndale New Testament Commentaries
TJ	*Trinity Journal*
WBC	Word Biblical Commentary
WMANT	Wissenschaftliche Monographien zum Alten und Neuen Testament
WUNT	Wissenschaftliche Untersuchungen zum Neuen Testament
ZTK	*Zeitschrift für wissenschaftliche Theologie*

1

Paul, Supersessionism, and the Letter to the Philippians

[T]he apostle's real adversary is the devout Jew, not only as the mirror-image of his own past—though that, too—but as the reality of the religious man. . . . Paul sees this possibility realized in the devout Jew: inasmuch as *the announcement of God's will in the law is here misunderstood as a summons to human achievement and therefore as a means to a righteousness of one's own. But that is for him the root sin* . . . . Right and righteousness can only be ours in so far as God gives them anew every day—i.e. in faith.[1]

Adherence to Torah, in the ways that Paul's opponents are advocating it, is no better than pagan idolatry. To undergo circumcision is, in effect, to give in to the principalities and powers. *It is a step back into a scheme of blood, soil, race and tribe.*[2]

The argumentation of Philippians . . . can be more precisely discussed in terms of the rhetorics of unity and sameness and the rhetorics of hierarchy and modeling. The letter seeks to establish the authority of a series of model figures, especially Paul, while *fashioning a vision of the community unified by both their sameness and their subjugation in a hierarchical pattern.*[3]

THESE THREE SEEMINGLY DISPARATE quotations from Ernst Käsemann, N. T. Wright, and Joseph A. Marchal do well in collectively synopsizing the matter that this volume seeks to address. What these characterizations of

1. Käsemann, *New Testament Questions*, 184–85; italics mine.
2. Wright, *Saint Paul*, 162; italics mine.
3. Marchal, *Hierarchy*, 194; italics mine.

1

Paul and his first-century Jewish context have in common is a prevailing assumption impacting a great deal of contemporary scholarship, regardless of the otherwise wide-ranging interpretive conclusions that have been drawn. With a relative minority of contrary voices, it is generally understood that Paul's letter to the Philippians presupposes a notion in which uniformity is intrinsic to the Christ movement, and, further, that the Christ movement seeks to replace Jewish identity (as well as all other social identities) and concomitant Torah[4] obedience. However else the character of the letter is construed, the idea that Jewish identity is rendered, for Paul, effectively obsolete "in Christ" is largely taken for granted.[5]

In my view, supersessionism, correctly understood, is this very idea that "Christian" or "Christ community" identity[6] is ultimately irreconcilable with Jewish identity. One can legitimately expand this definition by suggesting that supersessionism means *all* prior identities are to be abandoned upon entrance into the Christ community.[7] Thus, the question occupying this study is whether Paul's theology, as represented in his letter to the Philippians, can be accurately characterized as supersessionist.[8] And, if not,

---

4. I generally translate νόμος in Paul more accurately as "Torah," rather than "law." I will thus do so throughout the following, unless in reference to other scholars' views.

5. Though the vast majority of contemporary scholars would explicitly assert that the Christ movement consists of both Jews and gentiles, as will be pointed out below, the implications of their respective interpretations may not properly allow for the continuation of Jewish identity within the Christ community in any meaningful sense.

6. The name "Christian" does not appear in the Pauline corpus, and unless referring to other scholars' views I will generally refer to the "Christ allegiant" or "Christ community," etc., when interpreting Paul in his own historical context.

7. What supersessionism—in any sort of pejorative sense of the term—does *not* mean is that the "church" has replaced "Israel" as God's people. Despite the popularity of this definition in both popular and scholarly discussions, this definition makes absolutely no sense of the sociocultural and theological context from within which the Christ movement arose. I suggest, moreover, that interpreting the markers of covenant identity to have been in some sense, for Paul, transformed in Christ *neither* represent a problematically understood concept of supersessionism. I will propose instead that the transformation of the markers of covenant identity is fully compatible with a post-supersessionist view. As I will discuss further below, covenant identity, for Paul, was always fundamentally defined by God's faithfulness, and, in this respect, has not changed. What has changed by virtue of the Christ event is the content of that faithfulness, and the appropriate response to it among God's people. Further, this change in the appropriate response to God's final expression of covenant faithfulness in and through Jesus Christ does not function to eradicate the identity-shaping function of the former covenant requirements, but only serves to re-contextualize them.

8. The definition of "post-supersessionism" implicit in this study includes the

2

how can Paul be faithfully read in ways that move beyond this traditional Christian paradigm, which dates back at least as far as the writings of Justin Martyr in the middle of the second century CE,[9] and continues to have proponents in contemporary Pauline scholarship.

The Question of "Identity"

A basic definition of "identity" may include the following elements:

1. Identity indicates who/what individuals and groups believe they are, and also what they do.

2. Identity is affected by human agency as well as social structures, and thus may involve a number of both internal and external factors.

3. Persons and groups invariably possess multiple, nested identities.

4. Identity can be a dynamic phenomenon, subject to negotiation (and influenced by, e.g., various discursive strategies), though it may also contain both malleable/open (i.e., constructed) and more stable/closed (i.e., essential/primordial) aspects.

5. Constructed and evolving identities are sometimes perceived, or otherwise affirmed, as if they were essential/primordial, and therefore not having undergone any change, and neither being permeable.

6. Whether an identity is understood to be constructed or essential (or in some sense both)—and thus whether it is ultimately open or closed—may be a contested matter for insiders and/or outsiders.

---

following four points: (1) the irrevocable character of God's covenant relationship with the Jewish people; (2) the Jewish people's unique role and priority in God's redemption program; (3) the continuing distinction between Jew and gentile within the Christ community; and (4) the continuing function of full Torah observance as an appropriate expression of covenant faithfulness to God for Jews in Christ. I would draw attention here to the first point, which is the primary one generally evoked by New Testament scholars employing some form of a post-supersessionist paradigm. Since claims regarding the irrevocable character of God's covenant with Israel (understood as strictly the Jewish people according to conventional ethnic/socioreligious norms) can be rather ambiguous, and, as pointed out in n. 7 above, often (and unnecessarily) employed in ways that beg problematic notions regarding the relationship of church and Israel (including how these entities properly correspond to the covenant), I have decided to more explicitly focus the issue as it is stated here, which thus represents the central concern of this study.

9. E.g., *Dialogue with Trypho,* ch. 11.

In view of, though moving beyond, these basic considerations of identity, at several points this study will utilize insights from contemporary social-psychological theory, including Social Identity and Self-Categorization theories (SIT and SCT, respectively). Simply stated, SIT is a theory that seeks to predict intergroup behavior vis-à-vis social identity. SCT is a related theory that concerns the matter of how individuals understand themselves and others in relation to groups to which they respectively belong.[10] "Social identity" is defined as "that part of an individual's self-concept which derives from his [sic] knowledge of his [sic] membership of a social group (or groups) together with the value and emotional significance attached to that membership."[11] The importance of social groups is especially significant to the study of the New Testament. As Sergio Rosell Nebreda points out,

> People of the Mediterranean in ancient times tended to view themselves as mirrored in others. Membership in a group is, therefore, a must in such corporate societies, and one of the prime values that characterized people of the Mediterranean. And this is crucial, since the groups to which people belong, whether by assignment or by choice, will be massively significant in determining their life experiences.[12]

An aspect of SIT/SCT that will be integral to my reading of Paul (and which especially relates to #3 above) concerns the role of *superordinate* social identities. A superordinate identity is a higher aggregate identity category to which persons may belong in addition to possessing other group affiliations. Such larger social identifications function in creating a common in-group social identity, which may, in turn, reduce inter-group bias, and thus promote greater harmony and a basis for unified action among subordinate groups. Contemporary social-scientific research has evidenced the success of creating a common in-group social identity, particularly when a superordinate identity is made salient while simultaneously allowing (in some fashion) for group members' continued identification with and commitment to their respective subordinate group affiliations.[13]

10. Turner, "Self-categorization Theory."

11. Tajfel, "Social Categorization," 63.

12. Nebreda, *Christ Identity*, 109–10.

13. Cf. Stone et al., "Superordinate and Subgroup Identification." They conclude: "One of the key findings of our studies is that although high subgroup identification has a negative impact on intergroup relations following recategorization, superordinate identification has a positive impact. These findings fall nicely in line with research from the immigration/acculturation literature, which similarly assert that dual identification is a

It is my contention that Paul understood Christ-movement identity as a superordinate identity that allowed for the continuing saliency, however transformed, of subgroup identities, particularly that of Jew and gentile. He thus utilizes several higher aggregate identity descriptors for his addressees, as relevant to the particular occasions and rhetorical demands of his respective letters. What I will attempt to demonstrate in this study is that through various discursive measures Paul fundamentally seeks to intensify the saliency of the Philippians' "in Christ" identity. Yet he does so in a fashion in which their prior ethnic identities—though subordinated, relativized, and transformed—nevertheless remain salient and enduring in light of the Philippians' offering of allegiance to Jesus Christ as Lord and Savior, and consequent entrance into the people of God.

First-century Jewish Identity

It is important to clarify that Judaism in the first century represented not foremost a "religion" (especially not one in competition with a religion called "Christianity"), but what perhaps can best be described (however in etic fashion) as an ethnicity defined by various cultural indicia, including a shared myth of ancestry, geographic origins, history, beliefs, customs, etc., which thus functioned to demarcate Jews from other social groups of the period.[14] Some scholars, such as Philip F. Esler, prefer to utilize the geo-ethnic designation, "Judean," as the appropriate English translation for Ἰουδαῖος, to emphasize both the ethnic character of first-century Judaism, and also its discontinuity with later groups self-identifying as Jews.

Notwithstanding Esler's important insights on the matter, I have chosen to utilize the conventional English translation, "Jew," both because there is a strong religious component to Paul's discourse concerning Jewish

---

potentially beneficial strategy for the encouragement of harmonious intergroup attitudes in multicultural societies. Like Huo et al. (1996), we found that high identification with a subgroup is not necessarily always a barrier to positive intergroup attitudes. Rather, if there is simultaneous attachment to a superordinate group, the potentially negative effects of subgroup identification can be regulated by the counteractive effects of commitment to the inclusive group (see also Bizman & Yinon, 2001)" (509). See similarly, Esler, *Conflict*, 143–44.

14. For a similar explanation of ethnic boundary markers, see Hutchinson and Smith, *Ethnicity*, 6–7; cf. Mason, "Jews," 457–512; Esler, *Conflict*; Cohen, *Beginnings*. On the significance of Jewish identity as an ethnicity, interacting especially with the work of Cohen, Esler, and Mason, see further the discussion in Zoccali, *Whom God Has Called*, 4–8.

identity, and also in light of the significant continuity between first-century Judaism, and later forms.

Additionally, it is in my view critical to recognize that reference to "Judaism" in the first-century would necessarily *include* the Christ movement, as this was a decidedly a *Jewish* movement, though, as I will argue below, it consisted of gentiles qua gentiles alongside Jews qua Jews.

The Philippians as God's Holy People

In order to demonstrate my view, it will be helpful to first examine the basis for Paul's construction and negotiation of the Philippians' identity, as the founder and leader of their community.[15] Accordingly, in the next chapter I will be asking: who are the "holy ones" (ἁγίοις) (Phil 1:1; cf. Rom 1:7; 1 Cor 1:2; 2 Cor 1:1; 1 Thess 3:13; see also 2 Thess 1:10;[16] Col 1:2, 12; Eph 1:18), and how exactly is it that an ethnically-mixed, though largely (if not entirely) non-Jewish group in Philippi can be identified by a title used in the LXX to refer, if to human beings (rather than angels; see p. 21 n. 4 below), exclusively to Israel (Dan 7:18, 27; cf. Exod 19:5–6; Lev 19:2; Deut 14:2; Pss 16:3; 34:9; Wis 17:2; 18:9; 1 Macc 1:46; 3 Macc 2:6; 6:9; Tob 12:15; see also *Jub.* 2:24; 16:19; 1 En. 93:6; 99:16; 100:5)?

The short answer here is that the holy ones in Philippi are those who have embraced Paul's gospel of Jesus Christ, and have thereby given allegiance to Jesus as Lord and Savior (cf. Phil 2:9–11; 3:20–21).[17] But, by

15. Esler's explanation of "leadership" is particularly relevant here: "In short, leaders must be 'entrepreneurs of identity', capable of turning 'me' and 'you' into 'us' in relation to a particular project in a particular context that will bestow on the shared social identity meaning, purpose, and value" (Esler, *Conflict*, 38). This is not to suggest that only Paul's voice is of importance, and that the Philippians themselves are not integral to the shaping of their own identity. Indeed, a central matter at stake in the letter concerns Paul's attempt to persuade the Philippian Christ community to "see" things as Paul does, and thus to be likeminded with him, which presupposes that there were alternative visions for what the community should be like from those within. However, the aim of this study is fundamentally to understand Paul's perspective in light of not only its historical value, but also its abiding significance to contemporary Christianity self-understanding.

16. I understand 1 Thess 3:13 and 2 Thess 1:10 to refer to human and not celestial beings.

17. By "Paul's gospel" I refer to God's anticipated, faithful eschatological intervention in the world through Jesus Christ, his life, death, and resurrection, which calls for, and enables, the appropriate human response of faithfulness, and according to which God is setting right all creation, reconciling it to God's self. The gospel thus presupposes both judgment and salvation. It should also be noted that even here there are important

doing so, is it Paul's view that Christ allegiance simply usurps the traditions of Israel and the legitimate claim of the Jewish community to be the people of God? Though nuanced in a myriad of ways, scholars have generally interpreted Paul along these lines. G. Walter Hansen's commentary on Philippians is illustrative. He writes:

> The community in Christ is the new people of God. Paul draws a strong contrast at the beginning of chapter 3 between the people of God identified by belonging to the Jewish people and the people of God identified by belonging to Christ. . . . This radical redefinition of the community of believers in Christ as the true people of God gives the church a clear understanding of its identity before God and of its mission in the world.[18]

While I would not entirely invalidate Hansen's comment, I would seek to provide significant qualification to it. The necessity of such a qualification is demonstrated, for example, by Hansen's enthusiastic citation of Ralph P. Martin and Gerald F. Hawthorne, who propose that Paul understood the "church" (ἐκκλησία/ekklēsia) as the "new Israel, the true heir and successor of God's chosen people and so the universal society."[19] In my view, any language of the ekklēsia[20] as a "new Israel" is fraught with problems, and betrays the all-too-common caricature that the universalism/inclusivism of the gospel has overcome the particularity/exclusivity of first-century Judaism. I do not believe Paul's theologizing fundamentally represents a clash of worldviews on these sorts of terms.[21] Thus, a more accurate and nuanced

---

interpretive decisions that are debated in contemporary scholarship, namely, what exactly is entailed in accepting Paul's gospel of Jesus Christ? Does acceptance mean mere intellectual assent, i.e., "belief"? Or, does it also involve, as I suggest in my definition, a commitment to conform one's praxis in accordance with the demands of covenant membership, as revealed in Torah, i.e., faithfulness? This matter will be discussed further below.

18. Hansen, *Philippians*, 34.

19. Ibid., 228. He quotes here from Martin and Hawthorne, *Philippians*, 187.

20. While I believe the issue is sometimes overstated (cf. p. 57 n. 13 below), I will generally utilize the transliteration, *ekklēsia*, rather than the standard translation, "church," in keeping with the growing concern among Pauline scholars to avoid anachronism when referencing these first-century assemblies.

21. As I will discuss below, first-century Judaism as a whole contained elements of "inclusivism," that is, mechanisms in which non-Jews could be deemed "righteous," either as a present or future reality, and/or, could become full members of the covenant community, as would be the case with normative Jewish proselyte conversion. Moreover, as this study will argue, the Pauline mission did not seek to eradicate all difference

understanding will require a careful construction of Paul's underlying theology according to which he understands the import of the Christ event,
and consequent formation of the Christ community. It is my view that
Paul's theology evidences a fairly complex and layered rationale for how
these non-Jews in Philippi (normatively defined[22]) can affirm with him that
they are "the circumcision" (Phil 3:3), while also remaining in some sense
gentiles, as distinguishable from Jews.

Excursus:
The "Church" of Philippi (Phil 4:15)

Though Paul only references the Philippians by the title "church" (ἐκκλησία/
ekklēsia) indirectly in Phil 4:15, it should be pointed out that this name
is similarly adopted from the LXX, which translates עדה (*ʿēdă*) and קהל
(*qāhāl*) with the term, as likewise referring to the congregation, assembly,
or community of God's people.[23] "*Ekklēsia*" is employed by Paul both in
reference to (a) local congregations of Christ allegiants—either in an entire
region/city collectively, or, as in the case of Romans, more specific groups,
i.e., house/tenement *ekklēsiai* (cf. also Phlm 2), which possessed some affiliation with one another (cf. Rom 16:5),[24] and (b) the Christ community in

---

between members, but preserved the subgroup identities of "Jew" and "gentile"—that is,
"Israel" and "the nations" (e.g., Rom 1:16; 2:25; 3:30; 4:12; 9:24; 11:11–32; 15:7–12; 1 Cor
1:23–24; 7:17–20). Further still, the Christ movement in its entirety could be similarly
characterized as exclusionary, in that membership was predicated singularly upon allegiance to Jesus Christ as Lord and Savior. Thus, inclusive and exclusive elements existed
in *both* the greater Jewish community *and* the Christ movement in particular.

22. Notwithstanding the certain complexity surrounding the question of what makes
one "Jewish" over against "non-Jewish," I will refer throughout this study to these respective statuses in terms of their traditional, generally recognized meaning within the larger
first-century Jewish and Greco-Roman milieu. This is what is meant here by the qualifier,
"normative." See further on this matter below.

23. E.g., Deut 4:10; 23:1–3; 23:8; 31:30; Josh 8:35; Judg 20:2, 5; 21:5; 1 Sam 17:47;
1 Kgs 8:22, 55; 12:3; 1 Chr 13:2, 4; 28:8; 2 Chr 6:3, 12–13; 10:13; 23:3; Ezra 10:1, 8, 12, 14;
Neh 13:1; Pss 22:22; 26:12; 40:9; 68:26; 89:5; 107:32; 149:1; Lam 1:10; Joel 2:16; Mic 2:5;
1 Macc 4:59; Sir 50:13, 20.

24. I would briefly mention here that it should not be inferred that Paul only considers the group in Rome meeting in the home of Aquila and Priscilla as an *ekklēsia*. Rather,
any group of Christ allegiants could be readily designated accordingly; cf. Rom 16:4: "the
ekklēsiai of the nations"—those communities founded by Paul throughout the Diaspora
(see also Rom 16:1, 16, 23).

total, particularly when he adds "of God" (τοῦ θεοῦ) (Gal 1:13; 1 Cor 10:32; 15:9; see also, however, 1 Cor 1:2; 1 Thess 2:14).

Though I believe Paul's primary source for this language is the LXX, and while I'm reluctant to read too much into Paul's use of the term (including, e.g., counter-imperial, alternative-polis, and/or pro-democratic ideological connections), I nevertheless do not deny that he also intended the term to resonate with his audience on the basis of its usage within the contemporary Greco-Roman milieu, in which it referred to voluntary associations, including its contemporary Jewish usage in reference to the synagogue.[25] As Ralph John Korner postulates, "self-designating as *ekklēsiai* gave Paul's multi-ethnic communities the potential to present both as *intra muros* Jewish synagogue communities and as Greco-Roman voluntary associations, with a civic ideology that is both pro-*demokratia* and counter-oligarchic."[26]

Anders Runesson has similarly argued that Paul presupposes the continuity between the *ekklēsia* and the synagogue. He writes,

> [S]ince *ekklēsia* in Jewish settings was used to designate synagogue institutions beyond those run by Christ-believers, Paul specifies for his non-Jewish addressees that what he is referring to are the assemblies, or synagogues, of those who, like the addressees, were "in Christ." Far from denoting non-Jewish institutions, Paul's use of *ekklēsia* indicates that as "apostle to the nations" he is inviting non-Jews to participate in specific Jewish institutional settings, where they may share with Jews the experience of living with the risen Messiah, of living "in Christ."[27]

"Judaizers," Paul's Own Discarded Jewish Identity, and the Irrelevancy of Torah

Secondly, a post-supersessionist reading of Paul's letter to the Philippians will have to contend with chapter 3, a passage that has led many scholars to interpretive conclusions properly deemed supersessionist. Hawthorne's comments on the passage are indicative of this understanding:

25. For a detailed analysis of these layers of meaning to *ekklēsia*, along with the implications for interpreting Paul, see Korner, "Before 'Church.'"

26. Ibid., 19. See also esp. Runesson, "Terminology," 68–76.

27. Runesson, "Terminology," 73.

These opponents of the gospel of grace that Paul preached appear to be visitors from abroad who were threatening to undo the work of the apostle at Philippi. Apparently they require that men be circumcised before they could acceptably worship God. According to Paul their religion was a ritual of externals that fostered pride in their own achievements instead of a boasting in Christ Jesus, and that encouraged a confidence in themselves instead of reliance upon the Spirit. Who are these opponents? It is not possible to say with certainty, but everything we know about them points to the assumption that they were Jews—evangelistically oriented Jews who had their own missionaries (cf. Matt 23:15), who were insisting on physical signs of initiation, priding themselves on their privileges of pedigree (vv. 5–6), and proclaiming a message of righteousness and perfection that was attainable *now* simply by submitting to circumcision and complying with certain food laws.[28]

Hawthorne's reading is different than most in that he does not understand the assumed Jewish "opponents" alluded to in the passage as being Christ allegiants. However, his characterization of their agenda is essentially the same as most scholarly interpretations of the text. Evidently, in his view, Paul's gospel finds its meaning squarely in terms of why it is *not* like Judaism—described in terms that I suggest are quite inaccurate. That is, while Paul's gospel is predicated on grace, genuine spirituality, and humility, Judaism is portrayed as being consumed by human achievement, external ritual, and arrogance. This sort of characterization of Judaism has been tempered some in more recent Pauline scholarship, though there still remains a good measure of such ideas in the interpretation of Paul, and specifically his letter to the Philippians, especially chapter 3. Thus, the question remains whether Judaism is the inevitable foil for Paul's teaching to the Philippian Christ community in this passage.

Before attending to my own analysis of both Paul's underlying theology that informs his instruction to the Philippians, and his discourse in chapter 3 of the letter in particular, I will summarize, albeit briefly, the relevant contemporary scholarly positions that my reading of Paul will seek to critique. These summaries will provide a contextual basis to explore the question at hand. I will categorize these positions as "Old Perspective," "New Perspective," and "Imperialist Perspective."

---

28. Hawthorne, *Philippians*, 123.

Scholarly Views Vulnerable to Supersessionism

Old Perspective

With the rise of the New Perspective on Paul, and its reassessment of first-century Judaism, few contemporary scholars would advance such stark exegetical comments as those of Ernst Käsemann quoted above.[29] Indeed, most would condemn such language as implicitly anti-Semitic, even if not intentionally so in light of Käsemann's own social-theological context.[30] Nevertheless, though now holding the minority position within Pauline scholarship as a whole, there are still scholars who remain self-consciously committed to the "Old Perspective." Though doing so in a more informed fashion, these scholars continue to largely uphold a "Lutheran Paul" who is thoroughly concerned with combating a notion in which divine favor and vindication could be merited through rigorous obedience to the law.[31] Paul's assertion in Phil 3:8–9 would be understood by Old Perspective scholars as indicative of this conflict:

> I regard everything as loss because of the surpassing value of knowing Christ Jesus my Lord. For whose sake I have suffered the loss of all things, and I regard them as rubbish, in order that I may gain Christ and be found in him, not having a righteousness of my own that comes from the law, but the one that comes through faith in Christ, the righteousness that comes from God on the basis of faith. (NRSV)

It is generally concluded from this passage that Paul directly equates his past in Judaism with a futile attempt to merit God's favor, and proceeds from there to point to his eventual discovery of God's grace found in Jesus Christ—apart from "good deeds"—as the true basis of salvation. Again,

29. For an analysis of this paradigm shift in Pauline scholarship, see Zoccali, *Whom God Has Called*, 1–22.

30. Käsemann's (a) supreme commitment to the Lutheran emphasis on salvation by God's grace through faith, (b) "apocalyptic" theological orientation, over against existential and, in large part, salvation-historical interpretations of Pauline soteriology, and (c) staunch opposition to the ideology of the Third Reich, leading him to denounce in no uncertain terms any claims to ethnic superiority, were formative to such exegetical claims, however problematic they ultimately are.

31. Cf. esp. here the two-volume work: Carson, O'Brien, and Seifred, eds., *Justification*. Beyond the editors of this work, prominent advocates of the Old Perspective include scholars such as Stephen Westerholm, Simon Gathercole, Thomas Schreiner, and Seyoon Kim.

this interpretive conclusion raises the question as to whether Paul fundamentally defines the Christ movement *over against* the Judaism of his day. Further, it portrays first-century Judaism as a "religious system" fundamentally defined in terms of "works-righteousness" apart from divine grace, and thus directly *contrary* to the redemption available through *believing* in Jesus Christ, apart from *doing* the law.

New Perspective

Among advocates of the New Perspective, such as N. T. Wright, it is understood that Paul's main point of contention with the greater Jewish community is not a fallacious notion of "legalism" or "works-righteousness," but rather "ethnocentrism": the conviction that Jews, and Jews alone, are in possession of right standing with God. Wright refers to this presumed Jewish worldview as "automatic national privilege," which was propagated by a "misuse of the Torah," as if it were a national "charter" of sorts.[32] Consequently, it is believed that first-century Judaism should be largely characterized in terms of an ethnic exclusionism, which acutely guarded the boundaries between Jews and gentiles, ruling out any possibility of divine favor for those outside of the Jewish community.

In such New Perspective interpretations of Paul, the idea that nearly everything he states in his letters should be construed in opposition to first-century Judaism carries over largely unabated from the Old Perspective. In all, the New Perspective's perceived antithesis between the universality of the gospel of Jesus Christ and the particularity of Judaism—preeminently manifest through rigorous Torah obedience—leaves little room for the continuation of Jewish identity in any meaningful sense within the Christ community. Philippians 3:4–7 would be interpreted in just such a fashion by scholars committed to this paradigm:

> If anyone else has reason to be confident in the flesh, I have more: circumcised on the eighth day, a member of the people of Israel, of the tribe of Benjamin, a Hebrew born of Hebrews; as to the law, a Pharisee; as for zeal, persecutor of the church; as to righteousness under the law, blameless. Yet whatever were gains I had, these I have come to regard as loss because of Christ. (NRSV)

32. Wright, *Climax*, 240.

Imperialist Perspective

For other contemporary scholars, such as Joseph A. Marchal,[33] an aggressive hermeneutic of suspicion[34] is employed in the interpretation of Paul. It is thereby suggested that throughout his letters, and not least in Philippians, Paul's fundamental purpose in writing is to elicit the submission and obedience of his addressees to himself. Though Paul's communal vision is of a different order than Rome,[35] it is no less imperialistic and hierarchical. Accordingly, Marchal understands Paul's primary rhetorical goal in Philippians to be the engendering of "sameness" within the community, while

33. See Marchal, *Hierarchy; Philippians.*

34. For an argument advocating resistance to the so-called "hermeneutics of identification" in Paul, in preference to one of suspicion, see, e.g., Schüssler Fiorenza "Politics of Interpretation," 40–57. She writes: "In short, an ethics of interpretation that does the work of a public health department in Pauline studies would require that scholars problematize the hermeneutics of identification with Paul and critically investigate the 'public health' aspects of Paul's rhetoric and politics of meaning" (51).

35. A central problem that I find in Marchal's extensive work on Philippians is that he never really adequately judges the *content* of Paul's message, but merely the form. This raises the question of whether any agenda that seeks to persuade others of its unequivocal rightness—even if authentically good—can escape the charge of suppression, domination, and imperialism, etc., particularly when such attempts at persuasion employ standard rhetorical forms and techniques that have elsewhere been used for demonstrably oppressive ends. While structure is inseparable from content, it is highly problematic to simply ignore the latter, as if structure alone can be determinative of the character of one's discursive agenda. Additionally, Marchal's ideological presupposition that hierarchy and calls for obedience are entirely incompatible with leadership that authentically seeks the goals of liberation and an egalitarian community is in my view fundamentally misguided, as it seemingly assumes that power and authority must always be absolute rather than functional and flexible; cf. Ehrensperger, "Be Imitators," 247; Park, *Submission.* This sort of methodology easily becomes self-refuting once it is recognized that its own totalizing critique betrays its own hierarchical structure, which are inevitable in any discourse (Ehrensperger, "Be Imitators," 247), and thus that it can be just as easily characterized as a form of suppression and domination (thus, my somewhat intentionally ironic characterization of this viewpoint as the "imperialist perspective").

In all, Marchal's analysis, while important and insightful at many points, in the end strikes me as largely an exercise in character assassination, assigning to Paul the most negative of intentions (albeit in light of a history of New Testament scholarship that has largely assigned only the best intentions to Paul). While some undoubtedly find such an exercise illuminating, and while, indeed, a hermeneutics of suspicion should be given its due consideration, I would suggest that ultimately a hermeneutics of trust, which is, as Hays, *Imagination,* 197–98, points out, "a faithful struggle to hear and discern," and "a readiness to trustingly receive," provides for a more fruitful analysis of the letter, and will be the general approach taken in this study.

13

establishing his incontestable authority over them. Philippians 3:15–18 is read by Marchal precisely along these lines:

> Let those of us then who are mature be of the same mind; and if you think differently about anything, this too God will reveal to you. Only let us hold fast to what we have attained. Brothers and sisters, join in imitating me, and observe those who live according to the example you have in us. For many live as enemies of the cross of Christ; I have often told you of them, and now I tell you even with tears. (NRSV)

In this construal of Paul, "difference" can only exist in terms of differentiating Paul from the community. That is, he is the supreme model the community must emulate, though all such attempts will ultimately prove unsuccessful, leaving the community in a perpetually subordinate position to him.[36] Of particular importance to the present study is this emphasis on "sameness." It would seem that, if interpreted along these lines, Paul's teaching to the Philippians completely rules out the continuation of Jewish identity, along with all other prior social identities upon entrance into the Christ community. In other words, to be "in Christ" is wholly incompatible with and thus renders obsolete *all* other social particularities possessed by Christ allegiants.

A Non-Supersessionist Paul[37]

Once again, it is the aim of this study to demonstrate that none of the above scholarly viewpoints adequately captures Paul's underlying convictions,

---

36. Drawing especially upon the work of Castelli, *Imitating Paul*, Marchal suggests that integral to this imitation rhetoric is the idea that such imitation can never be fully achieved, thus rendering the audience in a permanently subordinate position to the model. For a thorough critique of Castelli, see Park, *Submission*, 82–116; also esp. Ehrehsperger, "Be Imitators," 241–61. Ehrensperger rightly concludes "that imitation language rather than being an instrument of domination and control serves as a means to guide members of the Christ-believing movement into life in Christ; this implies a deconstruction of the thought and value system of the dominant Greco-Roman society. Inherent within it is the tendency to guide in a way which coheres with the content of imitation, that is, in a way which actually demands the creativity and self-responsibility of Paul's converts in the formation of their lives in Christ" (258).

37. I am aware that in contemporary Christian theology "non-supersessionism" finds a somewhat different meaning than "post-supersessionism," generally pointing to either some form of two-covenant soteriology, or a Dispensational theological perspective (as popular among many Christian fundamentalist groups). What I am referring to here,

goals, and message to the Philippian Christ community. I will suggest, rather, that Paul's vision of the Philippian *ekklēsia* is one that stands in historical continuity with God's people "Israel"—sharing in the Jewish symbolic universe (e.g., 1 Cor 10)—*and* which consists by necessity of multiple people groups.[38] On both counts, the *ekklēsia* is for him emphatically *not* a "third race" that is neither Jewish nor gentile, nor even less an entity altogether void of ethnic ascription. Rather, the *ekklēsia* is in one sense *entirely* "Jewish." In other words, it is an orientation of Judaism—a Jewish movement according to which the participants follow a largely Jewish lifestyle, even though non-Jews remain as such (and do not, then, undergo the rite of circumcision as the culmination of the process of proselyte conversion to normative Judaism; see below). In another sense, it is *both* Jewish *and* gentile,[39] according to which these subordinate groups, equal and unified in Christ, affirm and respect the continuing saliency of subgroup identity, and thus of differing, culturally-informed expressions of covenant faithfulness to God (cf. esp. Rom 14:1—15:7).[40] As especially pertinent to Phil 3, then, *Paul's gentile converts to his gospel must in an important sense remain as they are—members of the nations who have given uncompromising allegiance to the God of Israel and to Christ Jesus in light of the coming kingdom of God.*

---

and throughout this study, is not such contemporary Pauline theologies, but rather a critical-historical construct of Paul and his teaching, which cannot be properly characterized as "supersessionist," according to the definition I have presented above.

38. Non-Jews (a descriptor that I will use interchangeably with "gentiles," or "nations"/"*ethnē*" throughout this study) almost certainly represented the vast majority of the Philippian congregation, and, in my view, much of Paul's admonition in his letter to them concerns the status and praxis of gentiles in particular. However, Paul does not view local assemblies of Christ allegiants as autonomous; thus, in principle (if not in actuality), every *ekklēsia* he addresses in his extant letters is a "Jew and gentile" one, with the latter social category consisting in itself of multiple people groups (cf. nn. 39, 40 below).

39. It should be recognized that Paul clearly thinks and operates within a Jewish worldview that understands humanity in terms of the oppositional categories of "Jew" and "gentile." However, the significance of each category, and how each corresponds to the other is where Paul, though firmly grounded in existing Jewish tradition, creatively develops a new significance for each in light of the Christ event. See further here below.

40. As I will be employing the phrase "multiethnic" with respect to the *ekklēsia* at large, I am affirming that the self-perception of early (i.e., first- and second-generation) Christ allegiants was *not* one in which prior ethnic identities were thought to be wholly transcended, nor one in which ethnicity itself had become irrelevant—i.e., "non-ethnic" (this latter notion in particular being a literal impossibility, despite the assertion of such in later Christian writings).

The Fundamental Coherence of Paul's Theology

Though this study is focused on Paul's letter to the Philippians, any adequate construction of Pauline thought, in my view, needs to draw from the entirety of Paul's writings.[41] Of course, the immediate context of the letter itself must be given primacy. Further, it is clear to me that similarity of language and/or concepts from letter to letter do not in themselves indicate identical meaning. Certainly, the contingent qualities of each of Paul's letters must be carefully considered in their respective interpretation before any holistic construal of Pauline theology can be formulated. I fully agree, therefore, with the assertion of William S. Campbell that

> for Paul, the best way to do theology, to theologize, was to address local issues in the light of the gospel message of Jesus Christ, and thereby create the theological statements, contextually rooted, but with the potential to be reinterpreted in other contexts and even applied to other issues in ever-changing circumstances. The letters of Paul are not to be considered as theology in and by themselves but as raw material for creating theology for new situations and new issues in other contexts.[42]

In the following study, I will presuppose that, while given expression in various contingent circumstances, Paul's thought is nevertheless grounded upon fundamental, reasoned convictions, and is therefore fully coherent, rather than ad hoc, opportunistic, irrational, or otherwise contradictory. Additionally, as I find no compelling evidence to believe otherwise, I will also assume that his teaching is largely consistent—that is, *not* having undergone significant evolution over the course of the writing of his extant letters. Given that he wrote to at least five groups of Christ communities (in Philippi, Thessalonica, Corinth, Galatia, and Rome), it would seem to me to be both problematically reductionist, and methodologically negligent to isolate Paul's assertions in any particular letter in an attempt to discern what Paul may have intended to communicate to the community in question.[43]

41. This study will largely concede to the majority scholarly view regarding the seven undisputed letters of Paul, though I will also reference the disputed texts, especially Ephesians and Colossians, as being instructive to Pauline theology, and even the historical Paul's thought, regardless of authorship. I do not find any real theological/ideological contradictions in these, so-called, second-generation Pauline texts, as compared to what is found in the undisputed letters.

42. Campbell, *Unity & Diversity*, 205.

43. The question of "meaning" is a complex one, involving an intersubjective,

Except in the case of the Christ community in Rome, Paul founded these communities, having taught and otherwise communicated with them beyond the letters that we now possess. It is abundantly reasonable to conclude that Paul shared similar, fundamental ideas with each of the communities he founded, with certain of these notions, if perhaps absent from one letter, being elsewhere expressed, as the respective contexts of his occasional letters demanded. In the absence of single, comprehensive treatise from Paul on all things having to do with his gospel, his occasional letters, collectively, may offer the next best thing in an attempt to construct the fullest description of both his thought, and what the Philippians themselves would have understood him to mean, having had greater access to Paul's views beyond the letter to them that we now possess. Again, in agreement with Campbell, discerning Paul's theology from the entirety of his letters will necessarily entail careful consideration of the respective contexts in which his teaching is embedded, rather than through abstraction of his various assertions, as if they represent free-standing, universal propositions for all people of any time.

Interpretive Objectives and Outline of Following Chapters

In the chapters that follow I will attempt to demonstrate four key points:

1. Contrary to the Old Perspective view, the Christ event is for Paul the culmination of God's faithfulness to both Israel and all creation, which calls, in turn, for rigorous Torah obedience on the part of God's people, Jew and gentile alike, though such Torah submission is undertaken differently by each subgroup.

2. Contrary to many New Perspective readings, the universalism of the gospel ineluctably includes, and is thus not antithetical to, the continuation of Jewish identity, alongside the continuation of non-Jewish identity (normatively defined).

---

dialogical process, in which the alterity of the text, as well as the perspectival location of the interpreter play a critical role. Further, while authorial intent is not the sole criterion of "meaning," and how, e.g., Paul's historical addressees (who, of course, did not have access to Paul's other letters) understood these texts is also an important consideration, I affirm that it is nevertheless critical to discern what Paul may have meant by what he wrote, however tentative such constructions may be. For a fuller explanation of this interpretive dynamic, see Zoccali, *Whom God Has Called*, 10–16.

3. Respect for difference is essential to the unity of God's people, and is therefore central to Paul's apostolic message to the Philippian Christ allegiants.

4. Paul's call for conformity is not all-encompassing, but centrally concerns the need to remain steadfast in the gospel of Jesus Christ, even if one's "in Christ" identity will make one vulnerable to suffering.

Taken together, these four points mean that (a) the Philippians must remain, in an important respect, as they already are, and *not* then become like Paul, and (b) *any* influences that would seek to undermine the community's commitment to God through Jesus Christ must be understood as wholly contrary to the appropriate community ethos.[44] In all, I will conclude that Paul's gospel is *consistent with* the Judaism of his day, and seeks to supersede neither it, nor *any* previous ethnic identities in terms of their fundamental significance.[45]

In the next chapter I will examine what I understand to be the three most basic premises of Paul's theology through which he interprets the significance of the Christ event and consequent formation of the multiethnic *ekklēsia*. These are (a) the seminal basis of covenant identity, (b) covenant and creation renewal, and (c) the eschatological restoration of Israel and consequent pilgrimage of the nations. I will examine each of these separately, and then draw implications for the Philippians' identity as God's "holy ones."

As pointed out above, Phil 3:1–9 has commonly been read by Pauline scholars as representing an anti-Jewish polemic, in which Paul warns the Christ community about so-called "Judaizers." In chapter 3 I will assess the question of whether Paul is in fact critiquing Judaism, and, if so, (a) what

---

44. As Paul suggests in Phil 2:12–16, in order for the Philippians to serve the gospel mission to the world they must themselves take care to uncompromisingly represent an alternative pattern of life to the present world order, in anticipation of a new world order that will be fully consummate upon Christ's return (cf. Phil 1:6, 10; 2:15–16; 3:20–21). However, the new age does not wholly obliterate the old, but transforms it in accordance with God's original purposes for all creation, which necessarily includes the development of cultural and ethnic diversity.

45. I will be demonstrating, then, that Paul's vision for God's people accords with the apocalyptic imagery portraying the significance of the Christ event found in the book of Revelation: "They sing a new song: 'You are worthy to take the scroll and to open its seals, for you were slaughtered and by your blood you ransomed for God *(holy) ones from every tribe and language and people and nation*; you have made them to be a kingdom and priests serving our God, and they will reign on the earth'" (Rev 5:9–10; italics mine).

the rationale would have likely been for such a confrontation, and (b) what the implications are for correctly understanding Paul's premises and exhortation to the Philippians. I will hope to demonstrate that *if* indeed Judaism is in view, Paul's issue is solely on the matter of proselyte conversion to normative Judaism for gentiles. There would be here, then, no rebuke of the substance of Judaism in so far as there is anything inherently wrong with Jewish identity, including full Torah submission. Paul would only be suggesting that his gentile audience must take every measure to live true to the implications of their superordinate identity in Christ, regardless of the cost, and this means remaining as gentiles.

In chapter 4 I will continue in my analysis of Phil 3, highlighting the key interpretive points that while often used in support of supersessionist conclusions, actually point in the other direction. First, it will be demonstrated that Paul's concern is to maintain unity around the cause of the gospel, along with the continued stability and viability of the community, according to which both ethnic differentiation and commitment to Jesus Christ are preeminent. Thus, while Paul's gentile converts to his gospel are to retain gentile identity, it is no less incumbent upon them to avoid any idolatrous compromise in their allegiance to the God of Israel through the risen Christ. Second, the primacy of "in Christ" identity means that not only Jews, but also gentiles must strive to live out God's revealed will in Torah, even if not in identical fashion. "In Christ" identity fulfills—and is not then contrary to—a Torah-shaped identity. As such, God's grace revealed in Jesus Christ *fulfills*—rather than supplants—what it means to be a "righteous one."

In chapter 5 I will offer concluding reflections on Paul's call to the Philippian Christ community, especially in terms of the implications regarding the concept of salvation in Pauline/Christian theology, and in light of the need for unity within the community. First, "salvation" positively implies both discontinuity and continuity with the past. Second, both the preservation and transformation of previous social identities—and thus abiding difference *in Christ*—are required elements of Pauline/Christian theology if such theology is to represent an authentically liberating and ethical worldview.[46]

---

46. A final note: because of the considerable overlap in subject matter with some of my other published works, portions of the following book have appeared in print elsewhere. I would like to thank Wipf & Stock Publishers, as well as *Neotestamentica* and *Criswell Theological Review* for their kind permission in reproducing this material here.

2

Jews, Gentiles, and the "Holy Ones" (Philippians 1:1)

> I saw one like a human being coming with the clouds of heaven.
> ... To him was given dominion and glory and kingship, that all
> peoples, nations, and languages should serve him. ... [T]he holy
> ones of the Most High shall receive the kingdom and possess the
> kingdom forever. (Dan 7:18)

> But our citizenship is in heaven, and it is from there that we are
> expecting a Savior, the Lord Jesus Christ. He will transform the
> body of our humiliation that it may be conformed to the body of
> his glory, by the power that also enables him to make all things
> subject to himself. (Phil 3:20–21; cf. Matt 6:10)

Paul addresses the Philippians as "holy ones" (Phil 1:7), a title that he also
uses for the Christ communities in Corinth (1 Cor 1:2; 2 Cor 1:1), Thessalonica (1 Thess 3:13[1]), Rome (1:7), and Jerusalem (1 Cor 16:1; Rom 15:25,
31). Some scholars have suggested that this title, at least in some instances,
represents a subgroup identity descriptor, and refers to Jewish Christ
allegiants in particular.[2] I do not find such a view to be at all warranted.

The title almost certainly originated among the first Christ community
in Jerusalem. However, given Paul's application of it to not only an entirely
Jewish assembly (i.e., the Jerusalem Christ community), and mixed assemblies of Jews and gentiles (e.g., in Rome), but also, as here in Philippians,

---

1. In my view, the "holy ones" here represent God's people, rather than an angelic
entourage. See the arguments for this reading in King, "'Holy Ones.'" Though the reference would, then, apply to the universal Christ community, Paul clearly intends the
Thessalonians to especially see themselves included among this group.

2. Cf. Korner, "Before Church," 214–20, for a summary of this perspective, particularly in relation to 1 Cor 14:33b–35.

a largely gentile community with minimal interaction with Jewish groups at large, it seems clear to me that Paul extends this title in superordinate fashion to *any* local community of Christ allegiants, whether in Corinth, Thessalonica, Rome, or, of course, Jerusalem.[3] In short, to be "in Christ," is to be a "holy one," that is, a member of God's covenant people who will receive the kingdom of God, in distinction from those outside of the community (cf. Dan 7:13–27; Phil 1:27–28; 3:20–21; 1 Cor 6:9–11; 15:20–58; Gal 5:16–25; 1 Thess 4:13—5:11).[4]

As such, this chapter will explore the theological rationale that lay behind Paul's view of how gentiles are brought into (as well as how Jews are confirmed among) this group. Specifically, I will trace three interrelated and progressive aspects to his thought by which his gospel message and mission takes shape, and from which, then, he interprets the identity of the Christ community in accordance with the four-fold conclusion stated on pp. 17–18 above. These elements are as follows:

1. *The seminal basis of covenant identity.* What is and has always been, for Paul, the foundation of covenant relationship with God?

2. *Covenant and creation renewal.* Is Paul's theology predicated on salvation history—that is, the larger scriptural narrative of God's relationship to God's people, including preeminently the promises to redeem Israel along with all creation?

3. *The eschatological restoration of Israel and consequent pilgrimage of the nations.* Does Paul discern a basic pattern of redemption that involves Israel's eschatological restoration followed by the ingathering of the

---

3. In 1 Cor 1:2 Paul could hardly be clearer; the "*ekklēsia* of God," "sanctified in Christ," are "called to be holy ones." All three of these appositional descriptors refer equally to the Christ community in general.

4. On the transition of the descriptor "holy ones" from a reference, largely, to angelic beings, to its exclusive use (in my view) in reference to God's people in the New Testament, see Woodward, "'Saints,'" 107–16. Woodward locates the origins of this transition in significant part to the book of Daniel. He explains that according to the book's portrayal "before the arrival of the 'kingdom' earthly government apparently resides wholly in the hands of the celestial 'holy ones' (4:14–17). But at its inception much if not all of the rule passes to the earthly 'holy ones,' and indeed little else is said of angelic rule in this period. . . . Thus, with the coming of the 'kingdom' there is a shift in rule; a shift in prominence—men [sic] are royal regents of the 'kingdom'; and a transition in terminological usage—men [sic] are now worthy to be called by the heavenly designation of the angels. In this respect the old distinction has been weakened significantly" (112).

other nations qua nations to participate in the worship of the God of Israel, the Creator God?

Each of these elements will be examined separately below.[5]

The Seminal Basis of Covenant Identity

Do not say in your heart, "It is because of my righteousness that Yhwh has brought me in to occupy this land." . . . It is not because of your righteousness or the uprightness of your heart that you are going in to occupy their land. . . . Know, then, that Yhwh your God is not giving you this good land to occupy because of your righteousness." (Deut 9:4–6; cf. Hays, *Echoes*, 78; see also esp. Rom 10:6; Dan 9:18; Ps 143:1–2; Isa 64:5–9)

Blessed are those whose transgression is forgiven, whose sin is covered. Blessed are those to whom Yhwh imputes no iniquity, and in whose spirit there is no deceit. . . . Many are the torments of the wicked, but *ḥesed* surrounds those who trust in Yhwh. Be glad in Yhwh and rejoice, O righteous, and shout for joy, all you upright in heart. (Ps 32:1–2, 10–11; cf. Rom 4:6–8)

So it depends not on human will or exertion, but on God who shows mercy. (Rom 9:16; cf. 9:23–24)

I am confident of this, that the one who began a good work among you will bring it to completion by the day of Jesus Christ. (Phil 1:6)

Paul asserts in Phil 3:3a: "For *we* are the circumcision." Despite the ambiguities it presented for women, in post-Maccabean Judaism in particular the Torah ordinance regarding circumcision took on preeminent importance in defining Judaism in distinction to the surrounding cultures. While it would be in error to assume that Jewish identity was defined in a monolithic fashion throughout first-century Judaism, and without attempting to gloss over its complexity, it is safe to conclude that most orientations of Judaism viewed circumcision as a primary marker of it, and inextricable from other aspects of Jewish identity.[6] In any case, there should be no ques-

5. Much of this section is taken with permission from Zoccali, "What's the Problem with the Law?"

6. See Cohen, *Beginnings*, 109–39, for a discussion on the preeminence of circumcision

tion that Paul believed this to be so, given his use of the term as a synonym for Jewish identity in his letters to the Romans, Galatians, and Corinthians (e.g., Rom 3:30; 4:9, 12; 15:8; Gal 2:8; 1 Cor 7:18), as well as his explicit reference to the rite, as per the presentation of his Jewish credentials in Phil 3:5. Clearly, the import of Jewish identity vis-à-vis circumcision in Philippians is in terms of membership among the covenant people, the children of Abraham, God's "holy ones." Paul's point to the Philippians is thus unmistakable: the Christ community *is* the covenant people of God (e.g., Rom 2:28–29; 9:7–8, 23–26; see also Col 2:9–12).[7]

But how, exactly, can this be the case if the majority (if not the entirety) of the Philippians are gentiles, and have therefore not actually undergone this rite (after birth or in proselytism to normative Judaism)?[8] I suggest that, for Paul, the fundamental basis of covenant identity is and has always been God's חסד (*ḥesed*)—God's covenant love and faithfulness.[9]

---

in Jewish self-understanding, beginning in the second century BCE. See also Nanos, *Irony*, 88–91. Circumcision on the eighth day for native born Jews, or circumcision as the completion of the rite of proselyte conversion for Jewish proselytes, will be assumed in reference to "normative Jewish identity" throughout this study.

7. It has been proposed that Paul does *not* in fact understand gentile Christ allegiants as participating in the covenant relationship God established with Israel, but rather merely share in Israel's covenant *blessings*, and/or represent a separate (covenant) people that God established through Jesus Christ; i.e., the so-called two-covenant view, as advanced by Gaston, *Paul and the Torah*; Gager, *Reinventing Paul*; Gager, "Apostle of Judaism," 56–76; Johnson Hodge, *If Sons*, et al. I find either interpretive variant to be wholly unpersuasive; for a fuller critique of two-covenant readings of Paul, cf. Zoccali, *Whom God Has Called*. Yet, importantly, though Paul understands covenant membership to now be defined in terms of God's act in Christ, as pointed to in Phil 3:3 and elsewhere, this does *not* mean that Israel has forfeited their place in the covenant. Rather, Christ is the means by which God's covenant promises *to Israel qua Israel* are fulfilled, and, *because of this*, the nations qua nations can now enter into the people of God.

8. The matter of proselyte conversion to normative Judaism will be discussed further below.

9. For the meaning of God's *ḥesed* in terms of God's loving and faithful commitment to God's people, and thereby the fundamental basis by which the covenant will continue, see Routledge, "Ḥesed." Commenting on Ps 89, Routledge states, "*Ḥesed* precedes, and indeed gives rise to the *bĕrît* ["covenant"], which then provides additional assurance that God's promise will not fail (vv. 34–37). . . . [W]e may conclude that when God entered into a covenant with Israel he bound himself to show *ḥesed* to them. It was because of his covenant with Abraham that God demonstrated his *ḥesed* in delivering Israel from Egypt (Exod 2:24) and, in the light of the special relationship established through the Sinaitic and Davidic covenants, God's people could expect God to go on showing *ḥesed* to them. It was this unfailing and enduring divine love [he notes here: 1 Chr 16:34; 2 Chr 5:13; 20:21; Pss 107:1; 118:1–4, 29; 136; Jer 33:11] [on which] God's servants based their

Though always requiring the appropriate response of faithfulness to God
(cf. Mic 6:8; Hos 6:6–7), God's *hesed* is primary to the covenant relationship
(cf. esp. Rom 3:3; 11:28–29). It is what secures one's status among God's
people,[10] and is therefore the basis for redemption and reconciliation (cf.
Rom 5:10–11; 2 Cor 5:18–19). Paul reflects this covenantal dynamic in
Phil 2:13. In exhorting the Philippians to "work out [their] salvation," he
simultaneously affirms that "it is God who is at work in [the community]
enabling [them] both to will and to work for his good pleasure" (cf. Phil
1:6).[11] As Paul implies here, covenant relationship with God has *never* been

confidence and their appeal for deliverance in times of trouble [he notes here: Pss 6:4;
44:26; 86:5–7; 89; 107; 119:88, 159; 143:12; Mic 7:20]" (187–88).

10. E.g., Gen 24:27; 32:11; Exod 15:13; 34:6–7; Num 14:18–19; Deut 5:10; 7:9, 12;
1 Kgs 8:23; 2 Chr 6:14; Ezra 9:9; Neh 1:5; 9:17, 32; Pss 25:7–10; 32:10–11; 33:4–5; 36:5,
7, 10; 51:1; 85:4–13; 85:15; 89; 98:2–3; 103:8–18; 106:45; 130:7–8; 136; 143; 145:8–21;
Isa 16:5; 54:8–10; 55:3; 63:7; Jer 9:23–24; 31:3; Lam 3:22–23, 31–32; Dan 9:4–19; Hos
2:19, 23; Joel 2:12–13; Jonah 4:2; see also esp. Jer 16:5. Regardless of authorship, 2 Tim
2:13 succinctly expresses this very notion: "if we are faithless, he remains faithful—for
he cannot deny himself."

11. There is a range of thought in early Judaism regarding the relationship of human
and divine agency vis-à-vis salvation and/or divine favor (analogous in many ways to
various streams of later Christian tradition). However, though the relevant texts may
stress (a) the human responsibility of obedience, (b) it being the basis of God's judgment, and thus (c) having salvific or reward-based consequences, generally presupposed
in some fashion is the crucial involvement of God's sovereign and enabling grace and
mercy in all three areas. Outside of his locus on Christ, this is not qualitatively different
than what Paul suggests here in Philippians, and throughout his other letters. In addition
to the covenant renewal texts cited in p. 32 n. 30 below, e.g., Wis 2:18; 3:9; 4:15–17; 6:6–8;
7:15; 8:21; 9:6, 11; 11:23; 12:16, 19, 22; 15:3; Sir 2:6–11; 18:13–14; Bar 3:7; 4:21–24, 29;
5:9; Jub. 5:12; 12:20; 1QS 10.11; 11.2–3, 11–17; 4 Ezra 6:25–28; 9:7–13; 11:46; 12:34;
13:23; 14:34; 2 Bar. 75:1–6; 84:11; 1 En. 1:8; 27:4; 92:4; see Das, "Paul and Works," 797–
801, for a discussion on this issue surrounding the texts cited from Wis, 1QS, and Jub.
Further, contrary to a number of more traditional readings, I find little evidence to
suggest that Paul believed it even necessary to understand the precise relationship of
divine and human agency involved in salvation, beyond recognizing the priority of God's
grace and mercy (preeminently in the provision of Christ and the Spirit), and some consequent human response/cooperation. It would seem he was content to emphasize (in
the context and/or alongside of common grace and mercy) either one or the other as the
circumstances demanded, in the belief that the two mysteriously work together as part
of the same salvific process (cf. Rom 11:33–36). This is probably consistent with Pharisaic thought in general, though not without some apparent resonance with the Qumran
community as well; cf. Gal 1:15; 3:2–5; 5:7, 13; 6:4–5; Rom 2:6–8; 6; 9:22–24; 11:22–23;
1 Thess 1:4–10; 2:13; Phil 2:12–13; 1 Cor 15:10; see also Josephus, *J.W.* 2.162–63; *Ant.*
13.172; 18.13; 1QH 6.5–10; 15.13–19; 16; 1Q14 frg. 10, 7. For a full discussion on divine
and human agency in Paul vis-à-vis early Judaism, see the collection of essays in Barclay
and Gathercole, eds., *Divine and Human Agency*.

initiated or maintained in the first place by the performance of Torah, or any particular set of requirements, including the rite of circumcision (cf. Rom 3:27–31; 4:4–8; 9:11–16; see also Ps 32:10–11).[12] This same dynamic finds expression in other of Paul's letters, especially those that have particular concern for the relationship of Jews and gentiles in the people of God, namely, Romans and Galatians.

Illustrative, Paul concludes his letter to the Galatians in 6:16 with a petition for "mercy" on the "Israel of God," which refers here to the multiethnic community of God's faithful people, "the *ekklēsia* of God" (cf. Gal 1:13).[13] The term ἔλεος (mercy) is the normal translation in the LXX of חסד (*ḥesed*), and such petitions predicated on God's *ḥesed* are otherwise ubiquitous.[14] *God's ḥesed* is the heart of the message of Isa 54 (cf. v. 10), and

12. The critical implications of the primacy of God's *ḥesed* are twofold. First, as evidenced in both Paul and the relevant Jewish literature (cf. n. 11 above; p. 32 n. 30 below), salvation is always *ultimately* predicated on God's grace and mercy, rather than righteous human activity, which is itself dependent on God's gracious and merciful initiative and empowerment. Second, while there are elements that are continuous and unvarying, the content of what it means to be faithful to God, as formative to covenant identity, is not fixed or necessarily uniform, but varies according to the progress of God's salvific program; a conclusion that can be drawn from the Hebrew Bible itself (e.g., Deut 23:1–4 with Isa 56:1–8). This notion was seminal to the apostolic decree not requiring gentiles to be circumcised in order to participate in the Christ community, and, of course, to the Pauline mission itself (cf. Acts 15; Gal 2:7–9; see also esp. Rom 14; and further below).

Note further that God's sovereign and faithful resolve as the very basis of the human-divine relationship vis-à-vis salvation history is central to Paul's argument in Rom 9–11; cf. esp. 9:6–8, 11, 15–16, 18, 23–26; 11:5–6, 26–29; see similarly esp. 1 Cor 1:23–25. Indeed, Paul could not be more explicit on this matter than in Rom 9:11–16: "Even before they had been born or had done anything good or bad (so that God's purpose of election might continue, not by works but by God's call) she was told, 'The elder shall serve the younger.' . . . What then are we to say? Is there unrighteousness on God's part? Absolutely not! For he says to Moses, 'I will have mercy (Ἐλεήσω) on whom I have mercy (ἐλεῶ), and I will have compassion on whom I have compassion.' So it depends not on human will or exertion, but on God who shows mercy (ἐλεῶντος)."

13. Cf., Zoccali, *Whom God Has Called*, 78–89. A significant problem in much Pauline scholarship is, in my view, a failure to recognize the multivalent nature of the identity category of "Israel," and, moreover, Paul's willingness and ability to articulate the implications of his gospel along different tracks of thought, relative to the particular context to which he is attending. Such varied ways in which the significance of the gospel is articulated by Paul—particularly as it relates to both the Torah and historical Israel—ultimately cohere quite well once the contextual nature of his thought is sufficiently appreciated (contrary to, e.g., much of the interpretive conclusions reached by Räisänen; cf. Räisänen, *Paul and the Law*).

14. E.g., Isa 54:8–10; 63:7; Lam 3:22–23, 31–32; Pss 85:4–13; 103:8–18; 130:7–8; 136; Dan 9:4–19; Amos 5:15; Mic 7:18–20; Ezra 3:11; Hos 2:19, 23; Joel 2:12–13; see also

Paul both cites Isa 54:1 in Gal 4:27, and alludes to the greater context of Isa 54 throughout much of that letter.[15] But further, it would seem that Paul takes up the theme of God's *ḥesed* as foundational to his entire theological program, which envisions the redemption of gentiles qua gentiles alongside Jews qua Jews (cf. Gal 3:8, 13–14; Rom 1:16–17; 3:27–30; 10:11–13), with both groups united as one *ekklēsia* in worship of the God of Israel through the risen Christ (cf. Phil 2:10–11; 3:20–21; Gal 3:16, 20, 28–29; Rom 15:8–12).[16] Isaiah 54:5, 15 LXX anticipates just such an eschatological scenario:

> For it is the Lord who is making you; the Lord of hosts is his name; and the one redeeming you, he himself is the God of Israel, and he will be called so by the whole earth. . . . "Behold proselytes[17] will

Pss 40:11–12; 51:1; 69:13–16; Jonah 4:2; Ezek 39:25; Pss. Sol. 4:29; 6:9; 8:33–34; 9:19; 11:9; 17:51; and Ps 109:26–31, which is also relevant here. For a discussion on the close connection of *ḥesed* with *raḥamim* (mercy) and *ḥen* (grace) in the MT, see Routledge, "Ḥesed," 190–93. Clearly, *not only mercy, but the parallel centrality of God's grace in Paul's gospel is likewise a reflection of his complete dependence on this seminal attribute of God*; cf. Gal 1:6, 15; 2:21; 5:4; Rom 3:24; 4:16; 5:2, 15, 17, 20–21; 6:14–15; 11:5–6; 1 Cor 15:10; 2 Cor 4:15; 6:1; 8:1; 9:14.

15. Cf. Beale, "Peace and Mercy," 204–23. Beale notes Isa 53:1 in Gal 3:2; Isa 64:10 in Gal 3:10; Isa 44:1–3 and 59:21 in Gal 4:4–6; Isa 54:1 and 66:6–11 in Gal 4:25–26; and the Spirit's fruit of Isa 32:15–18 (as well as Isa 27:6; 37:31–32; 45:8; 51:3; 58:11; cf. 55:10–13 with 56:3; 60:21; 65:8, 17–22) in Gal 5:22–25 (cf. Phil 1:11). He observes in summary, "Isaiah 40–66 contains the same major themes which Paul develops in Galatians: the Abrahamic covenant, Abraham's seed, the inheritance, the return of a sinful people to God, and the new creation" (218). All of these ideas are grounded in a conviction regarding God's *ḥesed*.

16. The prophecy of Isaiah, esp. chs. 40–66, is fundamental not simply to Paul's letter to the Galatians, but to his entire gospel program. As pointed out by Wagner, *Herald*, 342, both direct citations as well as allusions to Isaiah also permeate Paul's letter to the Romans; cf. Rom 2:24 (Isa 52:5); 3:15–17 (59:7–8); 9:27–28 (10:22–23; 28:22); 9:29 (1:9); 9:33 (28:16; 8:14); 10:11(28:16); 10:15 (52:7); 10:20 (65:1); 10:21 (65:2); 11:8 (29:10); 11:26–27 (59:20–21; 27:9); 14:11 (45:23); 15:12 (11:10); 15:21 (52:15); and the following allusions: Rom 2:9 (Isa 8:22); 4:25 (53:6, 11–12); 8:32 (53:6, 12); 8:33–34 (50:8); 8:35 (8:22); 9:6 (40:7–8); 9:20 (29:16; 45:9); 9:30–31 (51:1); 10:18–19 (40:21, 28); 11:8 (6:9–10); 11:34 (40:13); 13:11 (56:1); 14:13, 21 (8:14). In the letter to the Philippians, the Christ hymn of 2:6–11 most probably finds its primary source in Isa 52:13—53:12, and it culminates with a citation of Isa 45:23 (see further below).

17. Though the original context of Isa 54 LXX may seem contrary to any idea of gentile *qua gentile* inclusion in the covenant, it seems likely, nevertheless, that Paul would have equated the "proselytes" envisaged here with gentile Christ allegiants, who would represent, then, *gentile* proselytes to the covenant community—a community that has been transformed into a multiethnic one centered around God's act in Christ, in fulfillment of the promises (cf. Gal 3:8, 14). In Paul's reading of Scripture, these righteous gentiles (cf. Rom 4:17–18) who have joined God's historical covenant people (cf. Rom

come to you through me and they will sojourn with you, and they will run to you for refuge."

Paul succinctly expresses this inclusive salvific phenomenon predicated on God's *ḥesed* in Rom 11:30–32: "For God has imprisoned all [both Jews and gentiles] in disobedience so that to all he may show ἐλεήσῃ [mercy]" (Rom 11:32).[18] And it is also explicitly affirmed as the very conclusion of the main theological discourse of Romans: "For I tell you that Christ has become a servant of the circumcised for the truthfulness of God in order to confirm the promises to the fathers, and as a result the gentiles may glorify God for (God's) ἐλέους [mercy]" (15:8–9; cf. Rom 9:14–26; Gal 3:22; 2 Cor 4:1; 5:17–21).

It is important to observe, then, that while Paul's conclusion regarding gentile qua gentile inclusion in the covenant community may move beyond the norms of first-century Judaism, his premise regarding the priority of God's covenant faithfulness would no doubt find agreement from other Jews. The concession that Israel's righteous status as God's people

---

4:11–12) were already anticipated in the Torah in the person of the righteous *uncircum-cised* Abraham who initially received the covenant blessing (cf. Rom 4:9–10). In this way, I suggest that Paul's theology is informed by the eschatological pilgrimage tradition, which was one of the major forms of soteriological inclusivism in late Second Temple Jewish thought; see further on this point below.

18. In the context of Rom 11:26–32 (as well as 3:9–26) πᾶς refers to all *groups*, that is, Jews and gentiles, who are both, interdependently, the recipients of the salvation that God has provided in Christ. Though having precedent in their covenant history (cf. Rom 2:17–24; 7:7–24; 10:1–21), the disobedience of Israel pointed to here is their failure (in large part) to give allegiance to Jesus as the Christ (cf. Rom 10:1–4; 11:7, 23; Gal 4:21–25; 1 Thess 2:14–16), whereas the disobedience of the gentiles has to do with their former exclusion from the covenant (cf. Gal 2:15; 4:8; Rom 1:18–32; 1 Thess 1:9). It is the defeat of sin's power and the enabling of obedience for Jews and gentiles in Christ (cf. Rom 5:17, 19; 6:5–7; 8:1–2; 1 Cor 15:20–21, 56–57), as intrinsic to the covenant's fulfillment (cf. Rom 11:25–27), that *makes full and permanent what was formerly only partial and ephemeral among God's people* (cf. 2 Cor 3:7–11); a new order of life wholly free from that which frustrated God's original purposes for all of creation (cf. Gal 6:15–16; Rom 8:18–30).

This salvation-historical context mitigates the notion of Paul's anthropological pessimism. That a concept of "originating sin" comparable to Paul's may have been absent in most forms of early Judaism is not, in my view, especially critical to the intra-Jewish debate in which Paul is engaged. An acute awareness of the pervasiveness of sin and its negative consequences was shared by Paul and most other Jews of the period, irrespective of how Paul develops the idea of sin in relation to his conviction regarding Christ. In any case, I do not find the Augustinian view of original sin to accurately represent Paul's perspective.

was ultimately secured by God's faithfulness to Israel rather than Israel's faithfulness to God is overwhelmingly demonstrated in their Scriptures, and is also well-attested in the relevant extrabiblical literature. Thus, the proposition that it is only in the context of God's prior *ḥesed* that any Israelite could truthfully claim a status of righteousness would easily meet with little controversy among the greater Jewish community (cf. Phil 3:6b; see also 1 Cor 15:10).

The central point of disagreement between the Pauline mission and Jews outside the Christ movement would therefore lie strictly in the matter of *how* God's *ḥesed* is presently being revealed, and *what faithful response is now required* for those in covenant relationship with God as a result of this revelation. Non-Christ-allegiant Jews would have observed no change in either the content of God's faithfulness, or that of the faithfulness required on the part of God's people. In contrast, for Paul, the Christ-event signals a dramatic and culminating shift in both: as the final expression of God's *ḥesed*, the coming of Jesus Christ makes possible an expression of faithfulness indicative of covenant membership that does not require full Torah submission, that is, normative Jewish identity. This new expression of covenant identity that is nevertheless predicated upon God's enduring, sovereign mercy and grace is straightforwardly indicated in Rom 11:5–6, as Paul refers here to the present body of Jews who have become allegiant to Christ:

> So then also in the present time, a remnant of grace has come into being. But if it is by grace, it is no longer on the basis of works, otherwise grace would no longer be grace.[19]

Though inseparably involved, the priority of God's covenant faithfulness does not, however, provide a complete justification for this new form

---

19. This also raises the question of whether various Jewish groups believed gentiles could at all participate in the covenant—that is, whether Jewish proselytism was considered legitimate, or if instead Jewish identity was perceived to be primordial rather than constructed, and thus impermeable/closed. This question was answered differently by different Jewish groups in the first century (cf. p. 65 nn. 37, 38; p. 82 n. 90 below).

Note as well here that "full Torah submission" does *not* mean "perfect obedience." Rather, in view is the full body of ordinances contained in the Torah, thereby including those laws that, for Paul, continue to distinguish Jewish identity from gentile identity, including preeminently circumcision, and also, e.g., kashrut and Sabbath observance. As will be discussed further below, when Paul refers to the ἔργων νόμου (works of the Torah), he has in mind specifically normative Jewish identity as made manifest through Torah obedience.

of faithfulness to God. Even if Paul could convince that God's faithfulness has reached its fullest expression in the Christ event, how exactly does it follow that God no longer requires full Torah submission as the appropriate expression of covenant faithfulness to God among God's holy ones? It is one thing to claim that being a Jew does not in itself secure covenant identity (which, again, would not be a point of controversy). It is quite another thing to claim that God has in fact expanded covenant identity such that it is no longer coextensive with normative Jewish identity, as especially signified in first-century Judaism by the rite of circumcision. Understanding how Paul is able to connect the necessity of gentile inclusion in the covenant, and thus their identity alongside Jews as holy ones, with God's *ḥesed* revealed in Jesus Christ calls for an investigation into Paul's eschatological worldview as both informed by and informative to his reading of Scripture.

Covenant and Creation Renewal

The days are surely coming, says YHWH, when I will make a new covenant with the house of Israel and the house of Judah. . . . I will put my Torah within them, and I will write it on their hearts; and I will be their God, and they shall be my people (Jer 31:31, 33).

A new heart I will give you, and a new spirit I will put within you; and I will remove from your body the heart of stone and give you a heart of flesh. I will put my spirit within you, and make you follow my statutes and be careful to observe my ordinances (Ezek 36:26–27).

For I am about to create new heavens and a new earth; the former things shall not be remembered or come to mind (Isa 65:17).

In my view, Paul is deeply grounded in the larger scriptural narrative according to which the coming of Jesus Christ represents the culmination of God's purposes for Israel and all creation.[20] Only such a "promise and

20. Building in large part from the work of Käsemann, arguments in Pauline theology characterized by the term "apocalyptic," including those found in, e.g., Beker, *Triumph*; Martyn, "God's Invasion," 160–79; Martyn, *Galatians*; Martyn, *Theological Issues*; de Boer, *The Defeat of Death*; ed. Gaventa, *Apocalyptic Paul*; Campbell, *Quest*; Campbell, *Deliverance*; Harink, *Postliberals*, et al., have proposed that Paul's theology represents a radical break with the past, such that the Christ event ushers in a new era *wholly* discontinuous with all that went before. While my understanding of salvation

fulfillment," salvation-historical schema makes any adequate sense of Paul's own sociohistorical context,[21] as well as his use of Scripture throughout the majority of his letters. Demonstrably, the Hebrew Bible as a whole, as understood in at least some strands of late Second Temple Judaism, is occupied in large part with the matter of God's work to bring all creation, and Israel in particular, into conformity with God's will, in the conviction that neither Israel nor the entire created order fully represents such a state in the present order of things.[22] Thus, unless one is prepared to argue that Paul simply fabricated a predicament for which Jesus Christ is the solution, as E. P. Sanders has famously suggested,[23] and/or that he merely "plunders" the Hebrew Bible for convenient language that function as useful proof

---

history in Paul's letters is not at the expense of his equal emphasis on the dramatic, "apocalyptic" in-breaking of the eschatological age in and through the Christ event, it is the very continuity of God's purposes in creation and election that provides the basis of meaning and anticipation for the revelation of Jesus Christ. Without the calling of historical Israel, set apart by virtue of the Torah, there would be no Christ to fulfill the promises, redeeming God's good creation from the enslaving power of sin and death, and thus making all things new—a conclusion that surely did not escape Paul (cf. Rom 1:2–4; 9:4–5; 15:8–12). Stated succinctly, for Paul, the apocalypse of Jesus Christ singularly fulfills and illuminates salvation history; it is *not* contrary to it (contra esp. Martyn, "God's Invasion;" *Theological Issues*, 161–75). This matter will be taken up further in ch. 5 below. For an overview on this question of continuity/discontinuity in Pauline scholarship, see Zoccali, *Whom God Has Called*.

21. While over-generalizations of the significance of the Babylonian exile should be avoided, I nevertheless find it an almost impossible conclusion that most Jews of Paul's time (with few exceptions; e.g., the sect of the Sadducees, who did not hold to the prophetic literature) believed that the prophetic hope of Israel's final restoration had been fully consummated, and thus that there did not exist a strong perception in most Jewish communities that Israel was still awaiting the (entirety of) fulfillment of the exilic promises in Scripture; see further below.

22. E.g., Phil 2:15–16; Rom 1:18–32; 2:17–24; 3:9–20; 8:18–25; 1 Cor 2:6–9; 3:18–23; 7:31; 2 Cor 4:4–6; Gal 1:4; 1 Thess 5:1–11. To the extent, then, that Paul's worldview is significantly influenced by late Second Temple Jewish apocalyptic thought, it is important to recognize that Jewish apocalyptic texts themselves do *not* reject Israel's salvation history. Rather, "an apocalypse was . . . a way of reaffirming the continuity of the past with the future as both God's." And such a reaffirmation was of crucial importance when Israel found herself "suffering persecution and could see no other way for the covenant and its promises to be sustained" (Dunn, "How New Was Paul's Gospel?" 383). Further, as Wright points out, Paul's "new creation" language is found precisely in covenantal contexts (Wright, *Saint Paul*, 152–53; cf. esp. 2 Cor 3–5). Indeed, the origin of such language found in Isaiah (e.g., 43:18–21; 65:17–25) is concerned in the first place with the fulfillment of God's covenant promises to Israel (cf. 54:9–10).

23. Sanders, *Palestinian Judaism*, 442–47.

texts for the legitimacy of his gospel,[24] then we have to contend for the fact that Paul situates his gospel as the very fulfillment of the promises in Scripture (cf. esp. 1 Cor 10:11; 15:3–4; 2 Cor 1:20; 3:14–16; Gal 3:22), and thus in a context for *both* Jews and gentiles as fundamentally characterized by a lack of such fulfillment up until that time.[25]

Accordingly, in Phil 3:3b Paul continues by exclaiming that the Philippian Christ community "serve/worship (λατρεύω) by the Spirit of God and claim honor (καυχάομαι) in Christ Jesus."[26] Integral to Paul's theology and apostolic mission is the belief that, as the very basis for the fulfillment of the Abrahamic blessing and promises, the renewal of Israel's covenant,[27] along with the entire created order,[28] has now been inaugurated "in Christ." In this eschatological renewal, the Spirit implants the Torah within God's people, giving them a new capacity for faithfulness.[29] It is this phenomenon

---

24. Wagner, *Herald*, 356.

25. In basic agreement with the overarching thesis of Wright, I suggest that Paul's theology is informed by the metanarrative of sin-exile-return. For a fuller treatment of this matter, cf. Zoccali, *Whom God Has Called*, 150–70.

26. Cf. esp. Rom 8:13–14; Gal 5:16; see also 1 Cor 2.

27. Cf. Rom 11:27; 1 Cor 11:23–26; 2 Cor 3:3–18; Gal 4:24–28; see also Col 2:11

28. Cf. Gal 6:15; 2 Cor 5:17; Rom 4:13, 17; 8:18–25; 1 Cor 3:21–23; 6:2; 15:20–28; see also Col 1:15–20; Eph 1:7–14.

29. Cf. Rom 2:14–16, 25–29; 7:6; 8:1–11; Gal 3:2–5; 4:6; 5:5; 1 Cor 2:12; 2 Cor 3:6. Thiessen, *Gentile Problem*, 129–60, argues that Paul's connection of the blessing of Abraham to the promise of the Spirit in Galatians (3:14), implicit elsewhere in his letters (cf. esp. Phil 2:14–15; 1 Cor 15:48–49), is found in a *qualitative* understanding of the promise to Abraham that his descendants would become like the stars, which were understood in the ancient world as angelic, pneumatic beings. This view has also recently been argued by Burnett, "'So Shall Your Seed Be,'" 211–36. While I appreciate this insightful observation, which aligns with the characterization of the resurrected righteous in Dan 12:2–3 that is echoed in Phil 2:14–15 (cf. p. 97 n. 29 below; see also, e.g., [as largely noted by either Burnett, or Ware, *Mission*, 130] 1 En. 38:4; 104:2–6; 2 En. 66:7–8; 2 Bar. 51:1–11; Test. Mos. 10:9; 4 Macc 17:5–6; 4 Ezra 7:97, 125; Wis 3:7–8; Matt 13:43; 17:1–3), it seems to me that such an understanding is, nevertheless, secondary to the prophetic promises of the Spirit that are inextricable to the inauguration of the eschatological age of Israel's restoration—the renewal of the covenant and all of creation, which are, in turn, inseparable from the explicit promises to Abraham of land (i.e., the renewed creation), offspring (i.e., the multiethnic Christ community who fulfill the Torah), and the extension of blessing to the other nations through him (i.e., the inclusion of the gentiles in particular). In this respect, Thiessen's argument strikes me as reductionist, as if Paul's thought is not shaped by a larger narrative of God's dealings with Israel, and through Israel, the rest of the world, as per the full sweep of the Hebrew Bible (cf. esp. Isa 42:1–6; 49:5–13; 52:13—53:12).

Further, as I will discuss below, while Paul clearly held that the resurrection body of

of renewal that Scripture had prophesied would happen as a result of a fresh act of divine intervention motivated by God's *ḥesed* towards God's people.[30]

Christ allegiants is an exalted, glorious, and pneumatic one, in keeping with a qualitative understanding of the Abrahamic promise, I do not agree that the resurrection state is, for Paul, supra-earthly. Paul's echo of Daniel 12:3 in Phil 2:14–15 points explicitly to an inaugurated reality for the Philippians, which suggests that the association of the Christ community with the "stars" does *not* connote a celestial existence (cf. esp. Rom 6:4–11). Indeed, in contradistinction to some strands of Jewish tradition suggestive of "astral immortality," that Christ allegiants have already received the Spirit in the present order, and are accordingly Abraham's offspring, indicates that fully realized pneumatic existence for human beings occupies no less the earthly—rather than the heavenly—realm (cf. esp. Rom 8:9–30; Gal 3:1–5; and ch. 5 below). In all, for Paul, the kingdom of God, along with its king, Jesus Christ, comes *from* heaven *to* earth, and *not* the other way around (e.g., Phil 3:20–21; 1 Thess 1:9–10; 4:14–17; 1 Cor 15:23; p. 97 n. 30 below).

30. For the renewal of Israel's covenant, cf. Deut 30:1–6; Isa 32:15; 44:3; 59:21; Jer 31:31–40; 32:39–40; Ezek 11:19–20; 36:22–32; 39:29; Joel 2:28; Zech 12:10; see also Bar 2:30–35; Jub. 1:21–24; 22:15, 30; CD 3.10–20; 1QS 1.16—2.25; 1QH 5.11; 7.6–35; 9.32; 12.12; 13.23–25; 14.3, 8–13; 16.7–15; 1Q34 2.5–7; 4Q504 5.6–16. Paul's description of the gospel in Rom 1:2–4 in terms of the messianic hope is an integral part of covenant renewal. While Davidic messianic expectations (derived from texts such as, e.g., Isa 9:6–7; 11:1–12; Jer 23:5–8; 33:14–26; Ezek 34:23–31; 37:24–28; Amos 9:11–15; Hos 3:4–5; Mic 5:2–3; Zech 3:8; 6:11–13) are by no means monolithic in the extrabiblical literature, Fuller, *Restoration*, 184, points out that when such a figure is envisaged "it is usually within the exilic model of restoration. For those Jews who sustained the hope for his coming, the messiah's arrival was understood to be pivotal to Israel's restoration" (cf. Pss. Sol. 17–18; 1 En. 37–71; 4 Ezra 7:25–44; 12:31–34; 13:25–50; 2 Bar. 26:1—30:5; 36:1—40:4; 53:1—76:5; 4Q252 5.1–6; 4Q161 3.11–22; 4Q285 frg. 5; 4Q174 1).

For the renewal of all creation, cf. Isa 2:1–4; 9:6–7; 11:1–9; 25:6–10; 27:6; 40:3–5; 42:1, 6; 45:8; 49:6; 51:4–6; 54; 56:6–8; 60; 65:17–25; 66:22–23; Zech 9:10; Sir 44:19–21; Pss 36:9, 11, 22, 29, 34 LXX; 72:8–11; Jub. 1:27–28; 4:26; 17:3; 19:21–25; 22:14–15, 27–30; 32:18–19; 1 QH 13.15–18; 17.15; 1 En. 5:6–7; 4 Ezra 6:55–59; 2 Bar. 14:13; 51.3; Philo, *Moses* 1.55; *Somn.* 1.175; and in the New Testament outside of Paul: Heb 1:2; Acts 3:17–21; Matt 5:5; 6:10; 2 Pet 3:10–14; Rev 21–22.

As found in Isa 40–66, and likewise understood by the author of Jubilees (cf. 1:23–29; 4:26; 19:21–25; 22), *inextricably linked for Paul are the fulfillment of the promises to Abraham, the renewal of all creation, and the renewal of Israel's covenant.* Paul refers to this faithful act of eschatological renewal (in and through Jesus Christ) in fulfillment of the promises as (with some variation) the δικαιοσύνη θεοῦ ("righteousness from/of God") in Phil 3:9; Rom 1:16–17; 3:21–26; 10:3 (see further on this matter in ch. 4 below). Importantly, this key Pauline expression of divine faithfulness (cf. Rom 3:3) presupposes *both* salvation and "God's . . . wrath against all ungodliness and unrighteousness" (Rom 1:18; cf. 2:5–11, 16; 3:5–8; see also esp. Phil 1:27–29; and, e.g., Pss 9:8; 50:4–23; 96:13; 98:9; 143:11–12; Isa 11:4–5). While I do not follow all of his conclusions, for a similar understanding of δικαιοσύνη θεοῦ, see Wright, "Romans and the Theology of Paul." For the close connection between *ḥesed* and righteousness, see Routledge, "Ḥesed," 188–91; he notes here Pss 33:4–5; 40:10; 85:4–13; 89:14; 98:2–3; 103:17–18; Isa 16:5; Jer 9:23–24; Hos 10:12; see also esp. Ps 36:5–6, and further the LXX's translation of חסד as δικαιοσύνη

As a derivative of the inauguration of the (re)new(ed) covenant and creation, it would seem that Paul further understands the Torah's potential outcomes of "life" or "death" for God's people as being subsumed under God's final judgment, and as therefore centered around Jesus Christ (cf. esp. Deut 30:15–20 with Rom 6:23).[31] In Paul's eschatological reading of Scripture, then, the experience of blessing or curse set in motion by obedience or disobedience to God's covenantal commands ultimately remained an open matter that would be settled once and for all in the eschaton when God would again intervene to redeem God's people.[32] Thus, the gospel and its

in Gen 24:27; 32:11; Exod 15:13; 34:7.

31. Indeed, it should be observed that Paul's extensive dependence on both Isaiah (cf. p. 26 n. 16 above) and Deut 27–32 in Romans reveals that he "locates himself and his fellow believers" in both Isaiah and Deuteronomy's "larger three-act 'plotline' of rebellion, punishment, and restoration" (Wagner, *Herald*, 354). With respect to Deuteronomy, quotations in Romans include: 29:4 (11:8); 30:12–14 (10:6–8); 32:21 (10:19); there are also allusions to Deut 32:31 (11:11–14) and Deut 32:4 (9:14). Concerning Rom 9–11, Wagner notes that of "particular significance is the fact that three times Paul links a citation from the last chapters of Deuteronomy to a passage from Isaiah": Deut 32:21 and Isa 65:1–2 (10:19–21); Deut 29:4 and Isa 29:10 (11:8); Deut 32:43 and Isa 11:10 (15:10–12). "This interpretive strategy suggests that Paul understands Isaiah and Deuteronomy to be telling the same epic story of the triumph of God's faithfulness over Israel's unfaithfulness" (Wagner, *Herald*, 355). I would further suggest that this theological conviction is implicit throughout Paul's letters, and given further explicit representation in Galatians and Philippians. In Galatians, in addition to the Isaiah references in p. 26 n. 15 above, Paul cites Deut 27:26, likely merging the verse with Deut 28:58, 61; 29:20–21, 27; 30:10, in Gal 3:10 (cf. p. 34 n. 33 below). In his letter to the Philippians, Phil 2:6–9 is dependent on Isa 52.13—53:12; Phil 2:10–11 on Isa 45:22–23; and Phil 2:14–15 on Deut 32:5 (cf. p. 96 n. 25 below). As is clear in all three letters, for Paul, the triumph of God's faithfulness means not only Israel's salvation, but that of the entire world.

32. Cf. esp. Ezek 20:1–39 with 36:22—37:28; see also Gal 1:4; 3:22; 4:4–5; Rom 3:21–26; 10:21—11:5, 25–27. For the significance of God's final judgment in Paul, cf. Rom 1:18; 2:2–6, 16; 4:15; 5:9; 9:22–23, 28; 14:11; 16:17–20; 1 Cor 1:8; 4:5; 2 Cor 5:10; Phil 1:28; 3:18–19; 1 Thess 1:9–10; 5:9; see also Col 3:5–6; Acts 17:20–21. A delay in this judgment in order to provide a space of time for repentance and salvation in Christ seems to be assumed in Rom 2:2–11, and also 3:21–26, where Paul refers to God's divine forbearance, in which God "passed over the sins previously committed" (Rom 3:25). I suggest that such delay in judgment is also the basic premise for what Paul argues in Rom 11 in regard to the purpose of Israel's hardening (cf. 11:11–24). As Wright explains, in an apocalyptic context hardening is understood as befalling those who do not accept God's forbearance as an opportunity to repent. As a result, once judgment finally does come upon them it will be seen as just (cf. 1 Thess 2:14–16; 2 Macc 6:12–16; Wis 12:9–27; 19:4–5; Gen 15:16). This period of hardening happens, then, "during a temporary suspension of God's judgment that would have otherwise fallen," allowing time for some to escape (Wright, *Romans,* 639, 677–78; *Climax,* 271). Thus, by the paradoxical means of Israel's partial hardening, God is restoring Israel, and also saving the nations through the

acceptance have become for Paul the final substance and import of the call to obedience in the Torah, and thereby the means to life—interpreted by him in terms of resurrection or eternal life—for *all* people (cf. Rom 10:5–13).[33] Failure to properly respond to the final expression of God's faithfulness/righteousness in Jesus Christ will ultimately mean death/destruction.

This eschatological dynamic is explicitly demonstrated in Phil 3:18–21:

> For, as I have often told you before and now tell you again even with tears, many live as enemies of the cross of Christ. Their destiny is destruction, their god is their belly, and their glory is in their shame. Their mind is set on earthly things. But our citizenship is in heaven. And we eagerly await a Savior from there, the Lord Jesus Christ, who, by the power that enables him to bring everything under his control, will transform our lowly bodies so that they will be like his glorious body [cf. 1 Thess 4:13—5:11].[34]

---

gospel of Jesus Christ; cf. Zoccali, "'All Israel'"; Zoccali *Whom God Has Called*, 91–117.

33. As I have argued in Zoccali, "What's the Problem with the Law?" Paul asserts in Gal 3:10–12 that the perseverance in the Torah demanded by God is ultimately fulfilled in the gospel of Jesus Christ (cf. Rom 2:12–16, 25–29; see p. 52 n. 80 below). In this sense, I suggest that Israel and Israel's covenant relationship with God poses representational significance for Paul in terms of God's dealing with all of humanity. That is, what was fundamentally true for Israel, e.g., the requirement of fidelity toward God under warning of judgment, is also *now* true for all humanity in the dispensation of Christ, as consistent with the story of creation in Gen 2:15–17 (cf. Rom 3:21–26; 5:16–21; 7:7–25; 9:30—10:13; see also esp. 1 Cor 10; n. 34; p. 45 n. 58 below). Correspondingly, Ware, *Mission*, 75–76, importantly observes that "[t]hroughout Isaiah 40–55, the obligation of exclusive devotion to Yahweh incumbent Israel on the basis of the Mosaic covenant (e.g. 43:10–13; 48:4–5; cf. Isa 2:6–11; 17:4–11; 30:22; 57:3–13; 65:2–12; Ex 20:3–6; Jer 2:2–13; Hos 13:4) is expressly applied to the gentiles as well, as a consequence of Yahweh's unique identity as the only true God (e.g. Isa 41:24; 44:9–11; 45:16; cf. Isa 2:12–21; 16:12; 21:9; 37:15–20; 66:22–24; Ps 33:8–9). Previously in Isaiah 40–55, the outcome of this universal claim is judgment upon the nations (cf. 41:24; 44:9–11; 45:16). However, in Isaiah 45:20–22, the claim expressed in 45:21 that Yahweh alone is God leads in 45:22, remarkably, to an invitation to conversion."

34. Notwithstanding his assertion that gentiles do not "by birthright" (φύσει) possess the Torah (Rom 2:14), and, outside of Christ, continue to be "lawless" (cf. 1 Cor 9:21), Paul understands *all* people as ultimately responsible to its ethical demands, despite the fact that it had been given to Israel in particular (cf. Gal 3:22; Rom 2:2–11; 3:19–20). As pointed to in Davies, *Rabbinic Judaism*, 168–71; Donaldson, *Paul and the Gentiles*, 206–7; and Gaston, *Paul and the Torah*, 26–28, the association of Torah with Wisdom in Jewish tradition (cf. Sir 24:8, 23; Bar 3:37—4:1; T. Levi 14:4; Sib. Or. 3.195; Sipra 86b; see similarly Paul's association of Christ with wisdom: 2 Cor 4:4; Col 1.15–16; Phil 2:6 [cf. Wis 7:26]; 1 Cor 1:24; 8:6; 10:4 [cf. Philo, *Leg.* 2.86; Wis 10:17; 11:4]; Rom 10:6 [cf. Bar 3:29–30]) contributed to a view in which the Torah was universally applicable to all nations (cf., e.g., 4 Ezra 3:28–36; 7:19–24, 37–38, 79–82; 8:55–58, 9:10–12; Pseudo-Philo

This same dynamic is found, moreover, in Phil 1:27–28. I submit that Paul's programmatic phrase appearing in Phil 1:27, "the faithfulness of the gospel" (τῇ πίστει τοῦ εὐαγγελίου), presupposes the fulfillment of God's revealed will in the Torah vis-à-vis the transformative hope of covenant and creation renewal (cf. Phil 3:9; see also Rom 3:27). Indicating the Philippians' obedient allegiance to Jesus Christ and concomitant praxis (cf. Rom 1:5; 10:16; 16:26), "the faithfulness of the gospel" is, then, both enabled by, and the very manifestation of God's *ḥesed* to Israel and the nations (cf. Phil 1:6; 2:13). But as all do not properly respond to God's faithfulness, the destiny of the Philippian Christ community is set contrast in 1:28 with their "opponents." The Philippians' opponents—by the fact of their faithlessness/disobedience—forfeit their place in God's gracious future, receiving "destruction" rather than "salvation" (Phil 1:28)—that is, the "life" that God offers to all humanity, Jew and gentile alike (cf. Rom 5:15–21).

The Eschatological Restoration of Israel and Pilgrimage of the Nations

Along with Isaiah 54:15 LXX, there are a number of other texts in the Hebrew Bible/LXX that foresee the eventual salvation of the nations as a consequence of Israel's restoration following God's judgment that had led them into exile from the land of promise; a tradition commonly referred to in contemporary New Testament scholarship as the "eschatological pilgrimage of the nations." In some of these passages the nations are (seemingly) envisaged as becoming subordinate to Israel by virtue of such pilgrimages.[35] However, a more explicitly positive role for the nations vis-à-vis Israel is found in Isa 11:10 LXX; 19:18–25; 51:5 LXX; 54:15 LXX; 56:6–8; 66:18–21; and Amos 9:11–12 LXX.[36]

In other passages, notably Isa 2:2–5 (see below), the relative status of the nations in relation to Israel is ambiguous. Isaiah 11:1–10; 25:6–10; 42:1–9; 45:22–23; 49:6; and 51:4–6 portray the destiny of the nations in such ambiguous terms, as do also Jer 3:17; 16:19–21; Mic 4:1–3; Hab 2:14; Zeph 3:9; Zech 2:11; 8:20–21; 14:9; Tob 13:11–14; 14:5–7 (see also

11:1–2; 2 Bar. 48:40–47; 13:1–12, esp. v. 8; 1 En. 63:1–12, esp. v. 8; Apoc. Ab. 31:6).

35. Cf., e.g., Isa 14:1–2; 18:7; 45:14; 60:1–22; Hag 2:6–7, 21–22; Zech 14:16–19; Pss. Sol. 17:29–35; Jub. 32:19; Sir 36:11–17; Tg. Isa. 25:6–10; 55:5; 1 En. 90:30; 2 Bar. 72:2–6.

36. This LXX passage from Amos is cited in Acts 15 as the scriptural basis for the Jerusalem council's decision that gentile Christ allegiants do not have to undergo the rite of circumcision, as per the process of proselyte conversion to normative Judaism.

Pss 22:27–28; 67; 86:9; 102:15–16, 21–22; 138:4–5). In the relevant extra-biblical literature, there are comparable assertions concerning the role of the nations in Israel's restoration.[37]

It may be asked to what extent, if any, Paul draws upon this tradition, and what the implications are for his theology. While a good number of scholars virtually take it for granted that Paul's gospel of gentile inclusion is informed by the prophetic notion of the eschatological pilgrimage of the nations, several other scholars have questioned its significance in Paul's thought.[38] However, I do not find the common objections to this tradition's import to Paul to be especially convincing.

First, as James P. Ware has pointed out, as indicated by the frequency of which it is cited throughout the New Testament, the book of Isaiah was of particular importance to the early Christ movement, and not least to the Pauline mission. This is almost certainly because of "the attention which that book devotes to the place of the nations in God's salvation. The relationship of the God of Israel to the nations is in Isaiah, to a greater degree than in any other book of the Old Testament, a prominent and consistent theme."[39] Representing a programmatic oracle for the book as a literary whole is Isa 2:2–5:

> In days to come the mountain of YHWH's house shall be estab-
> lished as the highest of the mountains, and shall be raised above
> the hills. And the nations shall stream to it, and many peoples shall
> come and say, "Come, let us go up to the mountain of YHWH, to
> the house of the God of Jacob; that he may teach us his ways, and
> we may walk in his paths." For out of Zion will go forth teaching,
> and the word of YHWH from Jerusalem. He will bring about justice
> between the nations, and render judgment for many peoples. And

37. Cf., e.g., 1 En. 10:21—11:2; 48:4–5; Sib. Or. 3.556–72, 710–23, 757–75; T. Levi 18:2–9; T. Naph. 8:3–4; T. Jud. 24:4–6; 25:5; T. Zeb. 9:8; T. Benj. 10.3–11; Philo, *Moses* 2.44; also possibly 4 Ezra 6.25–28.

38. As set forth in his 1997 monograph *Paul and the Gentiles*, and, more recently, in "Paul within Judaism," 284–93, Donaldson has suggested that the eschatological pilgrimage tradition is *not* significant in Paul's thought, though he originally argued for this very thesis in "The Curse of the Law," 94–112. My position is not dependent on the exegetical arguments made in that article, as I do not hold that Paul distinguishes between Jewish and gentile Christ allegiants in his use of first-person plural pronouns in the letter; cf. Zoccali, "What's the Problem with the Law?" 406 n. 55. In any case, see below for counter-arguments to Donaldson's critique of the eschatological pilgrimage tradition as being influential to Paul.

39. Ware, *Mission*, 59.

> they will hammer their swords into plowshares, and their spears
> into pruning hooks; nation will not lift up sword against nation,
> and they will no longer learn war. O house of Jacob, come, let us
> walk in the light of Yhwh.[40]

But even if Isaiah's influence on Paul is granted, an initial objection is that
it does not seem Paul directly quotes or otherwise alludes to such eschatological pilgrimage texts in his letters. This objection is incorrect. In his letters most occupied with the question of gentile inclusion in God's covenant
people, the eschatological pilgrimage tradition can be clearly discerned
in Paul's respective arguments. First, as pointed out above: (a) at the very
conclusion of the main theological discourse of Romans, in 15:12, Paul
cites Isa 11:10, which reflects the eschatological pilgrimage tradition seen
throughout Isaiah; and (b) Isaiah 54 LXX, a passage that likewise reflects
the tradition, is cited (Gal 4:27) and strongly echoed throughout Galatians. Again, we find these scriptural references/allusions *exactly* where we
should expect them—in arguments occupied with the relationship of Jews,
gentiles, and God's act in Christ.

Yet, it is suggested that in most of the eschatological pilgrimage texts
the relationship between the nations and Israel is completely ambiguous.
Do the nations remain distinct from Israel, or do they become (in a first-
century reading) Jewish proselytes? For example, in Isa 2:2–4 the nations
are explicitly said to embrace the Torah, and so it is difficult to understand
how Paul could arrive at a "Torah-free" gospel if indeed the tradition was
formative to the apostolic message he proclaimed to the nations.[41]

This criticism fails on the fact that Paul's gospel is clearly *not* Torah-
free in any sort of unmitigated sense (see below). Paul only maintains that
gentiles should not undergo the rite of circumcision as per the process of
proselyte conversion. And the reason for that is simple: if gentiles must
continue in proselyte conversion to normative Judaism in order to participate in the covenant, as Paul seemingly believed prior to his Christ conviction and apostolic calling (cf. Gal 5:11), this would imply that nothing has
in fact changed—that the Christ has not come, and that the new age has
not dawned, which would be precisely signalled by the ingathering of the
nations to join God's historical covenant people, Israel.

Second, we have good reason to understand why Paul would not
directly cite eschatological pilgrimage texts, even if the tradition was

40. Ibid., 59–60 (trans. with some modification here).
41. So Donaldson, "Paul within Judaism," 286–88.

informative to his gospel. Since a number of the passages in question from the Hebrew Bible are either ambiguous on the matter, or present the nations in a subordinate role to Israel, we should expect Paul to shy away from explicit references, since in his theology the nations are brought into the covenant on *equal* terms with Jews. Of course, some might suggest that this is exactly why the tradition is of little use to Paul. However, I submit that, as especially found in Isaiah (again, a text that is fundamental to Paul's understanding of the gospel), the eschatological pilgrimage passages are most unlikely to have simply been ignored by him, given that they are (a) numerous and integral to the theological import of the book as a whole, (b) generally associated with future expectations regarding the Davidic dynasty, which are integral to the messianic expectations that Paul associates with Jesus Christ (cf. p. 32 n. 30 above), and (c) inseparable from the envisaging of a renewed creation in which peace between Israel and the nations will reign supreme. Further, the appropriation of this tradition in various relevant Jewish sources seems to indicate that the idea of the eschatological salvation of the nations, consequent to God's restorative work on behalf of Israel, was one of the main forms of soteriological inclusivism in late Second Temple Judaism. There is little reason to conclude that Paul failed to negotiate with any of these strands of inclusivism, irrespective of how he creatively transformed each of them around his experience of the risen Christ.

Excursus: Jewish Soteriological Inclusivism

As I have argued in *Whom God Has Called*, the three major forms of Jewish soteriological inclusivism, however re-worked, can all be discerned in Paul's extant writings. In agreement with most scholars who hold to the significance of the eschatological pilgrimage tradition in Paul's theology, I suggest that Paul combines this idea with the concept of the "righteous gentile." The idea of the righteous gentile is suggested in the relevant literature according to two fundamental patterns categorized by Terence L. Donaldson as "sympathization" and "ethical monotheism."[42] The category of sympathization consists of texts depicting some measure of attachment to Judaism among gentiles whereby they could positively relate to God.[43]

42. Donaldson, *Judaism and the Gentiles.*
43. Ibid., 469–82. Donaldson notes the following examples: Dan 4:34; 6:26–27;

The category of ethical monotheism consists of texts "in which Jews consider it possible for Gentiles to acquire accurate and adequate knowledge of the one true God, or to relate to this God in appropriate ways, without any knowledge of Judaism or association with the Jewish community."[44] Accordingly, this notion was arrived at through an appreciation of natural theology, and either its alignment with or independence from the Torah.[45]

Paul's almost certain awareness of such ideas, along with the corresponding first-century reality of gentile synagogue associates (i.e., "God-fearers"), was surely instructive to his understanding of the identity of gentiles who have responded to his gospel—that they indeed remained non-Jews, but, having attached themselves to the God and people of Israel, they were no longer "pagan" idolaters. Yet, their complete cessation from idolatry (in contrast to the typical experience of gentile synagogue associates) would have been Paul's (subversive) innovation of this otherwise well-known socioreligious phenomenon (in combination with their righteous status as having its locus in relationship to Jesus Christ).

Regarding proselyte conversion to normative Judaism, as pointed out in p. 26 n. 17 above, it seems to me that Paul could have readily conceived of his gentile converts to his gospel as righteous gentiles who have been gathered into the people of God, as per the eschatological fulfillment of the promises, and, *simultaneously*, as also "proselytes" to the (renewed) covenant community, who, nevertheless, fundamentally maintain a non-(normatively) Jewish subordinate identity. Their righteous status is thus inextricably connected, for Paul, to their anticipated place in the covenant (cf. Rom 4:9–11). This transformed "proselyte" status is indicated by Paul's assertions that the non-Jewish converts to his gospel were *formerly* gentiles (cf., e.g., 1 Thess 4:5; 1 Cor 5:1, 9–13; 10; 12:2)—that is, "gentiles" in the

Josephus, *J.W.* 2.201, 340–41, 409–17; 4.181, 275; 5.15–18, 562–64; *Ant.* 3.318–19; 8.116–17; 11.3–5, 87, 103, 120–32, 331–36; 12.11–18; 13.69–71, 78, 242–44; 14.110; 16.14; 18.122, 286, 288, 309; 20.195; *Ag. Ap.* 2.45, 48, 279–84; 2 Macc 3:1–3, 12, 33–39; 5:16; 9:11–18; 13:23; 3 Macc 1:9; 4 Macc 4:11–12; 2 Bar. 68:5–6; Let. Aris. 4–7; Philo, *Embassy* 157, 291–320; *Mos.* 2.17–43; Luke 7:2–5; Acts 10:1–33; 13:16–50; 16:13–14; 17:4, 11–12, 16–17; 18:4–7; John 12:20.

44. Donaldson, *Judaism and the Gentiles*, 493.

45. Ibid., 494–98. Donaldson notes the following examples: Esth 16:15–16 LXX; Wis 1:1–2; 6:9–11; Eusebius, *Praep. ev.* 13.12.6–7; Let. Aris. 16, 140; Sib. Or. 3.545–50, 624–31; 4.24–39; On Jonah 216–19; Philo, *Spec. Laws* 2.42–48; *Good Person* 62, 72–74; *Embassy* 245, 291, 294–97, 309–10, 317–20; Josephus, *Ant.* 12.22; *Ag. Ap.* 2.168, 255–57.

sense of being estranged from God's covenant people (cf. 1 Cor 6; see also Eph 2:11—3:6[46]).

Moreover, it should not be underappreciated that Paul is writing occasional letters rather than theological treatises that might articulate how, exactly, he had come to formulate his gospel vis-à-vis God's prior revelation to Israel. In such letters we should expect a great deal of his reasoning to be only implicit, and it is, then, no great surprise that when Paul is addressing issues related to the relationship of Jews and gentiles, Rom 9–11 notwithstanding, he is far more focused on the practical implications of this relationship, and not the articulation of every aspect of his scriptural reasoning that lay behind those implications (cf., e.g., Gal 4:8–9; 1 Thess 1:9–10).

Third, the servant songs in Isaiah strongly resonate with the eschatological pilgrimage tradition, and do so in a way that emphasizes the vocational dimension of God's election of Israel *on behalf of* the rest of creation—a vocation that is for Paul taken up and fulfilled by Jesus Christ, and, by extension, the body of Christ allegiants.[47] Ware remarks on the first servant song of Isa 42:

> From a traditional-historical standpoint, the depiction of the Servant in 42:1–4 draws heavily on language and imagery associated with the eschatological pilgrimage of the nations (cf. Isa 2:2–5; 51:4–5; Psalm 67:3–5 [Eng 67:2–4], 96:7–13; 98:4–9). . . . [T]hese motifs reflect traditions of conversion, and describe the salvific and illuminating activity of Yahweh on behalf of the nations.

46. Note that contrary to many readings of it, the letter to the Ephesians does *not*, in my view, establish the abolishment of the Torah, but expresses, rather, that in Christ gentiles have joined God's historical covenant people without themselves adopting full Torah submission, as per normative Jewish identity. The letter is otherwise clear that the Torah still forms a basis for covenant community praxis; cf. Eph 2:10; 5:3–5; and esp. 6:2.

47. Cf. esp. Gal 3:6–9; see also Gen 18:18; 22:18; 26:4; 28:14; Exod 19:5–6; Deut 4:5–8; 10:19; Isa 2:2–4; 11:9–10; 42:1, 6; 49:6; 52:13—53:12; Tob 13:11; 14.6; Sib. Or. 3.195; Wis 18:4; 1 En. 105:1; T. Levi 14:3–4; 1Q28b 4.27; Rom 2:17–20; 3:2. If Paul also aligned himself with the servant of YHWH, as per Isa 42:6–7, 11, and 49:1, 6 (cf. Gal 1:15–17; 2 Cor 4:4–12), this would resonate with his understanding that he along with other Jewish Christ allegiants represent the righteous remnant of Israel (cf. Rom 9:27; 11:5) who as such are fulfilling Israel's task to be "a light to the nations," particularly in view of the dawn of the eschatological age when, according to the prophets, the nations would turn in worship of Israel's God. See further here Kim, *New Perspective*, 101–12.

The verb יְחֵל ["wait"] with which the stanza closes expresses the trust-filled hope of the nations in Yahweh, and thus brings these motifs to a remarkable and climatic conclusion. Moreover, within the literary presentation of the book of Isaiah in its final form, a striking number of thematic and lexical connections link 42:1–4 to Isaiah 2:2–5, and thus portray the Servant's work as bringing about the conversion of the nations envisioned in the programmatic passage.[48]

It is abundantly clear that Paul was heavily influenced by the Isaianic servant songs, particularly the fourth song in Isa 52:13—53:12.[49] A number of scholars have asserted that the Christ hymn (or story)[50] in Phil 2:6–11 is dependent upon the fourth song as its primary source, even perhaps representing "a conscious interpretation of the passage."[51] In keeping with this observation, I contend that Paul understood the passage in the context of

48. Ware, *Mission*, 79. Ware further points out with respect to Isa 42:6: "While several alternative meanings for בְּרִית [*berît*] in this passage have been proposed, it is more likely that the word here retains its usual sense of 'covenant.' The Servant is thus depicted in this passage as the embodiment of God's redemptive covenant with all humanity. The phrase 'light to the nations' in 42:6 is clearly related, within the final composition of the book of Isaiah, to the imagery of light associated with the conversion of gentiles in Isaiah 2:2–5, 8:23b–9:1, and 51:4–5" (80–81).

49. As demonstrated by Wagner, "Heralds"; Wagner, *Herald*; Hofius, "Servant Song," 175–83; Watson, "Hermeneutics of Salvation," there is a great deal of evidence suggesting that Isaiah 53 had a significant influenced on Paul. He directly quotes from the LXX passage in Rom 10:16 and 15:21 (cf. Gal 3:2). Further, textual echoes from it are found in Paul's ὑπὲρ ἡμῶν formula (cf., e.g., 1 Thess 5:10; Rom 5:8; 8:32; Gal 3:13), his understanding of Christ's vicarious death for "our sins" (ἁμαρτιῶν ἡμῶν) (cf. Gal 1:4; 1 Cor 15:3; and similarly in Rom 4:25), as well as his language of Christ being "given up" (παρέδωκεν) (cf. Rom 4:25; 8:32; 1 Cor 11:23). Although Paul's use of this text denotes an association of the servant with Jesus Christ, surely he was well aware of the identification of the servant as Israel elsewhere in Second Isaiah (cf. Isa 44:1; 45:4; 49:3; see also 42:18–28) and was thoroughly considerate of this relationship (cf. n. 52 below).

50. Whether Phil 2:6–11 is a pre-Pauline tradition or not is irrelevant to this study; I remain uncommitted to any particular argument for or against such an understanding. Further, while I may refer to this section of the letter as a "hymn," in keeping with the majority of Philippians scholarship, I am likewise ambivalent on the question of whether the genre of 2:6–11 should even be classified as such, or whether it is better understood as prose narrative, as recently argued by Weymouth, "The Christ-Story." Even if a hymn there is surely here a storyline, and, despite some scholarly arguments favoring one intent over the other, it quite clearly functions *both* as the fundamental hope for the Philippian Christ community's salvation, and also the chief paradigm for their identity and praxis (note that discussion on this twin function of the passage is ubiquitous in the secondary literature, and the great majority of contemporary scholars recognize it accordingly).

51. Ware, *Mission*, 224; cf. the list of exemplary scholarly works in 224–25 n. 80.

Isaiah, and in light of the Christ event, along the lines of Paul D. Hanson's remarks:

> [I]t is through the Servant's humiliation and suffering that God accomplishes the redemption of God's people from bondage to sin. . . . Even that act, though, is preliminary. Israel's redemption prepares the way for God's salvation to reach the ends of the earth. For by being restored to spiritual wholeness Israel becomes the fitting instrument through which God can teach the torāh to all nations as a reliable basis for universal peace. The Servant Songs of Second Isaiah thus complete the picture in the second chapter of Isaiah of the nations streaming to Zion to learn God's way as the basis for an alternative to war. God has now appointed the teacher who will instruct the nations in this path to universal harmony. The teacher is the Servant.[52]

Fourth, beyond the lack of explicit citations, another common objection to the importance of the eschatological pilgrimage tradition in Paul is because of his supposed reversal in Rom 11 of the salvation-historical order, in which the nations' salvation is predicated upon Israel's prior restoration.[53] This objection is based upon a misunderstanding of the passage. As suggested in p. 33 n. 32 above, Paul does not intend here to forecast a future redemptive event for Israel only after that of the nations, but rather to demonstrate that Israel's partial hardening has paradoxically opened up a space of time prior to the eschaton and final judgment for the salvation of gentiles—as well as more Jews—and that the redemption of both groups are interdependent upon one another, as per the mysterious process that Paul

---

52. Hanson, *Isaiah 40–66*, 166. In view of the "many nations" referred to in the opening of the fourth song in Isa 52:15, Ware, *Mission*, 86, suggests that "the depiction of 'nations' and 'kings' beholding the glory of Yahweh belongs to the eschatological pilgrimage tradition (Isa 60:3, 10, 11, 16; Ps 47:8–9; 102:15–16; 102:22; 138:4–5; cf. Ps 22:27–28; 66:1–4). Moreover, from a literary standpoint the phrase 'many nations' (גוֹיִם רַבִּים), within the final composition of the book of Isaiah, recalls the first two Servant passages (42:6; 49:6), as well as the eschatological pilgrimage oracle in Isaiah 2:2–5 (עַמִּים רַבִּים)." See also esp. Seitz, *Isaiah 40–66*, 462: "The dual mission of the servant—restoration of the survivors of Israel and as 'Israel,' a light to the nations (49:6)—is here confessed . . . as fully accomplished . . . [I]n this poem the servants come to acknowledge the life and death of the servant, as an individual, as expiatory for themselves. But because the servant, as an individual, has understood himself as the embodiment of 'Israel, in whom I will be glorified' (49:3), especially with a vocation to the nations, the poem functions at yet another level. The individual servant's suffering and death are Israel's on behalf of the other nations."

53. So Donaldson, "Paul within Judaism," 288–93.

outlines in vv. 7–24, and summarizes in vv. 30–32.[54] The passage, then, presupposes that Israel's restoration has *already* been inaugurated in Christ's resurrection (cf. esp. Rom 11:1–5), and this, in turn, makes possible the consequent salvation of the gentiles alongside the Jews all the way up to Jesus Christ's return as Lord and Savior, who will "make all things subject to himself" (Phil 3:21).[55]

Finally, Paul's exclamation in Phil 2:10–11, based on Isa 45:23, "that at the name of Jesus every knee should bend, in heaven and on earth and under the earth, and every tongue should confess that Jesus Christ is Lord, to the glory of God the Father" assumes the eschatological pilgrimage tradition that forms the greater context of the Isaiah passage, which Paul surely knew well. Ware asserts:

54. For a detailed analysis of Rom 11, see Zoccali, "'All Israel'"; and Zoccali, *Whom God Has Called*, 91–117. The "mystery" (μυστήριον) that Paul reveals in vv. 25–26 is what he has just explained in vv. 7–24, and then summarizes in vv. 30–32: Israel's stumbling/hardening/disobedience allows for the gentile mission, and the gentile mission will spur Israel to jealousy, resulting in their salvation as well. Thus, God's promise to save Israel happens precisely "in this way" (οὕτως), that is, as a paradoxical result of their partial hardening (rather than immediate judgment), and thus *interdependence* with the salvation of the other nations. For the sake, then, of *both* Israel and the other nations, Paul conceives of this phenomenon of "partial hardening" (πώρωσις ἀπὸ μέρους τῷ Ἰσραὴλ) as enduring "until" (ἄχρι οὗ) the end of the age, when the "fullness of the gentiles arrives" (πλήρωμα τῶν ἐθνῶν εἰσέλθῃ), and thus both the other nations and "all Israel" (πᾶς Ἰσραὴλ) are once and for all saved through the gospel of Jesus Christ in fulfillment of the covenant, as God had promised (vv. 26–28) (cf. p. 48 n. 69 below).

55. I believe it is important here to differentiate between Paul's perspective formed in light of an imminent Parousia, and the historical reality that such an event did not occur in the first-century. I have argued that the partial hardening is an intensification of a chosen course not to embrace the Christ, which is, nevertheless, humanly surmountable (cf. 2 Cor 3:14–16). If this hardening is viewed primarily in negative terms (however paradoxically and ultimately beneficial to Israel), as taking the place of immediate judgment, and in order to bring about the salvation of the nations alongside an ever-increasing body of Jews faithful to Jesus Christ, then—in terms of a contemporary Christian theology—it might be conceived of as something exhausted in the events surrounding the destruction of the Jerusalem Temple in 70 CE—an event imbued by the Gospel writers (and the author of Revelation, in my opinion) with theological import (cf. Mark 13, Matt 24, Luke 21, Rev 6–19). Alternatively, if one understands the partial hardening as having a more thoroughly positive dimension, in the sense of protection or preservation, and in anticipation of eventual healing, as per the argument of Nanos, "'Callused,'" 52–73, then the affirmation of such a continued state for the Jewish people might find a constructive place in contemporary Christian theology. Of course, this discussion must also contend with the relationship between the first-century group contemporaneous with Paul, and modern Jewish groups (including the intervening history of the Jewish people) in light of the evolution of the socioreligious boundaries that demarcate Jewish identity.

The conversion of the nations elsewhere in Isaiah ... is an expectation of the future (2:2–5; 11:9–10; 51:4–5; 55:5), and 45:18–25 envisions the response of the nations to Yahweh's coming redemption of his people through a new Exodus (44:24—45:22). In the wider literary context, the invitation to conversion in 45:22 does not function as an actual appeal to gentiles, but rather, like the invitations to praise and worship Yahweh addressed to gentiles in the Psalms (e.g. 66:4; 67:4–6; 96:1–2, 7–10; 98:4–6), anticipates the inauguration of Yahweh's universal reign, when the nations will turn to the God of Jacob (cf. 2:3; 51:4–5; Ps 66:1–8; 67:1–7; 86:9; 102:15–16, 21–22).[56]

The Christ allegiant gentiles in Philippi, as members of the nations living in the eschatological age, in embracing Paul's gospel are envisaged by him as those anticipated throughout Isaiah, and similarly understood elsewhere in the relevant Jewish literature. Namely, they are the recipients of God's redemptive work consequent to Israel's restoration, whereby the other nations of the earth would be brought into the (holy) people of God, in fulfillment of the promises to Abraham of a multiethnic family (cf. Rom 4; Gal 3).[57]

56. Ware, *Mission*, 77.

57. Cf. my treatments of Rom 4 and Gal 3 in Zoccali, "Children of Abraham," 253–71, and "What's the Problem with the Law?" respectively. Though I do not read Paul according to the sort of two-covenant soteriology she employs, I largely agree with the conclusion of Johnson Hodge, *If Sons*, 79–91, that, for Paul, Christ allegiants find their identity *in* Abraham by being *in* Christ, and that he creatively reads Gen 15:6 and 12:3, such that he connects Abraham's response of faithfulness to God's promises to the ultimate fulfillment of those promises found in the multiethnic Christ community (cf. Gal 3:7–8, 16, 19, 26–29; Rom 4:16–17). Observing the similarity between Rom 4:13 and Sir 44:19–21, she comments: "both entail the fertility of Abraham, the inclusion of the gentiles in his progeny, and the ultimate inheritance of the earth for his descendents. This passage illustrates a point that is also true for Paul: the blessing and incorporation of the gentiles are necessary parts of this particular understanding of God's promise. The author of the Wisdom of Sirach sees an implicit connection between the ancestor Abraham (the 'father of many nations'), the incorporation of the gentiles, and universal inheritance. This same connection forms the basis of Paul's argument in Romans 4" (188).

However, in contradistinction to Johnson Hodge, and in answer to the final objection to the eschatological pilgrimage tradition in Paul put forward by Donaldson, "Paul within Judaism," 293–98, I contend that, for Paul, covenant identity has been transformed around Christ (as comparable to Donaldson's own view on the question). Because of this, Paul is not content to simply argue "that Christ was the means by which the promises made to Abraham—that he would the 'father of a multitude of *ethnē*' [nations] and that 'by [his] seed (*sperma*) all the nations of the earth shall gain blessing for themselves' (LXX Gen. 22:18; also 26:4)—was being fulfilled," as Donaldson points out. Yet,

Implications for a Non-Supersessionist Paul

There are at least four interrelated implications that stem from Paul's (a) understanding of the seminal basis of covenant identity, (b) conviction regarding covenant and creation renewal, and (c) appropriation of the eschatological pilgrimage tradition. First, though the traditional markers of covenant identity that also define normative Jewish identity have been transformed in the coming of Christ, such markers were never, for Paul, the fundamental basis of covenant membership in the first place, and do not ultimately demarcate God's holy ones. This basis has always been God's faithfulness toward God's people, which then called for the appropriate response of faithfulness from God's people toward God. Thus, it is only the specific content of this faithful response that has changed as a result of the climatic manifestation of God's ḥesed in Christ's death and resurrection; it has become allegiance to Jesus Christ (Phil 2:9–11).

But, secondly, the Christ event is not an arbitrary "apocalyptic" event that is detached from, extrinsic to, and/or runs roughshod over, Israel's scriptural traditions. Rather, for Paul, God's act in Christ is the very mechanism through which God is fulfilling God's promises to God's people. Accordingly, the Philippian Christ allegiants are among the very ones who have had Torah written on their hearts via the Spirit (cf., e.g., Rom 2:15, 29; 2 Cor 3:3). God's revealed will in Torah is not done away with in Christ, as it is the very substance of the renewed creation that Paul explicitly envisions as having been inaugurated in Christ's resurrection from the dead, and the grounds, then, for the inheritance of God's holy people, Abraham's family, the children of God (cf. esp. Rom 8:1–39; 9:7–8, 23–26; p. 32 n. 30 above).[58] Paul's conviction in this respect is made quite clear in Phil 1:6 and 3:21:

Donaldson goes on to assert that, "[i]nstead, he makes an exegetical move that lands him on untenable ground. He attempts to square the covenantal circle by applying to uncircumcised *ethnē* an identifier to which non-Jews were not entitled unless they ceased to be *ethnē* and became proselytes" (297). However, as I have argued elsewhere and above, Paul was perfectly capable of creatively combining elements of different traditions, and do so in a fully coherent and reasonable fashion. As Donaldson would surely agree, it is not only legitimate, but, in my view, necessary to allow for some degree of innovation on Paul's part (as with other contemporaneous Jewish groups) that would not itself indicate a departure from Judaism. Indeed, there is sufficient continuity between Paul's view and others found in late Second Temple Judaism to suggest that Paul stands *within* the greater Jewish tradition (in all its various orientations)—certainly so from his own perspective (cf. Rom 3:31), and that of most of the converts to his gospel.

58. Though all people living at the time were, of course, subject to the previous dispensation, only Israelites/Jews participated in the covenant; gentiles were ἀνόμως (cf.

> I am confident of this, that the one who began a good work in you will bring it to completion by the day of Jesus Christ. . . . He will transform the body of our humiliation that it may be conformed to the body of his glory, by the power that also enables him to make all things subject to himself.

Paul is emphatic here that the return of Christ will usher in the full consummation of this universal transformation, in which Christ allegiants, restored in the image of their God, and thus having become like Christ (cf. Phil 2:6; see also esp. Col 1:15–20), will be finally equipped—that is, morally perfected—in order to engage in the task of faithful dominion as God's true multiethnic humanity, experiencing the fullness of life that God intended in the original act of creation, and the calling of Israel in particular.[59]

Rom 2:12). Thus, it is Israelites/Jews who were specifically "under Torah," as per the identification of God's son in Gal 4:5 (a position still occupied, for Paul, by non-Christ allegiant Jews, in contrast to non-Christ allegiant gentiles, whom he designates as ἄνομος in 1 Cor 9:21). This is notwithstanding the fact that Paul addresses his gentile audience as currently members of the covenant/God's (holy) people who, though entering in at the time and as a result of the eschatological fulfillment of the promises, stand, alongside Christ-allegiant Jews, in continuity with God's people of any time/dispensation. Thus, Paul can say to the Galatian and Roman Christ allegiants that they are not "under Torah" (Gal 5:18; Rom 6:14) because they live in the dispensation of Christ and the coming of the Spirit (cf. Gal 3:21–29; Rom 10:4), though he clearly expects them to live in accordance with Torah-based ethics; to do otherwise would mean jeopardizing their part in the kingdom of God (cf. Gal 5:16–26; 1 Cor 6:9–11; see further pp. 49–52 below). As suggested above, I would additionally point out here that since the Torah serves to explicate and convict of sin, in the eschatological age, outside of Christ, it can only ultimately function as an instrument of God's wrath (cf. esp. Rom 4:15).

59. Cf., e.g., Gal 3:26–27; 4:19; 5:5, 21b; Rom 5:17; 8:18–30; 1 Cor 6:2; 15:20–28, 50–58; 2 Cor 3:18; see also Col 3:1–14. The radical "renewedness" of the eschatological age and concomitant restoration of human identity, effected by the Spirit (as per the very promises of covenant and creation renewal), and already inaugurated within the present order by virtue of Christ's resurrection (cf. esp. 2 Cor 1:20–22; 5:5; see also Eph 1:13–14), is characterized by Paul in terms of a new birth, or specifically as "sonship/adoption" (υἱοθεσία). Paul utilizes "birthing" language in relation to the coming eschatological age *in toto*, as well as to Christ allegiants in particular (cf. Rom 8:22–23; Gal 4:19, 22–31; see also elsewhere in the New Testament: John 1:12–13; 3:3–10; Jas 1:18; 1 Pet 1:3, 23; 1 John 2:29). The idea of a new birth seems to lie behind Paul's discourse in Rom 4, where Paul refers to Christ allegiants as "those [born] from the faithfulness of Abraham" (τῷ ἐκ πίστεως Ἀβραάμ) (4:16; n. 57 above; see further Zoccali, "'Children of Abraham'"). In keeping with this general "birthing" language, Paul utilizes the term sonship/adoption in reference to those having joined the Christ movement (cf. Gal 4:1–7 [v. 5]; Rom 8:12–17 [v. 15]; 9:4; see also Eph 1:5; and further Zoccali, *Whom God Has Called*, 80–81, esp. n. 51). The salvific conception of new birth is perhaps implicit, moreover, in the ascription of himself as a father to his gospel converts at Corinth, in as much as the gospel is mediated through his apostleship (cf. 1 Cor 4:15; see also 1 Thess 2:7, 11). It

Excursus: Christ Allegiants' Pneumatic Existence—A Transformation Necessary for Jews and Gentiles Alike

Building especially upon the work of Stanley K. Stowers,[60] Matthew Thiessen has suggested that Paul's conception of the Spirit (πνεῦμα | *pneuma*) is shaped by the Stoic idea of *krasis* (κρᾶσις), which involves a complete interpenetration of one substance with another, and which further corresponds to the Stoic theory of *pneuma* as "[b]eing an extremely fine and rarified material substance . . . [that] can interpenetrate other coarser substances without either altering them or being altered by them."[61] Thiessen thus suggests that "it is this sort of peculiar mixture that shapes Paul's thinking about the reception of the *pneuma* in the human body. . . . The presence of the *pneuma* means that believers share the very substance of Christ and therefore share the shape of his life, death, and resurrection."[62] Paul's participatory theology does not function, then, on the level of mere metaphor for him, but is predicated, rather, upon "substantial ontology."[63]

This new pneumatic existence is not merely the means by which gentiles become children of Abraham/the promise—i.e., a form of identity hybridity Thiessen calls "gentile-Abrahamic son," according to which gentile Christ allegiants remain fully gentile while also becoming fully Abrahamic sons; a phenomenon he likens to the hypostatic union of Christ's human and divine identities in later Christian theology[64]—but it is also, contra Thiessen,[65] how *all* human beings, Jews *and* gentiles, become *truly human*— "bear[ing] the image of the man from heaven" (1 Cor 15;49), Jesus Christ, "the last Adam" (1 Cor 15:45a), and who will thereby exercise their faithful

---

is, in any case, clearly indicative of the various (contextually determined) superordinate identity categories he ascribes to Jewish and gentile Christ allegiants of "children of God/ Abraham/promise/light/the day" (Phil 2:15; Rom 8:14, 16, 17, 19, 21; 9:7–8, 26; Gal 3:26; 4:28; 1 Thess 5:5; Eph 5:1, 8; see also Ps. Sol. 18; and elsewhere in the New Testament: Matt 3:9; 5:9, 45; Luke 3:8; 6:35; 16:8; 20:36; John 1:12; 8:39; 11:52; 12:36; Heb 12:7–8; 1 John 3:1–2, 10; 5:2, 19; Rev 21:7), as well as the "household of faithfulness" (Gal 6:10; cf. Phil 1:27).

60. Stowers, "'Participation,'" 352–71.

61. Thiessen, *Gentile Problem*, 112.

62. Ibid., 112, 114.

63. Ibid., 116.

64. Ibid., 121–22.

65. Ibid., 148–50.

dominion on earth.[66] The "already/not" character of this transformation is indicated by Paul in Rom 6–8:

> Just as Christ was raised from the dead by the glory of the Father, so we too might walk in newness of life. For if we have been united with him in a death like his, we will certainly be united with him in a resurrection like his. (6:4–5)

> [W]e ourselves, who have the first fruits of the Spirit groan inwardly while we await for sonship/adoption, the redemption of our bodies. (8:23)

As argued above, Abraham's family is and always was fundamentally demarcated by God's covenant faithfulness to God's people, as then met by the appropriate response of human faithfulness to God, *rather than mere ethnic affiliation.*[67] And both divine and human faithfulness culminate in the eschaton, upon sin and death's final defeat, when the kingdom of God is manifest, and "God may be all to all" (1 Cor 15:28). Yet, "For as all die in Adam . . . all will be made alive *in Christ*" (1 Cor 15:22), who, through his own death and resurrection, "became a life-giving spirit" (1 Cor 15:45b; cf. Rom 5:9–21; 7:4–6). While both Thiessen and Stowers do hold that Paul believes Jews—like gentiles—need to accept the gospel of Jesus Christ and receive the Spirit, they assert that Paul does not really explicate what the problem is for Jews that requires the gospel.[68] It is here that both Thiessen and Stowers nevertheless share in the mistake of two-covenant soteriology in that they orient the significance of the Christ event for Paul in nearly the exact opposite way from which he understands it. In contradistinction to Thiessen's and Stower's assertion, I suggest that Paul is actually quite clear: Israel's promised and hoped for redemption is found in Jesus Christ, and it is *through Israel's redemption that the whole world is ultimately saved*:

> Out of Zion will come the Deliverer; he will banish ungodliness from Jacob. And this is my covenant with them, when I take away their sins (Rom 11:26–27 [quoting Isa 59:20–21; 27:9]).[69]

---

66. *Not* in heaven, as suggested by Thiessen, *Gentile Problem*, 152; see further on this point below.

67. Cf. esp. Rom 9:6–26; see also Num 15:30–31; Matt 3:7–10; Luke 3:7–9.

68. Thiessen, *Gentile Problem*, 120; Stowers, *Rereading of Romans*, 205.

69. Cf. 1 Cor 15:3; see also, e.g., Mark 1:14–15; Matt 1:21–23; 4:17; Luke 1:67–79; 4:17–21. As I have argued in *Whom God Has Called*, Paul suggests in no uncertain terms that it is only in Christ that Israel becomes *truly Israel* (cf. esp. Rom 9:6–8). Additionally, it should be pointed out that the fundamental nature of Israel's redemption—that it is

Third, as is widely recognized, Paul's moral admonition to the communities he addresses in his letters are derived from the Torah.[70] He demonstrates no reservation in requiring from Christ-followers strict obedience to God as inextricable from their salvation.[71] Obedience to God's commands is not optional in Paul's thought anymore than it is/was for other Jews, and remains equally critical to one's place among God's people in his gospel (cf. Phil 2:5–8, 12–15; Gal 6:7–8). Accordingly, Paul exhorts the Philippians in 2:12 to obey God whether or not Paul is present with them.[72] Indeed, the matter of redemption for Paul is not merely how God deals with sins having been committed (cf. Rom 3:25; 1 Cor 15:3), but ultimately how God has provided the means through which sin's power is once and for all broken,

---

integral to the redemption of the rest of the world—is *not* in conflict with Paul's claim that Israel's stumbling/partial hardening/disobedience has opened up a span of time to allow for the inclusion of the nations among God's people. Rather, it is the inauguration of Israel's salvation, as manifest in the faithful remnant of whom Paul is one (Rom 11:1–5), which initiates the proclamation of the gospel to the other nations. And, further, it is the consummation of Israel's salvation that signals the full arrival of the age to come (cf. Rom 11:15). Thus, as pointed out above (p. 43 n. 54), while Paul understands a salvific interdependence between Israel and nations (cf. Rom 11:30–32), the entire phenomenon of redemption hangs in the first place on the fulfillment of the promises of God to save Israel, in as much as Israel was God's chosen agent to bring blessing to the rest of the world (cf. Gal 3:8, 14)—ultimately accomplished through its Messiah, Jesus (cf. Rom 1:1–4, 16; 3:1–2; 9:5; 15:8–9).

70. Cf., e.g., Gal 5:6, 13—6:10; Rom 7:12; 8:4–11; 12:9–21; 13:8–10; 1 Cor 6:9–20; 7:19; 2 Cor 12:20—13:7; 1 Thess 4:1–7; see also Col 3:5, 10; Eph 5:11, 20; 6:11, 2.

71. Cf., e.g., Phil 2:12–13; 4:9; Rom 2:6–11; 6; 14:10–12; 1 Cor 4:1–5; 9:24–27; 11:27–32; 15:58; 2 Cor 5:10; 1 Thess 2:12; see also Eph 2:10. Certainly, commands are only given with the logical expectation that they *should* be obeyed, and in light of the fact that such instruction may not otherwise be followed. Yet, it has been suggested that Paul differentiates an underlying disposition of faith (i.e., belief) from faithful actions, with the former understood as fundamental to the gospel in contradistinction to the latter; cf. esp. Watson, *Hermeneutics of Faith*, 157–63 (however, Watson is also careful to remark: "there is no faith without faithfulness" [161]). I find such a proposal to be entirely unnecessary and quite misleading for rightly understanding Pauline theology.

72. The NRSV mistakenly translates Phil 2:12: "as you have always obeyed me," referring to Paul, which is not what the text says. Rather, Paul states, "as you have always obeyed." The obedience in question is obedience *to God*, as it is the case with Jesus Christ in 2:8, and as made explicit in v. 13: "For it is God who is at work in you, enabling you both to will and to work for his good pleasure." While God's commands were mediated through Paul to the community, they do not originate with him (cf. Paul's readiness to differentiate his own judgment from the "command of the Lord" in 1 Cor 7:25). Contra Marchal, *Hierarchy*, 136–38, who suggests that Paul intentionally blurs the distinction between himself and God in an effort to assert his incontestable authority over the community.

thus allowing for the very sort of *moral perfection ultimately indicative of what it means to be a member of God's holy people*—a phenomenon that is for Paul caught between the "already" of Christ's resurrection and the coming of the Spirit, and the "not yet" of the general resurrection of the dead, when sin and death's defeat will be consummated.[73] This eschatological tension is articulated by Paul in Phil 3:10–14:

> I want to know Christ and the power of his resurrection and the sharing of his sufferings by becoming like him in his death, if somehow I may attain the resurrection from the dead. Not that I have already obtained this or have already reached the goal; but I press on to make it my own, because Christ Jesus has made me his own. Beloved, I do not consider that I have made it my own; but this one thing I do: forgetting what lies behind and straining forward to what lies ahead, I press on toward the goal for the prize of the heavenly call of God in Christ Jesus.

In short, as he indicates here, *perfect obedience is not an obstacle Paul's gospel overcomes, but a goal that is thereby obtained.* This is why he can exhort the Philippians to "be blameless and innocent, children of God without blemish" (Phil 2:14), pray that "in the day of Christ [they] may be pure and blameless, having been filled with the fruit of righteousness" (Phil 1:10–11), and further call them to "live [their] life in manner worthy of the gospel of Christ . . . contending in one accord for the faithfulness (πίστει) of the gospel" (Phil 1:27). On this last point, a far more accurate translation of πίστις (*pistis*) and its cognates throughout the Pauline corpus, including here in Philippians (1:25, 27, 29; 2:17; 3:9[74]), should necessarily reflect this idea of "faithfulness," "fidelity," or "allegiance," rather than mere "faith" or "belief." *Both* acceptance of and life in Christ are *never* cast by Paul in terms of mere intellectual assent, or as an abstract disposition, as connoted by the latter English terms, but *always* ultimately in terms of action and obedience (at least in principle, and to the extent possible), in keeping with the meaning of the equivalent Hebrew term אמנה (*ĕmūnâ*) (cf., e.g., Hab 2:4; see further below).[75] Philippians 2:10–11 makes it quite clear that God's Christ

73. Cf., e.g., Rom 11:26–27; 6:5–14; 8:2–14; 1 Cor 15:20–28, 50–58; Gal 5:5; see also Col 1:21–22; 3:5–10; Eph 4:22–24.

74. Philippians 3:9 evokes the infamous *"pistis Christou"* debate. See ch. 4 below for my treatment of this passage.

75. For the semantic range of πίστις, and its almost certain meaning for Christ allegiants of faithfulness, fidelity, or allegiance (to God/Christ) in Paul, see Campbell, *Quest*, 178–88. Contra, e.g., Dunn, "What's Right," 221, who remarks that Paul's supposed

demands full and unequivocal allegiance, not simply intellectual agreement
that Jesus is risen Lord (see similarly, e.g., Jas 2:14–26).[76]

However, fourthly, the way in which the Torah is to be obeyed is not
univocal, as Paul unmistakably suggests in Rom 2:25–29; 4:11–12, 16;[77] and
1 Cor 7:17–20.[78] All covenant members must submit (as empowered by the
Spirit) to the overarching ethical vision of Torah—that is, the doing of justice and righteousness, which are inextricable to the commandment regarding love of neighbor (Lev 19:18). This Jew *and* gentile Torah-based praxis,
which is fulfilled in the (re)new(-ed) covenant and creation, is referred to
by Paul as "Christ's Torah" in his letters to the Galatians and Corinthians

objection to his "fellow Jewish believers . . . was that their 'faith' elided too readily and
quickly into 'faithfulness.'"

76. Contrary to much discussion in both scholarly and lay circles, there is in actuality
no disagreement between the canonical James and Paul, once their respective contexts
are fully appreciated (see further on this point esp. ch. 4 below). As Paul clearly points
out in Rom 2:6–11: "For [God] will repay according to each one's deeds: to those who by
patiently doing good seek for glory and honor and immortality, he will give eternal life;
while for those who are self-seeking and who obey not the truth but wickedness, there
will be wrath and fury. There will be anguish and distress for everyone who does evil,
the Jew first and also the Greek, but glory and honor and peace for everyone who does
good, the Jew first and also the Greek. For God shows no partiality" (cf. Jas 2:8–26; Rom
14:10–12; 2 Cor 5:10; Gal 6:7–10; see also Eph 2:10; p. 34 n. 34; p. 49 nn. 70, 71 above).

77. For Jews in Christ, full Torah submission continues to function as an appropriate
expression of ethnic identity and faithfulness towards God. Paul therefore refers to this
subgroup in Rom 4:16 as "those [born] from the Torah" (τῷ ἐκ τοῦ νόμου). The superordinate group, which consists of both Jews and gentiles, is referred to here as "those
[born] from the faithfulness of Abraham" (τῷ ἐκ πίστεως Ἀβραάμ), that is, the multiethnic family originally promised to Abraham (Rom 4:17)—a promise to which Abraham
responded in faithfulness (4:18–22), and which finds its ultimate fulfillment, for Paul, in
the Christ community (cf. p. 44 n. 57; p. 46 n. 59 above).

78. As Zetterholm, "Assumptions," 83–84, points out, the matter of Torah observance
is not and had never been monolithically understood within the Jewish tradition; that is,
what constitutes one's faithfulness to the Torah receives different answers among different Jewish groups. She explains: "Jewish law is more than just detailed prescriptions or
prohibitions concerning specific situations. . . . The foundation of Jewish law is the belief
in a moral God; thus, the law is interpreted and shaped by moral considerations. If a specific law is understood to violate the moral principles of the Torah, it may be necessary in
certain circumstances to suspend that particular law in order to preserve and safeguard
the Torah. . . . The idea that suspension of the Torah in the sense of a particular law may
serve to preserve the Torah in the sense of Jewish law as a whole draws attention to the
potential confusion caused by the fact that the word *Torah* has several different meanings. Although it can be used in the sense of particular laws, the word *Torah* signifies a
broader and more nuanced concept that in Hebrew refers to 'instruction,' 'teaching,' or
'guidance.'"

Reading Philippians after Supersessionism

(Gal 6:2; 1 Cor 9:21; cf. Rom 3:27).[79] The nonnegotiable commitment of the multiethnic Christ community to Christ's Torah is indicated in 1 Cor 7:19:

> Circumcision is nothing and uncircumcision is nothing, but keeping the commandments of God (is everything) (cf. Gal 6:15; p. 105 n. 52 below).

Yet, Paul naturally expects Jewish Christ allegiants to continue in full Torah submission, which therefore includes those specific laws that continue to distinguish Jewish from gentile identity, preeminently circumcision, and also, e.g., kashrut, and Sabbath observance.[80] He writes in 1 Cor 7:17, 20:

> Let each of you lead the life that the Lord has assigned you—as God has called you. This is my rule in all the *ekklēsiais.* . . . Let each of you remain in the calling in which one was called.

In all, as explicitly demonstrated in Rom 1:16; 2:25; 3:30; 4:12; 9:24; 11:11–32; 15:8–12; 1 Cor 1:23–24; and 7:17–20, Paul continues to differentiate between Jews and gentiles within the Christ movement, and this differentiation makes best sense in terms of the eschatological pilgrimage tradition that sees the nations qua nations joining a restored Israel in the eschaton.[81]

79. Cf. esp. Gal 5:6, 13–14; Rom 8:4–9; 13:8–10; see also Mic 6:8; Amos 5:21–25; Isa 1:17; 5:7; 42:1–9; 56:1; Jer 7:5–7; Mark 12:28–34; Matt 22:36–40; 23:23–24; Luke 10:25–28; 11:42.

80. Accordingly, normative Jewish identity remains a salient subordinate identity in Christ, and, outside of full submission, the Torah functions as a basis for covenant praxis in a way that is applicable to gentile Christ allegiants. Some would protest this view on the grounds that Rom 7 suggests Christ allegiants are no longer to submit to the Torah. However, as made quite explicit in Rom 8:1–2, the captivity to which Paul refers in Rom 7:6 (κατειχόμεθα) does not point to the Torah in an absolute sense, but to its role in condemnation (cf. Rom 7:10–11; 3:19–20). In view here is sin and death, which, while made manifest by the Torah (cf. Rom 7:7, 13; 5:20), could not be overcome by it (cf. Rom 7:14–24). The defeat of these powers (anticipated by the Torah) has once and for all been accomplished through Christ. It is the dispensation of Torah—the era of the old covenant and creation co-opted by the power of sin—from which Christ allegiants are "discharged" (cf. Gal 3:21–23; 4:4–5; 5:1, 13–18; Rom 6:12–14). They are *not* said to be released from the practice of Torah in the (re)new(ed) covenant and creation inaugurated by Christ—either in terms of a full submission for Jews, or a "limited" submission for gentiles (cf. p. 34 n. 34; pp. 49–51 nn. 70, 71, 76 77 above; n. 81 below).

81. As noted above (pp. 39–40), the necessity of gentiles in Christ to, in some sense, retain their original ethnicity is not withstanding Paul's assertion in 1 Cor 12:2, where he ostensibly refers to his addressees as *former* gentiles (cf. 1 Thess 4:5; 1 Cor 5:1, 9–13; 10). For Paul, all existing social identities, especially non-Jewish identities, are *transformed* in Christ, and no longer identical to what they were before. However, such identities are still

When these four elements are taken together it becomes clear how Paul can refer to the gentile Philippian Christ allegiants as holy ones, *without* dissolving the distinguishable social identities of gentile and Jew. "Holy ones" thus functions as a superordinate identity. This identity is the equivalent of other (contextually determined) descriptors for Christ allegiants, such as "children of God" (Phil 2:15; Rom 8:19; 9:8, 26; Gal 3:26), "children of Abraham" (Gal 3:7, 23–29; Rom 4; 9:7), "the household of faithfulness" (οἰκείους τῆς πίστεως) (Gal 6:10; cf. Phil 1:27), and "the *ekklēsia*/Israel of God" (Gal 1:13; 6:16), which allow for the continuation of subordinate identities found therein.[82] As being the recipients of—even representing in

fundamentally preserved within the Christ community (cf. 1 Cor 1:23–24; 7:17–20; Rom 9:24). Accordingly, Paul's gentile converts to the Christ movement, while still members of the "nations," are no longer "pagan" idolaters (cf., e.g., 1 Cor 6). They have been brought into the Jewish symbolic universe, and, without becoming Jews, have adopted a largely Jewish lifestyle; though I do not follow all of their respective observations, on this point see recently Nanos, "Paul's Non-Jews," 26–53; Fredriksen, "'Law-Free' Apostle?" 637–50. As argued here, these gentile Christ allegiants are thus representative of the righteous gentiles who, as prophesied in Scripture, would join a restored Israel in the worship of the One God (cf. esp. Rom 3:29–31; 15:8–12). In Paul's theology, this means that they are also members of the (re)new(ed) covenant and creation, and in this sense part of the "Israel of God" (Gal 6:16; cf. 1:13; see also Rom 2:29; for Paul's fluid use of the identity category of "Israel" see Zoccali, *Whom God Has Called*).

82. While I do not follow all of her conclusions, Ehrensperger, "Saints," 99–100, points out that the underlying concern in Rom 14 is "the impact [that the] food-related behavior of some Christ-followers has on others (and thus on the holiness of the community)." Rather than making "revolutionary" assertions that seek to undermine, and ultimately dissolve, Jewish-specific Torah ordinances, in Rom 14:14, 20 Paul is drawing upon standard Jewish notions regarding the holy/profane and pure/impure that do *not* understand these categories as representing ontological realities. Foods are determined to be impure, then, *not because they are intrinsically so*, but because God has determined them to be so for his people, Israel, even if not for the other nations. Moreover, the "nations in this [standard Jewish] perception are 'profane' because they are not part of God's covenant with his people and thus not 'holy', but . . . that in and of itself does not render them at fault and it certainly does not render them impure. . . . From a Jewish perspective Gentiles are 'profane', but they are not inherently 'impure'. Non-observance of food laws, and laws that are summarized as 'ritual laws', do not render Gentiles impure, since these are not meant for them. Gentiles become impure, as likewise do Jews, through immoral deeds, with idolatry at the centre of the problem, as Rom. 1.18–32 demonstrates." Accordingly, Ehrensperger rightly locates Paul's presupposition in this discourse not in the discontinuation of the Jew and gentile distinction vis-à-vis certain Torah ordinances, but that "[i]n Christ [gentiles] were now morally pure. As such, through being in Christ, there were now in a state in which they could come close to the realm of the holy without risk. . . . Evidence for this change of status is that they have turned away from idols and immoral actions" (103; cf. Rom 12). She importantly concludes: "This messianic community, which in its internal diversity lives in anticipation of the world

themselves—God's *ḥesed*, in Christ, both Israel and the ingathered nations have experienced covenant and creation renewal, and as such are together called and equipped to fulfill Israel's/humanity's vocation to bring blessing to the other—"shining like stars in the world," and holding forth the word of life" (Phil 2:15–16; cf. esp. 2 Cor 5:17–21; p. 31 n. 29; p. 40 n. 47 above).[83]

The following two chapters will investigate how the conclusions drawn here inform Paul's rhetoric in Phil 3, which, as discussed in chapter 1, has been traditionally understood in supersessionist fashion.

---

to come, is supposed to be holy, to live a life in holiness. Purity is an issue when one enters the realm of the holy, but it is an issue in different ways for people who are and remain different. Thus, the holiness of the community is under threat of being profaned not by food and drink, nor by the food laws for that matter, but by actions that harm the 'brother for whom Christ died'. Such actions render the doer impure and this defilement threatens the holiness of the community of saints. This is the focus of Paul's argument in 14.1—15.13" (109).

83. Cf. Ware, *Mission*, for this translation, and concomitant argument that Paul expected the Philippian community to engage in the gospel mission in response to the threat of persecution and suffering. See also on this matter Michael Gorman, *Becoming the Gospel*, 106–41.

3

"Rejoice, O Gentiles, with His People"
Paul's Intra-Jewish Rhetoric in Philippians 3, Part I[1]

> As for the remainder, my brothers and sisters, rejoice in the Lord,
> to write the same things to you is not a problem for me, and for
> you it is a safeguard . . . . (Phil 3:1)

THE ISSUE OF JEWISH identity in relation to the Christ movement is particularly pertinent to Phil 3. Contemporary scholars have largely understood Phil 3:1–9[2] as representing, at least in some respect, an anti-Jewish polemic, in which Judaism is presented as the necessary foil to Paul's "Christian" claims. It is commonly asserted that the "opponents" to whom Paul refers in 3:2[3] are so-called "Judaizers,"[4] or "Jewish Christian" missionaries, whose modus operandi was "dogging" Paul's own missionary efforts,[5] infiltrat-

1. Portions of this and the next chapter are taken with permission from Zoccali, "Rejoice" (author's revised version, ATLA electronic database).

2. The following will assume the literary unity of the letter; arguments in favor of this conclusion are ubiquitous in the secondary literature, with few recent dissenters; e.g., Reumann, *Philippians.*

3. In question is whether those referred to here are identifiable as those oppositional forces alluded to elsewhere in the letter: 1:15, 17, 28; 2:21. While there is a clear commonality in that all individuals/groups mentioned oppose in some way the Christ community (at least from Paul's perspective), I nevertheless do *not* think that the same specific group is being referred to in these various sections of the letter; see further below.

4. I find the continued use of the term "Judaizers" to describe Jewish Christ-allegiant missionaries who seek to persuade gentile Christ allegiants to be circumcised and follow other Jewish customs to be somewhat baffling, as the term can only rightly refer to gentiles taking on Jewish characteristics; cf. Cohen, *Beginnings,* 175–97; Nanos, *Irony,* 116–19. Beyond the semantic difficulties, I suggest there is not a single explicit reference to such a group anywhere in the Pauline corpus; see further below.

5. Fee, *Philippians,* 294; cf. Martin, *Philippians,* 125.

ing the Christ communities he founded, and attempting to persuade the gentile converts to his gospel to accept circumcision as the only means by which they could then gain full membership in the people of God.[6] Others have suggested that Paul is not at all referring here to any *actual* opponents posing a threat to the Philippians. Rather, he is utilizing Judaism (or the "Judaizers") as merely a negative example from which the *ekklēsia* is to understand the implications of Christ-faith, particularly the avoidance of "religious boasts," "spiritual arrogance," and "contempt for others."[7] A recent objection to readings such as these has been made by Mark D. Nanos, who argues that the target in this section of the letter represents not Judaism but some form of pagan influences.[8] This view has been similarly advocated by Robert Brawley. Brawley looks to the local pagan[9] cults that

6. Cf., e.g., Fee, *Philippians*, 293–97; Sanders, "Paul on the Law," 83–84; Witherington III, *Friendship and Finances*, 90; O'Brien, *Philippians*, 345–57; Marshall, *Philippians*, 78–80; Stowers, "Friends and Enemies," 116–17; Tellbe, "Sociological Factors," 98–100; Tellbe, *Synagogue and State*; Bockmuehl, *Philippians*, 182–91; Hooker, *Philippians*, 525; Ascough, *Associations*, 204–5; Silva, *Philippians*, 147–48; Watson, *Paul, Judaism, and the Gentiles*, 143–46; Reunmann, *Philippians*, 469–81; Hansen, *Philippians*, 217–20; Campbell, *Deliverance*, 898–99; Betz, *Philippians*, 53–54. Exceptions to this view, suggesting that the "opponents" in Phil 3 are non-Christ-allegiant Jews, include: Klijn, "Opponents," 278–84; Lohmeyer, *Philipper*, 124–26; Caird, *Paul's Letters*, 130–34; Hawthorne, *Philippians*, xliv–xlvii; Garland, "Composition," 167–69. Still others have suggested that Paul is confronting, e.g., gnostic missionaries, "divine-men," or spiritualists promoting a "libertinizing" message. However, such suggestions have fallen out of favor among more recent interpreters of the passage, as they are largely predicated on an overly-aggressive mirror-reading of the passage. On the question of the identity of "Paul's opponents," see additionally: Koester, "Polemic," 317–32; Holladay, "Opponents," 77–90; Jewett, "Conflicting Movements," 362–90; Gunther, *Opponents*; Tyson, "Opponents," 83–96; Ellis, "Opponents," 264–98; Grayston, "Opponents," 170–72; Sumney, *Opponents*; 'Servants of Satan'; Orepeza, *Opponents*.

7. Garland, "Composition," 166; cf. Park, *Submission*, 48–57. Much of this reading depends on the translation of βλέπετε in 3:2 as "observe," ostensibly as a "cautionary" or "admonitory" example, without any connotation of warning, as per an external threat; cf. Kilpatrick, "ΒΛΕΠΕΤΕ," 146–48; Caird, *Paul's Letters*, 131; Hawthorne, *Philippians*, 124–25; Garland, "Composition," 165–66; Stowers, "Friends and Enemies," 116; Park, *Submission*, 51–57. In any case, the term's precise meaning can only really be determined by the context in which it is used. As such, it seems clear enough that Paul intends to express with it some form of caution to the Philippians in 3:2, which sufficiently comports with my reading of the passage.

8. Nanos, "Reversal," 448–92; "Out Howling," 183–222.

9. I am aware that use of this term in such contexts has been called into question as an anachronism, but I find it helpful nevertheless.

were syncretized with the imperial religion of the Empire,[10] as the subject of Paul's warning to the Philippian Christ community.[11]

Paul's "Opposition"

As suggested in chapter 1 above, there are legitimate concerns to be had about the potential anti-Judaic overtones contained in the Pauline corpus, and not least in this text; concerns that are certainly informative to the readings proposed by both Nanos and Brawley.[12] And their respective arguments do bring needed attention to elements of the passage that have been largely ignored, as well as put to rest interpretive conclusions that have otherwise prevailed, in much scholarship. A key premise in Nanos' argument, and one with which I agree (though I would not articulate it against the language of "Christianity"[13]), is that the Pauline communities derived their identity from *within* Judaism rather than in opposition to it.[14] He explains:

10. See also Bormann, *Philippi*.

11. Brawley, "Reflex," 128–46.

12. Of course, there is an important difference between interpreting what Paul has written, and then making value judgments about such writings, the former being the central task of historical-critical biblical scholarship. However, the lack of sensitivity and hermeneutical distance that accompanies even many contemporary readings of Paul is disconcerting, especially in light of the history of both latent and explicit anti-Judaism that has pervaded much Christian interpretation.

13. While I understand and appreciate how the category of "Christianity," in addition to not being explicitly found in Paul (and thus my reason for not employing the term), carries with it 2000 years of historical "baggage" that is perhaps too easily anachronistically applied to the first-century, I would nevertheless suggest that there is sufficient continuity to conceive of the Pauline communities as being "Christian," in as much as early Christianity was a form of Judaism. I would no more suggest that it is *wholly* improper to refer to these communities as Christian ones, than I would suggest that first-century Ἰουδαῖοι are not really "Jews." Regardless of whether Judaism or Christianity is in view, there is always the danger of anachronism, and thus careful attention to the historical "otherness" of these first-century groups is imperative. Indeed, whereas Paul is embedded in an already-existing ethnic group and socioreligious tradition, Christianity as such is in its near point of origin. Notwithstanding, the characterization of later forms of Christianity as detached from the historical Paul and the communities to whom he writes is, in my estimation, unnecessary and unwarranted. Again, I refrain from use of the term "Christian" in my historical exegetical conclusions only because Paul does not use the term.

14. Though I am not convinced by his conclusions, one of the most cogent articulations of the view that Paul actively sought to separate his communities from the greater Jewish community is Watson's *Paul, Judaism, and the Gentiles* (cf. p. 63 n. 33 below). This

[I]f Paul writes from within Judaism, not Christianity, from and to those who understand themselves (non-Jews as well as Jews) to practice Judaism within (sub)groups that are distinguished by their convictions about Jesus but are otherwise still members of larger Jewish communities (which are themselves minority communities and, in the case of Philippi, probably very small in number), then it is logical to explore very different connotations for Paul's language than the traditional approaches have taken into consideration. When Paul's polemics as well as the rest of his message are read from this perspective, his concerns can be understood to express *his Jewish sensibilities and his commitment to the practice of (Jesus-as-Messiah-based) Judaism within his communities—even by those non-Jews whom he insists remain non-Jews.*[15]

Among the alternative possibilities for the referent of Paul's warning to the Philippian Christ community in Phil 3, Nanos favors the philosophical school of the Cynics.[16]

Brawley argues for the likelihood that Paul is referring to any one of the cults of Diana, Cybele, and/or Hecate.[17] All of these deities were associated in some way with dogs, as per the first epithet in Phil 3:2. The cult of Cybele also practiced castration, as per the third epithet. And it would certainly not be difficult to view Paul as labeling adherents to these groups as "evil workers" (κακοὺς ἐργάτας), as per the second epithet.

But it is the merger of these local cults in Philippi with that of the Empire that makes this reading all the more probable for Brawley.[18] He points to strong anti-imperial currents throughout the letter, including Paul's assertion that the Philippian Christ community already possesses an alternative form of citizenship to that of Rome. This new citizenship manifests itself in a new social identity and way of life "imprinted by the power of

---

idea is also assumed by Betz, *Philippians*, 53.

15. Nanos, "Out Howling," 185; italics original.

16. Nanos, "Paul's Reversal," 476–77; "Out Howling."

17. Brawley, "Reflex," 146.

18. Ibid., 142: "[I]mperial religion was the adjunct of Imperial power"; cf. Neil Elliot, *Arrogance*, 121–44. As exemplary, Brawley, "Reflex," 143, cites a coin minted in Philippi dated to the same period of the letter, on which there is an image of Augustus being crowned by a Philippian goddess. See also Tellbe, "Sociological Factors," 108–13 (esp. 109 n. 49); he points to several inscriptions in Philippi mentioning the Roman emperors in close association with the various pagan cults present in the city (e.g., Apollo, Silvanus, Cybele, and Isis).

God that is an alternative to imperialism."[19] And this anti-imperial theme comes to full expression in 2:6–11, which in Brawley's reading "is about God's astounding act to reverse the attempt of the imperial system to marginalize Jesus and ban him forever from the social order."[20]

Notwithstanding the important insights of Nanos and Brawley, I cannot entirely agree with their conclusion as to the identity of those of whom Paul cautions the Philippians. In my view, there are two, conceivably interrelated, groups that are likely candidates for whom Paul has in my in this section of the letter.[21] It is highly improbable that Paul is here warning the Philippians of individuals or groups that would *not* have some form of intimate contact with the Christ community. He has already pointed to those oppositional forces who *clearly* stand *wholly* outside the community (Phil 1:27–30; 2:15), and who pose an unambiguous present threat to them, requiring them to stand firm in the face of such opposition, and the potential for suffering that may, and likely has already, come about as a result. It is incomprehensible that he would then assert that it is a "safeguard" to implore the community to "beware" of these same persons. This sort of warning strongly implies a certain perceived ambiguity and potential influence upon the community that, however potentially attractive and/or pragmatic for them, Paul finds to be problematic, and ultimately inconsistent with the implications of his gospel. In short, the passage suggests a (potential) "danger within," which Paul finds necessary to expose.[22]

In this chapter I will explore one of those potential influences that he may have in mind, namely, those who would advocate that the members of the Philippian Christ community undergo proselyte conversion to

19. Brawley, "Reflex," 136.

20. Ibid., 141.

21. As will become more clear in the following chapter, that Paul may be speaking more generally about any negative influences *within* the community could overlap with the supposition that the interests of philosophical schools and/or local pagan cults are at play in Paul's warning, to the extent that they are themselves influential factors for the negative influencers within the Philippian *ekklēsia*. However, I do not believe Paul is specifically targeting either of these groups.

22. Even if Jewish missionaries proclaiming a form of the gospel in opposition to Paul's gospel are in view in Phil 3, such individuals would stand, then, not only *within* Judaism, but, further, an orientation of Judaism holding in some way that Jesus is the Christ. Thus, they would really not represent *prima facie* an out-group in the same sense of those oppositional forces referred to in chs. 1–2 of the letter. Notwithstanding the possibility of such missionaries, the discourse of Phil 3 may better suggest a potential scenario similar to what is found in 1 John; that is, an *intra*-communal dispute (regardless of the substance of the dispute in question); cf. 1 John 2:18–28.

normative Judaism. While this thesis would not necessarily exclude the possible presence of Jewish Christ-allegiant missionaries, as per the dominant reading of the passage, it does not at all require it. Indeed, there are very few grounds for assuming such missionary rivals of Paul who were in the habit of visiting the Christ communities he founded throughout the Diaspora with the goal of enticing his gentile converts to accept circumcision and normative Jewish identity. Only the Corinthian correspondence actually provides unambiguous evidence for the presence of Jewish Christ-allegiant missionaries visiting a church Paul founded (cf. esp. 2 Cor 10–13). But there is absolutely no clear indication that they attempted to convince gentile Christ allegiants to be circumcised, which the prevailing reading understands to be at stake in this passage.[23]

Thus, building especially off Nanos' work on Paul's letter to the Galatians,[24] it is my tentative suggestion that even if Paul has problematic "Jewish influences" at least partly in view, it would strictly concern the need

23. The fundamental difficulty in reconstructions such as these is (a) a certain mirror-reading of Paul's letters that assumes Paul's oppositional rhetoric—assigning negative actions and motivations to those whose influence on the Christ communities he disapproves—reflects an objective reality, in which the targets of this rhetoric understand themselves and act as Paul's opponents, and (b) that there existed in the first place an organized, uniform opposition to Paul's mission. Of course, Paul does suggest in 2 Cor 10–13 that these missionaries were explicitly opposing him (cf. esp. 10:10). But there is no real evidence of a similar exigency in any of his other letters. Regarding (a) in particular, I would emphasize that both here and elsewhere in Paul such aggressive mirror-reading strategies are fraught with problems. Barclay, "Mirror-Reading," 73–93, has pointed to several of these problems, though still conceding the importance of mirror-reading within certain methodological constraints (cf. Sumney, *Opponents*). Yet, more recent scholarship on the issue has pushed further, even to the extent of calling into question the very legitimacy of mirror-reading for both the purpose of reconstructing the identity of Paul's "opponents," and believing this to be necessary for the interpretation of his letters; an issue especially critical in Galatians scholarship; cf., e.g., Elliot, *Cutting Too Close*, 1–3; Heitanen, *Argumentation*, 102; Lyons, *Pauline Autobiography*, 75–121; Hardin, "Without a Mirror," 275–303; Heinsch, "Reassessing Mirror Reading."

While it may be argued that mirror-reading on some level is inevitable (cf. Carson, "Mirror-Reading"), I will minimally refrain from the more explicit forms of this as it has been employed in discerning the precise message and identity of Paul's "opponents." Notwithstanding, if one does *not* read the passage as focused entirely on Paul's prohibition against gentiles in Christ taking on normative Jewish identity, then it is perhaps more plausible that similar missionaries as those mentioned in 2 Corinthians are involved. However, I do not believe that Paul is primarily concerned here with external threats; see further below.

24. Cf. Nanos, *Irony*; "Inter- and Intra-Jewish Political Contexts," 396–407.

Paul understands for gentiles in Christ to maintain their own ethnic identity as distinct from Jews.

Excursus: The Galatian Exigency

In my view, the motivation that lay behind the Galatian Christ allegiants' desire to be circumcised concerns the function of this rite as culminating the path of proselyte conversion to normative Judaism. Proselytism would be necessary in order for them to participate as full members of the local synagogue community; a community upon which there was already very likely some measure of dependence. That the primary rationale for such a move was the prospect of conflict vis-à-vis the imperial cult (which was interwoven throughout multiple local cults and public activities) has, beyond the work of Nanos, also been advanced (with important differences in their respective views) by Bruce W. Winter[25] and Justin K. Hardin.[26] The basic contours of this historical construction, in which the local Jewish community plays an operative role, possess the greatest explanatory power for the exigency of Galatians, despite persistent critics.

Even assuming sufficient awareness of and concern over a largely non-Jewish community in Galatia (or any of the provinces in which Paul founded local Christ communities), it would seem implausible that any serious pressure could have been brought to bear on Paul's gentile converts to the gospel from Jewish missionaries or zealot party representatives independent of local Galatian synagogue communities. While it may be that the majority of the influencers are themselves Christ allegiants (perhaps indicated in Gal 6:12, though Paul's polemical rhetoric should not be uncritically accepted as automatically representing an objective reality), the traditional understanding that the issue of circumcision here represents an entirely "intra-Christian" and/or theological concern is highly problematic.

Could gentile Christ allegiants in Galatia be seriously persuaded only by itinerant foreign Jewish visitors to their meetings, or even existing (or former) local Jewish participants—in isolation from the local synagogue community—to reject the teaching of the founder of their community, and undergo the dramatic procedure of circumcision on purely theological grounds? Could they be convinced to take such a course of action on any conceivable grounds without the group pressure and potential for

25. Cf. Winter, *Welfare*; Winter, "Imperial Cult," 67–75; Winter, *Divine Honours*
26. Cf. Hardin, *Imperial Cult*.

communal support provided by, and thus prospect of full enculturation into, the local Jewish community? An answer of "yes" would seem to stretch the bounds of historical plausibility. Thus, that there existed at least some dependency upon the synagogue by the Christ community in Galatia, and that gentile Christ allegiants were publicly identifying with the greater Jewish community, makes most sense of the data found in that letter.

A potentially significant number of gentiles claiming a form of Jewish identity outside of the normal channel of proselyte conversion would naturally raise concern for synagogue authorities over the potential consequences the Jewish community could face if their non-Jewish neighbors perceived Jewish socioreligious boundaries compromised by the equal admission of gentiles qua gentiles, and understood this as an attempt to undermine the interests of the local polis, as expressed in various (pagan) cultic activities among its residents.[27] This social dynamic could have provided a rationale for local Jewish groups to actively seek and/or support the proselytizing of Paul's gentile converts to the gospel.

Moreover, proselytes would, as Nanos points out, "have a vested interest in guarding and facilitating the ritual process that negotiates hierarchical distinctions between righteous Gentiles and proselytes. Ritual circumcision defines their sense of self- and group identity; it governs their social interaction; it defines their social reality and political worldview."[28] Additionally, both proselytes and Jews by birth would be subject to negative repercussions from the synagogue authorities if failing to uphold the social boundaries of the larger Jewish community. The prospect of synagogue discipline would position any such individuals affiliated with the Christ community in a precarious situation, providing further motivation for them to encourage proselyte conversion (Gal 4:17; 5:11–12; 6:12–13).[29]

In this light, Phil 3 may (partly) represent an implicit dispute between rival Jewish factions: the Pauline mission over against other Jewish groups who have not recognized the dawning of the new age with the coming of the Christ, and the implications for their communities. As such, Paul's exhortation to "rejoice" throughout the letter (Phil 2:12–18; 3:1; 4:4) is especially relevant, as it undoubtedly corresponds to Paul's scriptural catena in

27. Cf. Nanos, *Irony*, 257–71.

28. Nanos, "Inter- and Intra-Jewish Political Contexts," 405.

29. Cf. Nanos, *Irony*, 219–24.

Rom 15:8–12. Here Paul cites Pss 18:49; 117:1; Deut 32:43; and Isa 11:10 LXX, which collectively present the nations *qua nations* joining God's historical covenant people, Israel, together in celebration and praise, as the *whole* community of the redeemed, in fulfillment of the promises to the Jewish ancestors (cf. Rom 11:28).[30] The connotation of "rejoice" in Phil 3 is almost certainly, then, inextricably connected to Paul's exhortation to the Christ community to "stand firm in the Lord" (Phil 4:1; see also esp. 1 Chr 16:27; Neh 8:10; Pss 5:11; 16:9; 21:1; 35:9; 40:16; 64:10; 81:1; 89:15–18; Isa 12:2–6; 55:12; 61:3, 10; Jer 15:6; Hab 3:17–19; Zeph 3:14–17; Zech 9:9; Matt 5:11–12; Jas 1:2–4; see also 4Q510 1.4–8; 4Q511).[31] That is, in recognition and praise of their place in salvation history (cf., e.g., Rom 1:16), the Philippian Christ-allegiant gentiles must remain steadfast as they already are: *members of the nations who have given allegiance to Israel's Christ* (cf. Rom 9:5).

The importance of this observation cannot be understated. For Paul, the gospel arises from *within* Judaism, and the Christ community is itself *a form of Judaism*. Paul could not possibly be denigrating Judaism—a Jewish way of life—nor portraying it as in any way inferior to, or the antithesis of, the Christ movement, lest he risk undermining the very movement of which he was a part.[32] Neither would he likely be implying that gentile Christ allegiants should sever any possible ties to the greater Jewish community.[33] Rather, Paul would only be, at most, expressing his adamant

---

30. As pointed out above (cf. p. 25; p. 52 n. 81), that Paul may also view the community of the redeemed in total as the "Israel of God" (Ἰσραὴλ τοῦ θεοῦ) (Gal 6:16)—in as much as Paul can think in terms of the continuity of God's people, according to which the identity category of "Israel" becomes synonymous with such—does not subvert or in any way inhibit Paul's equal sense that the *ekklēsia* of Jesus Christ consists of Israel and the nations together, as equal but distinguishable sub-groups.

31. Hansen, *Philippians*, 215; Bockmuehl, *Philippians*, 181.

32. Cf., Runesson, "Terminology," 59–68. He suggests the term, "Apostolic Judaism," to denote the form of Judaism represented by the early Christ movement, including the Pauline mission. See also esp. Nanos, "Paul and Judaism," 117–60.

33. Watson, *Paul, Judaism, and the Gentiles* suggests that Paul's goal, evident both here and in his other letters, was to promote a breach between the Christ communities he founded and Judaism, as generally characteristic of the sociological process according to which reform movements develop into sectarian groups. To the contrary, my view is that Paul remained a Jewish reformer and did not seek to separate the communities he founded from the synagogue, though he ardently demanded gentiles Christ allegiants remain non-Jews (normatively defined). I contend, moreover, that *the entire Christ movement itself was a decidedly Jewish (reform) movement* (cf. Zoccali, *Whom God Has Called*, 126–44). Neither in Luke's account of the early *ekklēsia*, nor in Paul's own letters

rejection of the prospect of gentiles in Christ taking on normative Jewish identity.[34] As explained in chapter 2 above, Paul's entire theological and missionary program rests on this very conviction, that *both* Jews *and* gentiles, while transformed in Christ, must nevertheless maintain their respective ethnic identities within the "*ekklēsia* of God" (Gal 1:13). In this limited sense, it may well be that the assertion of Francis Watson concerning Phil 3 is fundamentally correct: that it "is a postscript to Galatians."[35]

The Philippians' Motivation

Paul's entire discourse in Phil 3:1–9 *assumes that his audience would readily accept the high value of his Jewish background*, which would be necessary in order for his argument regarding the surpassing value of "in Christ" identity to have any force. The Philippian Christ community was founded by a Jewish apostle, had given allegiance to a Jewish messiah, worshipped the God of Israel, observed Jewish ethics, provided financial aid to Jewish groups in Judea, and, in all, adopted the Jewish symbolic universe. However, they did all of this while remaining members of the nations, and not by becoming Jews.

---

is there any indication that Christ allegiants should depart from the synagogue; nowhere does Paul assert that such a relationship between the greater Jewish community and the multiethnic Christ movement was intrinsically problematic. Further, Paul's own actions suggest that he was non-sectarian. His (a) continued attendance of the synagogue and, moreover, willingness to submit to its discipline (cf. 2 Cor 11:24; Sanders, *Jewish People*, 192 [Sanders notes: "punishment implies inclusion"]), (b) collection efforts for the Jerusalem *ekklēsia* (cf. Rom 15:25–28), and, if Luke is accurate on this point, (c) participation in the temple system (cf. Acts 21:26), are difficult to explain otherwise (cf. Campbell, *Christian Identity*, 47–48). What Paul *does* exhort his gentile gospel converts to do is to remain steadfast in the gospel he preached to them, regardless of the consequences; see further on this point below.

34. It is my understanding that Paul does use the name "Jew" for all Christ allegiants, Jewish and gentile, in Rom 2:29 (cf. Gal 6:16), but this is not at the expense of the traditional definition, which is otherwise assumed by him throughout his letters (contra Lieu, *Christianity*, 128). As pointed out above, while the boundaries of Jewish identity were not entirely fixed or univocal throughout the greater Jewish, or, more specifically, Diaspora community (cf., e.g., the discussion in Lieu, *Christianity*, 98–146), Paul clearly possessed a particular understanding of what makes one Jewish, explicitly referring to two primary aspects of this ethnic boundary: kinship and full Torah submission, both of which are, generally speaking and despite the ambiguities it presented for women, connected to the rite of circumcision, which he further uses as a synonym for Jewish identity.

35. Watson, *Paul, Judaism, and the Gentiles*, 137.

This state of affairs was an entirely unique phenomenon, with no precedent outside of the fledgling Christ movement. It differed significantly from the experience of gentile synagogue associates who, despite sympathizing in various degrees with Judaism, did not, as a rule, abandon their participation in the local polis, which involved pagan activities that would be irreconcilable with membership in the Christ community.[36] While there was likely only a small Jewish population in Philippi, there nevertheless may have existed at least a perception among some within the Christ community that there was inherent value found in possessing normative Jewish identity.[37]

Although not uniformly observed or accepted by all first-century Jewish communities throughout the Diaspora,[38] the ritual process of proselyte conversion to normative Judaism would mean departure from one's non-Jewish communal network, and full immersion into the local Jewish

36. Fee, *Philippians*, 294 n. 38, makes the puzzling assertion that gentile Christ allegiants would "not be attracted to becoming a Jewish proselyte, since that is what most of them avoided as God-fearers." This raises the question as to why, then, they would be attracted to the teaching of "Judaizers," requiring them to become circumcised and ostensibly adopt other Jewish practices. But, moreover, it fails to take into account the actual sociohistorical realities involved here; see below.

37. The concept of proselytism in Second Temple Judaism originates from the idea of the "resident alien" (גר), who is viewed in the Torah as a near equal to the native Israelite, being likewise subject to God's laws to Israel. The LXX renders the term גר as "proselyte" (προσήλυτος). As Donaldson, *Paul and the Gentiles*, 55, points out, "in rabbinic usage גר (sometimes with the addition of צדק) refers to the proselyte proper." He notes the wide distribution of references to proselytism in the literature of the period: Palestinian pseudepigrapha (e.g., Jdt 14:10; Tob 1:8; 2 Bar. 41:4); Josephus, referring to Fulvia in Rome (*Ant.* 18.82), Helena and Izates in Adiabene (*Ant.* 20.34–53); Philo (e.g., *Virt.* 102; *Spec. Laws.* 1.51–52; 4.178); Tannaitic sources (e.g., m. Bik. 1.4; b. Pesaḥ 87b; m. ʾAbot 1.12; b. Šabb. 31a; Sipre Num. 108; Mek. on Exod. 20.10; b. Sanh. 97b; the thirteenth benediction in the *Shemoneh Esreh*); Christian literature (e.g., Matt 23:15; Acts 2:11; 6:5; 13:43; Justin, *Dial.* 122); Greek and Roman authors (e.g., Dio Cassius, *Hist. Rom.* 37.17.1; 57.18.5; 67.14.1–3; Juvenal, *Sat.* 14.96; Horace, *Sat.* 1.4.142–43). The profile of proselytism that arises from these texts includes (a) exclusive devotion to the God of Israel, (b) incorporation into the people of Israel, and (c) circumcision as an entry requirement for male converts (57–58).

38. It should be noted that there is little to no evidence that the Jewish community at large prior to the very late Second Temple period accepted the notion of proselytism. Rather, as argued by Thiessen, *Contesting Conversion*, only eighth-day circumcision within native Jewish families was granted any covenantal significance. Further, even in the first century, it is important to recognize that not every Jewish group granted the legitimacy of proselytism, and in those that did it is not clear that proselytes were viewed in a uniformly positive way by other Jews; cf. Donaldson, *Judaism and the Gentiles*, 490–91.

community in question. Culminating this process for men was the rite of circumcision. The possibility of proselytizing to Judaism may have been potentially compelling to gentile Christ allegiants in Philippi as both a remedy for their perceived social ambiguity, possessing neither "pagan" nor Jewish identity, and for their experience of persecution and suffering as a result of their newly acquired and socially subversive praxis as members of the Christ community[39]—abstention from certain activities of the polis that would have been deemed as idolatrous, especially as these related to the imperial cult.[40]

While there may have been varying degrees of assimilation among Jews throughout the Diaspora,[41] that there were certain activities from which Jewish groups, as a general rule, refrained is unquestionably the case. It has been suggested that first-century Judaism did not possess the status of a *"religio licita,"*[42] and that the decrees issued by Julius and Augustus Caesar disbanding *collegia*, save those of long standing (cf. Suetonius, *Jul.* 42.3; *Aug.* 32.1–2; Josephus, *Ant.* 14.213–16; 16.162–66; 18.83–84), along

---

39. Das, *Romans Debate*, 190, has suggested that "[r]elations between Jews and their neighbors were often well-disposed. The same positive dynamic would likely have applied to fledgling Christian communities. As long as they did not draw excessive negative attention to themselves by provoking unrest, they would have enjoyed calm and peace." While this may have been the case in some respects, especially in very large urban centers like the cities of Rome and Corinth (where relative anonymity was possible), Das' assertion does not seem to adequately consider the critical differences between the social expectations of Jews as compared to non-Jews; a matter that may have become more salient for the Christ communities in the provinces of Macedonia and Galatia. Indeed, as pointed out by Oakes, *Philippians*, 71, "In Philippi, there was probably still a certain amount of anonymity, but much less of it. Individual shop-keepers, for example, would be known quite widely in the city and, if they got involved in any trouble, they would be unlikely to be able to sink quickly back into metropolitan anonymity. The same would be true, to a marked degree, of a broader group, such as the church."

40. Fee, *Philippians*, 31, has suggested that Philippi's status as a Roman colony "would have meant that every public event . . . and much else within its boundaries would have taken place in the context of giving honor to the emperor, with the acknowledgment that (in this case) Nero was 'Lord and savior.'" And it is here "where believers in Christ could no longer join as 'citizens of Rome in Philippi." While it is a question whether many of the members of the Philippian Christ community were Roman citizens, civic pressures were likely brought to bear on the entire populace to participate accordingly, lest the wellness of the community be jeopardized; see further on this point below.

41. E.g., Rajak, "Jewish Rights," 19–35; Barclay, *Diaspora*; Harland, *Associations*, 200–212.

42. E.g., Rajak, "Roman Charter," 107–23; Harland, *Associations*, 221–22; Das, *Romans Debate*, 181–90.

with similar policies of subsequent rulers, point to more limited actions attempting to quell political unrest rather than to control religious associations throughout the empire, to which Rome was largely indifferent.[43] However, Mikael Tellbe importantly points out that

> the Jewish rights and privileges repeatedly affirmed by the Roman authorities throughout the empire were not without legal force even after they were issued. As a matter of fact, the Roman measures contributed to the creation of a sort of "official" Judaism that was generally authorized throughout the empire. As things developed, Judaism in the first century CE was thus granted a legal standing in the Roman society that in practice seems to have been more specific than what is actually conveyed by the more general Roman expression *collegiums licitum*.[44]

Though official legislation enforcing participation in the imperial cult did not exist, significant social pressure would have likely been brought to bear on all members of the polis, including non-citizens, for failure to venerate the cult (a failure that would have been manifest through neglect of local civic cults, and various other aspects of public life), which could have been perceived as endangering the greater community.[45] Philip A. Harland remarks,

> Failure to participate fully in appropriately honoring the gods (imperial deities included) in cultic contexts was one of the sources of negative attitudes towards both Jews and Christians among some civic inhabitants. Jewish and Christian "atheism" could then be perceived by some as lack of concern for others ("misanthropy") and, potentially, as a cause of those natural disasters and other circumstances by which the gods punished individuals, groups, and communities that failed to give them their due (cf. Tertullian, *Apology* 40.1–5).[46]

An interrelated, perhaps even primary, form of social pressure experienced by gentile Christ allegiants in Philippi may have been economic in nature. Peter Oakes has explored this dynamic as the principal background for the letter. He explains,

---

43. Cf. Walters, *Ethnic Issues*, 16.
44. Tellbe, *Synagogue and State,* 59.
45. Ibid., 35.
46. Harland, *Associations*, 243.

> A distinction between first-generation Christianity and that in subsequent generations is that the complex of economic and other relationships within which the Christian will have lived the earlier part of his or her life will generally have been with people who were not (and did not become) Christians. ... [I]t would have been the breakdown of these relationships which constituted the most significant form of suffering. In that situation, what the Christians would need to do in order to survive is enter into a new set of economic and other relationships among themselves.[47]

In some difference, I suggest that, in light of potentially strained economic relations between gentile Christ allegiants and the greater Philippian community, another potentially viable option would be for such gentiles to seek entrance into the Jewish communal network, which, again, could have significantly mitigated potential difficulties otherwise arising from their praxis and general theological/ideological commitments.

But, given the lack of evidence for a substantial Jewish community living in first-century Philippi,[48] was there a large enough population of Jews in the region to render such an understanding plausible? Oakes estimates the size of the Philippian Christ community to be fifty to one hundred persons.[49] Richard S. Ascough suggests that the size was probably much smaller, at around twenty members.[50] Thus, if there was a relatively small number of gentile Christ allegiants, the fact that only a small Jewish community existed in Philippi does not discount the thesis that the Philippian *ekklēsia* may have looked their way as a means to obviate social opposition. In the narrative of Paul's visit to Philippi in Acts 16:13–21 there is mention of a *proseuchē* ("place of prayer"), which is a term generally synonymous with "synagogue," and denotes a regular gathering of those practicing Judaism.

47. Oakes, *Philippians*, 100. Oakes, 89–96, provides a detailed illustration of how the breakdown of these economic relationships could come about as a consequence of gentile Christ allegiants' newfound commitments, e.g., abstention from idolatry vis-à-vis guilds, associations, clubs, and the invariable conflicts that would result.

48. The absence of a formal synagogue structure in first-century Philippi—as probably indicated in the account given in Acts (see main text), as well as by the archeological evidence—points to a minimal Jewish presence in the area in the first century. On the archeological evidence, see Koukouli-Chrysantaki, "Philippensis," 28–35. A late third-century Jewish burial inscription does mention a synagogue in Philippi, which demonstrates at minimum a Jewish community existing there at that time, though any such evidence dating to an earlier period has failed to be discovered.

49. Oakes, *Philippians*, 62.

50. Ascough, "Broadening the Context," 100.

That this term is not Luke's usual way to refer to a synagogue (cf. Acts 6:9; 9:2; 17:1, 10, 17) may indicate a lack of a building, or formal structure more typical of the larger synagogue communities elsewhere referred to in Acts.

Too much should not be made of the fact that only women are referred to in Luke's account of Paul's visit to the city, in the supposition that there did not exist a regular gathering of Jewish persons living in the area.[51] As Craig S. Keener points out,

> Speaking with the women in a group would not have been considered inappropriate; women certainly attended synagogues, and we currently lack evidence that synagogues segregated them in this period.[52] ... Asian Jewish women sometimes held titles such as "ruler of the synagogue" (e.g., CIJ 2:10, §741, in Smyrna; 2:20, §756 in Caria). A wealthy proselyte sponsor could become "mother of a synagogue" (1:384, §523, in Rome). In some locations, we even read of women Jewish elders.... Early Judaism, like paganism and early Christianity, included a mixture of tendencies regarding gender. ... That Luke mentions women specifically in Philippi, Thessalonica, and Beroea (Acts 17:4, 12) probably also points to their relative freedom and prominence in Macedonian religion.[53]

On this matter, it is perhaps worth entertaining the possibility that, like the figure of Lydia in the account in Acts, the Philippian Christ community leaders, Euodia and Syntyche (Phil 4:2), were among the group of synagogue associates that Paul first evangelized upon his visit to the city, and who would have had, then, some existing attachment to Judaism prior to entering the Christ community.

In any case, Acts 16:19–22 suggest that there was clearly sufficient awareness of the Jewish community among the residents of Philippi, along with a perception that Paul's activity among these gentiles overstepped the social boundaries between Jews and non-Jews. It should also be taken into

51. The Rabbinic requirement of a "minyan," or quorum, of ten Jewish adult males for public synagogue worship dates well beyond the first century, and the notion was almost certainly not recognized in the time of Paul.

52. As judiciously suggested by Spigel, "Separate Seating," it should be observed based on the available literary and archaeological evidence that there was very likely a diversity of practice among the synagogue communities throughout the Diaspora regarding the matter of mixed/segregated seating.

53. Keener, *Acts 15:1–23:25*, 2388–90; cf. Abrahamsen, "Priestesses," 25–62. On the active role of women in the early synagogue, see also, e.g., Brooten, *Women Leaders*; Ehrensperger, "Gender," 249–59; Safari, "Synagogue," 39–50; Levine, *Synagogue*, 499–518.

consideration that traders such as Lydia would have had significant engage-
ment with the Jewish community at large, and would have been cognizant
of the social dynamic existing between Jewish and non-Jewish participation
in the guilds. Oakes points out that the wealth of the town's elite in Philippi
"strengthened the 'demand' side of the town's service economy. . . . One effect of this demand, particularly in the area of specialists luxury goods
such as purple, was the drawing in of further merchants and craftspeople
from other regions, in particular Asia."[54] Keener explains that

> Jewish sympathizers from Asia Minor might well have learned of
> Judaism through contact with other purple dyers there since at
> least in Hierapolis (in Phrygia, near Lydia) Jewish members of that
> profession seem to have been abundant; many Jews there belonged
> to its associations of purple dyers and tapestry makers. So many
> Jews were members of these guilds that they "were made respon-
> sible for memorial ceremonies for deceased Jewish members on
> Passover and Pentecost!" That these guilds also contained Gentiles
> also demonstrates that Jews were well integrated into, and wel-
> comed into, the city's economic life in that region at least.[55]

Accordingly, the potential influx of migrant service workers into
the Philippian Christ Community, some of whom may have been Jewish
sympathizers, could have provided a partial basis for Paul's concern that
such influences might spur at least a perception among some members
that becoming a Jewish proselyte could open up the possibility of relief
from the opposition they encountered, given that the Jewish community
elsewhere did not seem to experience the same sort of difficulties, despite
quite similar praxis and ideological commitments. It would not be difficult
to imagine that those encouraging in some way gentile Christ allegiants'
initiation of the path of proselyte conversion to normative Judaism would
point to such benefits that would accrue to them as members of the Jewish
community.[56] Ironically, this scenario might also indicate that some in the

---

54. Oakes, *Philippians*, 34.

55. Keener, *Acts 15:1—23:25*, 2396.

56. It would seem that the Philippian Christ community was comprised mostly from
those on the lower strata of the social scale (cf. Phil 4:19; 2 Cor 8:1–3), many perhaps
traders in the marketplace (possibly a reason for the abundance of Paul's commercial
metaphors, e.g., Phil 3:7–8; 4:14–20), who were generally viewed with contempt by the
elite classes. Oakes suggests that the *ekklēsia* consisted of 35–55 percent from service
groups (including traders), 20–40 percent poor, 12–25 percent slaves, 15–23 percent
commuting peasant colonists, and 0.5–1.5 percent elite (Oakes, *Philippians*, 59–63; also

Philippian *ekklēsia* already desired to "imitate" Paul, but in ways that Paul considers wholly inappropriate (see further below). Regardless, as Paul's letter to the Galatians demonstrates, any attempt to convince gentile Christ allegiants to deviate from their status as non-Jews (normatively defined) is a perverse attack on the implications of his gospel (cf. Phil 3:2; Gal 1:7).

Thus, given the social reality described above, Paul's rhetoric in Phil 3 may reflect, at least in part, his desire to prevent gentile Christ allegiants from initiating the path of proselyte conversion to normative Judaism; a path that he characterizes in Galatians as "a different gospel" (Gal 1:6).[57] That is, in the dispensation of Christ, the rite of circumcision as per the process of proselyte conversion is irreconcilable with membership in the Christ community; it should be viewed, therefore, as no more than mutilation of the flesh.[58] The Philippians are to accept, rather, any consequent marginality, social death, or even persecution, as Paul himself had endured (cf. Phil 1:13–17, 27–30; 2:17; 3:10; see also 1 Thess 1:6; 2:1–2; 14–16;

---

cited by Marchal, *Heirarchy*, 111). Marchal explains: "[W]e have a picture of a colony marked by distinct socioeconomic stratification. An oligarchic political structure was maintained by an elite in the severe minority, while the population was distinguished by significant diversity in ethnicity, economic and legal status, and potential loyalty. The history of the city has included up to three different colonizing forces (Thasian, Macedonian, and Roman). In the last of these colonizations, the settlement processes managed to marginalize both previous inhabitants and eventually some of those 'rewarded' for making this colonization possible" (Marchal, *Hierarchy*, 108). This aspect of the Philippians' social context, in which they already existed (at least in greater part) on the socioeconomic periphery, significantly amplifies the severity of Paul's exhortations throughout the letter to suffer for the advance of the gospel: "For [God] has graciously granted you the privilege not only of offering allegiance to Christ but of suffering for him as well—since you have the same struggle that you saw I had, and now hear that I still have" (Phil 1:29–30; cf. 2 Cor 4:17).

57. For a similar argument, see de Vos, *Conflicts*, 269–75. He asserts: "[B]y being seen as 'proper' Jews, who abide by the ancestral customs, they would be afforded a measure of acceptance and recognition. It would be a legitimate way of gaining exemption from the expectation to participate in the traditional cults, and especially the imperial cult" (296).

58. This is in stark contrast to the continued value Paul assigns to this rite for Jews (cf. Rom 2:25; 3:1–2; 1 Cor 7:18). If we accept the historicity of Acts' account of Timothy's circumcision (Acts 16:1–4), it should be noted that Timothy's ethnic status was ambiguous, possessing matrilineal, though not patrilineal, Jewish ancestry. Paul likely understood Timothy to be Jewish, and thus normalized his status by having him circumcised. His circumcision was also very likely a pragmatic matter that served Paul's missionary agenda to which Timothy partnered.

3:1–10; Gal 5:11; 6:12, 14, 17; 2 Cor 4:7–12; 7:5; 11:22–25), and in the pattern demonstrated by Christ himself (cf. Phil 2:6–8; see also 2 Cor 8:9).[59]

It should be emphasized here that such influencers would *not* have to be themselves Jewish (either by birth or proselytism). An initiative towards proselyte conversion could easily originate from non-Jews for the very reasons stated above. If indeed Paul labels those advocating such a move as the "mutilation," this would *not* be a reflection of their own circumcised stated, but of only their agenda. It is not incidental to the point that Paul affirmatively mentions his own physical circumcision on the eighth day, having been born into the people of Israel, the tribe of Benjamin, and that he is "a Hebrew of Hebrews" (Phil 3:5)—all clear descriptors of his native Jewish ethnicity in contrast to proselyte status; a status that, for Paul, should no longer be sought in the dispensation of Christ.[60] All of the epithets in Phil 3:2 would similarly reflect such a potential group's maneuvering, and *not* at all their own ethnic identity and cultural praxis (see further below).[61]

It was perhaps the belief among some in the Philippian *ekklēsia* that not merely relief from suffering, but a more honorable status[62] *in toto* could

59. Cf. Jewett, "Conflicting Movements," 367: "The letter [to the Philippians] repeatedly makes the point that suffering for Christ is the epitome of Christian experience." Paul refers to those within the greater Christ community who do *not* seem, at least from his perspective, as ready to adopt this rule in 1:17, and perhaps implicitly so in 2:21. Notwithstanding this insight, Ehrensperger rightly points out: "To describe suffering and hardship as part of a life in conformity with Christ under the conditions of 'this world,' as Paul does, has to be distinguished from a suffering mystique (Leidensmystik) which idealizes suffering as a path to Christ. Paul is not idealizing the cross, which would in fact mean trivializing it, but calling his converts back to the real world they live in. And here in this world, to live in conformity with this 'world to come,' can make the violence of the cross and the suffering of human beings inevitable. But rather than being taken as a sign and proof for failure, as was the case in the dominant value system, such sufferings should be regarded as signs of real life in Christ. In that sense the sign of the cross is turned upside down, from a sign of failure into a sign of life" (Ehrensperger, "Be Imitators," 254).

60. It seems evident, particularly in light of Gal 5:11, that Paul believed prior to the coming of Christ normative Jewish identity was in fact coextensive with covenant identity, and thus that he likely found proselyte conversion to normative Judaism a fully appropriate means for non-Jews to gain access to covenant membership prior to Christ's coming, and his subsequent apostolic call. It should be observed, however, that Paul's reference in Gal 5:11 to "proclaiming circumcision" has almost certainly *nothing* to do with formal proselytizing efforts (either before or after his apostolic call), but simply with a general affirmation of the necessity of circumcision for covenant membership.

61. In the next chapter I will provide more detailed exegetical conclusions regarding the epithets that appear in Phil 3:2.

62. See Nebreda, *Christ Identity*, 91–98, for a careful and succinct examination of the

be won by undertaking Jewish identity (cf. Phil 3:15; Gal 3:3). As I will elaborate upon in the next chapter, others may have been contemplating a move in the opposite direction—a more compromised disposition in regard to their civic and socioeconomic obligations under the belief that such a renegotiation of their "in Christ" and former pagan identities could prove more successful. Still others within the community may have scorned those even remotely considering either of these options. And this sort of disjuncture among the members of the community might have resulted in disagreements between the community's leadership and Paul, or among the leadership itself, as to what sort of praxis and/or response would prove more advantageous for the community (cf. Phil 4:2–3).[63] Thus, Paul asserts throughout the letter the need within the *ekklēsia* for humility, likemindedness, and a commitment to unity, demonstrating spiritual maturity in their consideration of these issues (cf. Phil 1:27; 2:1–4, 14–15; 3:15–17).

But even more fundamentally, Paul seeks to reverse the conventional understanding as to the basis for which honor is gained, paradoxically suggesting that it is found instead in the willingness to suffer loss of reputation and status (and corresponding rights and privileges), and even endure

---

various approaches in contemporary scholarship to understanding the value of "honor" (and its negative counterpart, "shame") in the ancient Mediterranean world. He judiciously concludes that honor was almost certainly a central, though not singular, ancient Mediterranean social value, and further remarks that "even in this so-called *agonistic* context of the Mediterranean, there was still the 'possibility of choice' [Potter, *Literary Texts*, 152–53]. So, rather than to consider honour as a unique and constant concept, it is better to see it as a conceptual framework which provides people ways to express their self-worth and esteem for others" (97).

63. Cf. de Vos, *Conflicts*, 266–67: "[T]he disunity within the church would have arisen because of differing opinions about how to deal with the conflict. In particular it appears that there was a tendency to try to avoid or minimize this conflict on the part of many of the Philippian Christians. This is suggested by Paul's reference to them being afraid of their opponents (1:28), by his assertion that their suffering was granted by Christ (1:29), by his emphasis in the 'hymn' on Christ's death on the cross (2:8), and by his stress on the importance of sharing the sufferings of Christ (3:10–11). Consequently, although it is seldom recognized by scholars, the problem of the opponents in Phil 3:2–21 should be understood within the context of this conflict with the wider civic community. More specifically, this conflict and suffering has left them afraid (1:28) and hence vulnerable to the arguments of these adversaries." He continues: "Some of them were tempted to be circumcised to assume the status of Jews who followed their ancestral practices. Others, because of a Roman religious mentality, were tempted to maintain their traditional religious practices, worship the Emperor, and join *collegia*. There were probably some who had already taken these options, whom Paul regarded as apostates, and who were trying to persuade the Philippian Christians to follow them in order to avoid the conflict they were experiencing" (275).

maltreatment for the benefit of the other (cf. Phil 1:1, 12–13, 20–21; 2:6–11; 3:7–8).[64] The "other" includes *both* those within the Christ community (cf. Phil 1:23–26; 2:1–4, 19–20, 25–30; 4:14), and ultimately those outside of the community as well (cf. Phil 2:15–16). Honor will not accrue to Christ allegiants who attempt to circumvent the prospect of suffering by means that run counter to the gospel they had received from Paul, and thus to the detriment of each other and the rest of the world.[65]

Of course, the members of the Philippian *ekklēsia* were well-aware that Paul was a Jew who was imprisoned for the cause of the gospel, and that Jesus Christ was a Jewish martyr of the Roman regime, which would seem to demonstrate *prima facie* that (a) becoming a Jewish proselyte would not, in any case, guarantee the avoidance of marginality and persecution—Jewish communities throughout the Diaspora were themselves marginal groups,[66]

---

64. Such a reversal of conventional values is particularly seen in Paul's self-designation as a "slave" (δοῦλος) of Christ Jesus in Phil 1:1, and, preeminently, the taking on of slave-identity by Jesus Christ himself in Phil 2:7. Nebreda, *Christ Identity*, 200, explains: "[W]hat Paul does here is a re-definition of terms to construct a new identity based on alternative values. This use of slavery is not novel, but the overall structure in which the apostle places [it] certainly is. Paul turns an institution devoid of honour into a 'title' of close identification with the God-in-the-flesh Jesus." He further remarks: "Far from seeing slavery as social death, the early Christ movement perceived it as a metaphor of salvation, so that Paul's self-designation acquires an important soteriological component. . . . If, for 'honour-seeking' eyes, this practice [of 'self-selling' on behalf of others] was not in accord with Roman *dignitas*, the early Christ movement, by contrast, had already looked at it through the example which nowhere was more clearly manifested than in the text of Phil 2.6–11: that of Christ, who becomes the ultimate model as well as the beginning of the group's identity" (205).

In keeping with the assertion of Ehrensperger in n. 59 above, I would emphasize here that an important distinction needs to be drawn between voluntary self-denial that *authentically* serves the gospel, and other motivations of self-denial/abasement that does not serve that purpose. Paul is clearly *not* advocating, e.g., a form of Cynicism (however else he may have been influence by this philosophical school), or, for that matter, masochism, but, rather, a life that prioritizes Jesus Christ and his Torah (cf. Phil 3:10–15; Gal 5:22—6:10; 2 Cor 5:15–21; pp. 49–51 above) above all else, in the conviction that this represents God's perfect and good will for all creation, which will be soon consummated in the coming kingdom of God (cf. Phil 1:6, 10–11; 3:20–21; 4:5).

65. For an extensive study on Paul's (re)definition of honor that subverts Roman *cursus* ideology, particularly demonstrated in the Christ hymn of Phil 2, see Hellerman, *Reconstructing Honor*.

66. Further still, as suggested in p. 65 n. 38 above, in some Jewish communities proselytes were not viewed as "true Jews." However, we simply do not know anything about the Jewish community in Philippi, and the degree to which would-be proselytes would be, in any case, aware of any such status differentiation between native born Jews and Jewish proselytes.

and (b), as the Christ hymn in Phil 2:6–11 clearly demonstrates, the Christ movement itself was predicated upon a reversal of the typical perception regarding the possession of divine approval within the larger Greco-Roman world (e.g., 1 Cor 1:26–31; 4:8–13; see similarly esp. Matt 5:1–12; and further below). However, some perceived distinction between their community and its circumstances with that of both the apostle who founded it, and the Lord to whom they had given their allegiance, along with a natural reluctance to accept (rather than obviate) negative repercussions as a consequence of their communal involvement, would not be unsurprising for a relatively new group experiencing intense dissonance between their own, newly appropriated intra-group norms over against those of the greater civic community to which they also belong.

If Paul understood this to be the case, it makes further sense of the emphasis he places on the paradigmatic nature of his own suffering, and also that of Christ, as necessarily applicable to this community consisting largely (if not entirely) of gentiles (cf. Phil 1:7). It also suggests that his imitation rhetoric (cf. Phil 3:17; 4:9) is not all-encompassing, but quite specific in its application. As Kathy Ehrensperger suggests of Paul's similar imitation language in his letter to the Corinthians, this rhetoric is intended to guide his converts "into a way of life in Christ," which is "an inversion of the dominating pattern of life, the seemingly static hierarchies are 'deconstructed' by Christ and to live in Christ means to live, not just believe, in this inversion of hierarchies. . . . This could imply hardships and troubles under the circumstances of this world, but it neither asks for nor idealizes these."[67]

Paul's Rhetorical Purpose

Effecting the Steadfastness of the Nations

Paul therefore desires the gentile Philippian Christ allegiants to emulate his own uncompromising commitment to the gospel, but in the state and circumstances that they already possess—as members of the nations, who, like those in Thessalonica, "turned to God from idols, to serve a living and

---

67. Ehrensperger, "Be Imitators," 255. Cf. Nebreda, *Christ Identity*, 227–28: "We cannot take from Paul the right to hold strong convictions about his particular way of understanding the Christ-like life: he is more than prepared to put his life at stake (both *living* and dying for it; cf. Phil 2:17) for the sake of it."

true God, and to wait for his Son from heaven" (1 Thess 1:9–10), and who "suffered the same things from [their] own compatriots as [the Judean *ekklēsiai*] did from the Judeans" (1 Thess 2:14; cf. p. 81 n. 87 below).[68] By doing so, they themselves would become models for imitation, as the Thessalonians had become (cf. 1 Thess 1:6–8), and Paul's work among them would be thereby validated (cf. Phil 1:26–27). This required him to seek the Philippians' *empowerment* in their allegiance to Jesus Christ,[69] which he knew quite well could only be sustained amidst counter-pressures to the degree that the community fully recognizes and lives out their own creative yet prototypical[70] identity as "holy ones" (Phil 1:1) and "children of God" (Phil 2:15–18; see also esp. p. 80 n. 86 below).[71] Philippians 1:9–11 articulates his desire accordingly:

> [T]his is my prayer: that your love may abound more and more with knowledge and full insight, to help you determine what is best, so that in the day of Christ you may be pure and blameless, having been filled with the fruit of righteousness through Jesus Christ—to the glory and praise of God.

Regarding Paul's prayerful expectations for the Philippians, Nebreda insightfully points out how the Christ hymn functions to exemplify the radical reorientation involved in their commitment to Christ. No illusions

68. Cf. Park, *Submission*, 103; she asserts that "the goal of mimesis for Paul in 1 Thessalonians is not to keep the copy perpetually in the inferior position, but precisely the opposite: to encourage the copy to strive and attain to the level of the model. Contra Castelli, Paul's mimetic injunction in 1 Thess 2:14 does not seek to retain power but shares power with others."

69. Ehrensperger, "Gender," 271–72, importantly observes: "To respond to the call of [Israel's] God means to live a way of life that corresponds to the One who called. It is a God who reminds his people that he freed them from slavery, which obliges them to care for those who are vulnerable in the community (Deut. 10:18–19; 24:17–18). Paul's Jewish tradition presents alternative perceptions to Greek and Roman notions of the use of power. There is a discourse of empowerment at the heart of this tradition, a discourse of trust in a God who hears the cries of those in need (e.g., Exod. 2:23–25; 3:7–9; Pss. 3:4; 9:12; 22:5; 32:7; 99:6; 106:44; 145:19; 1 Kgs. 8:51–53; Neh. 9:9; Isa. 19:20; 65:19)."

70. I think here in terms of SCT, according to which "people cognitively represent social groups in terms of prototypes. A prototype is a subjective representation of the defining attributes (e.g., beliefs, attitudes, behaviors) of a social category." Hogg et al., "Tale of Two Theories," 26; see further on this issue in the following chapter.

71. In other words, *within* the in-group boundaries of Christ-community identity there is room for diversity. Indeed, for Paul, the boundaries of appropriate communal praxis in themselves necessitate respect for subordinate identity salience, and thus varying, culturally informed expression of covenant faithfulness to God through Jesus Christ.

are cast by Paul as to the immediate cost of their membership in the community. He explains:

> Often we tend to think about group formation as a way of creating stability, but we need to remember that something dear needs to be displaced in order to accept the new. The newness of the Christ-hymn might present the Philippian community with an insurmountable challenge too radical to be accepted without regrets, especially when it is understood in its social context. After all, before people join groups there is a reconnaissance process, where people assess before deciding. One answer is that people join groups that will be "maximally rewarding and minimally costly" [Brown, *Group Processes*, 24–25]. However, it is clear that although the apostle does not put aside the rewards of membership (3.20–21), the radical call to an alternative life-style (2.5 τοῦτο φρονεῖτε) places the cost of discipleship up front. The hope of future reward, no doubt, outweighs present difficulties. The Christ-hymn plays a crucial part in this literary/social communication, since it introduces an alternative life-style at odds with current society which is moreover a guarantee of success and salvation in the face of this present "stable system," which is geared to destruction.[72]

The End *for* (and Not of) the Philippians

Paul's exhortation in Phil 3 and throughout the letter is *not*, then, fundamentally grounded upon an appeal to his authority and presumed domination over the community, which would almost certainly prove unsuccessful given especially what is at stake in the Philippians' membership within it. But—to the contrary—it is founded upon the eschatological orientation of the Philippians' *own* "in Christ" identity, and its salvific implications.[73] Along these lines, Hansen points out that in Phil 3:10 Paul makes the implicit claim that "knowing the power of Christ's resurrection provides

---

72. Nebreda, *Christ Identity*, 63.

73. Two points need to be made here. First, in the letter Paul does, of course, exercise his authority and influence over the community, but, as suggested in p. 13 n. 35 above, *any* discourse will inevitably contain hierarchical elements, and the presence of these elements says nothing in itself about the ethical substance of the discourse in question. Second, as suggested in pp. 47–48 above, "salvation" for Paul is not merely a promise of future deliverance, but the present and ongoing transformation, via the Spirit, into Christ-likeness, and thus in being made *truly human*, according to God's original purposes in creation (cf. n. 76; and further ch. 5 below).

incentive and strength to participate in the sufferings of Christ."[74] Similarly, M. Sydney Park suggests,

> The reference to the heavenly πολίτευμα [citizenship] in 3.20 as in 1.27ff. is not the result of imitating Paul, but the precedent for imitating Christ and those who follow Christ's example, Paul included. Conformity to Christ has no meaning for those who have not already been saved. As indicated by the present tense of ὑπάρχω (3.20), salvation is already in their possession.[75]

Thus, the primary motivation put forward by Paul for enduring any distress is the hope of Christ's soon return to fully establish his kingdom *from* heaven—of which the Philippians are *already* citizens—*on* earth (cf. Phil 1:6; 3:20–21; 4:5; Rom 8:18; 2 Cor 4:16–18; see also p. 31 n. 29 above). At which time *all things* would be made subject *to him*, not least the oppressive forces at work against them.[76] *This eschatological hope, which should inform the Christ community's praxis, represents, therefore, the very antithesis of the eschatology of the Empire, which understood its own absolute and universal power as the rightful culmination of human history; a final, and everlasting order.*[77]

The Philippians' present circumstances are to be interpreted not, then, from the vantage of the past, when they themselves were constituents of a "crooked and perverse generation" (Phil 2:15; cf. Gal 2:15), but from the perspective of what lies in the near future—their final redemption and glorious transformation as citizens of God's kingdom, who will share in Christ's final victory over sin and death (cf. Phil 1:6; 3:11–13; 3:20–21; 4:5;

---

74. Hansen, *Philippians*, 243.

75 Park, *Submission*, 109.

76. That is, the nature of the coming kingdom of God is one in which God's sovereignty, as mediated through Jesus Christ, makes possible the fullest expression of human integrity and flourishing, as per the royal status of all human beings as *imago dei*, and thus their fundamental calling to bring blessing to the other, as intrinsic to the task of faithful dominion (cf. Gen 1:26–28; cf. p. 40 n. 47 above). For a discussion of Paul's vocational and cruciform theology of election, grounded in the creational mandate of humankind as image-bearers of God, and preeminently expressed in the servant song of Isa 53, see Zoccali, *Whom God Has Called*, 158–70.

77. Cf. Tucker, *Remain in Your Calling*, 201–6. There is wide agreement in contemporary New Testament scholarship that Paul's gospel challenges the imperial pretenses of the Roman Empire, including, e.g., the ascription to Caesar Augustus of the titles, "son of god," and "savior of the world"—titles that, for Paul, rightfully belong to Israel's Messiah, Jesus of Nazareth (cf. Rom 1:2–4; see also esp. 1 Thess 5:1–11, which seems to allude to the *Pax Romana/Augusta*).

see also esp. 1 Cor 15:24–28, 50–58; 2 Cor 4:14—5:5; 1 Thess 4:15–17; Rom 6:4–5; 8:21–39; Col 3:4).[78] The ultimate vindication of the Christ community, patterned after that of Jesus Christ (cf. Phil 2:8–11; Rom 5:17; 1 Cor 6:2; see also Eph 2:6; 2 Tim 2:12), is in contradistinction to the "destruction" that awaits those outside the community (Phil 3:19;[79] 1:28). And while Paul does not base his exhortation on threat of expulsion, outside the community is where certain members of the Philippian *ekklēsia* would risk placing themselves if not heeding Paul's caution in 3:2, and choosing, rather, to distort or subvert their liberating identity found in Jesus Christ (cf. Gal 5:2–4), in collusion with the very oppressive forces opposed to not merely them but God's good purposes for all creation.[80]

Excursus: They Are Who They Will Be: The Temporal Aspect of the Philippians' Identity

As clearly evidenced in the letter to the Philippians, Marco Cinnirella has suggested that "[s]ocial groups will create shared 'life stories' or narratives of the group which tie past, present and predicted futures into a coherent representation."[81] Contemporary identity research in the theory of "possible selves," which includes both personal and social identity (the latter being especially pertinent in collectivist cultures, such as the one in which Paul and his addressees were embedded), may assist here in discerning the import of Paul's future-oriented rhetoric as it serves his efforts to strengthen the Philippians' identity in Christ. Shedding light on this rhetorical strategy,

78. There is a clear parallel here between the loss of "all things" in Phil 3:8 and the subjecting of "all things" to Christ in 3:21. Christ's future reign as "Lord" (κύριος) and "Savior" (σωτήρ) (Phil 3:20; cf. 2:10–11) will mean for the Philippians a sure reversal of the perception of shame in light of their present circumstances; the vindication and honor and they seek will at that time be accorded them (cf. Phil 1:20; see also 1 Cor 3:21–23).

79. The implication here is that these individuals/groups will also experience a reversal; ultimately, they will be shamed for that which they had once glorified.

80. See p. 33 n. 32 above for the centrality of God's judgment in Paul. The lack of clarity on the part of the Philippians (in Paul's estimation) regarding the full implications of the gospel leads him to exhort the community members who would be "perfect" (Phil 3:15)—that is, those who should desire to attain to the resurrection (Phil 3:11)—to, like him, first conform themselves to Christ's death, demonstrable in a willingness to suffer all things in obedience to God for the benefit of all (Phil 3:10; 2:8; see also esp. Gal 2:19–20; p. 95 n. 22 below).

81. Cinnirella, "Temporal Aspects," 235.

Cinnirella points out that "[w]here a substantial number of ingroupers become motivated to avoid or attain a shared possible social identity, then this is likely to lead to collective action."[82]

> The crucial link to motivation in the theory is afforded by the contention that individuals attempt to achieve positively valued (i.e. desired) possible selves, whilst hopefully avoiding other, negatively evaluated (i.e. feared) possible selves. Furthermore, it is supposedly through the process of manufacturing possible selves that individuals devise plans and strategies to achieve or avoid particular outcomes.[83]

Since the Philippians' present oppressive circumstances would conceivably hinder a positive self-esteem provided by their membership in the Christ community,[84] and thereby jeopardize their continued allegiance to Jesus Christ, Paul's rhetorical focus on the future success of the group over against the future demise of those remaining outside of the community can be viewed as a discursive strategy that seeks to provide the necessary motivational needs critical for each member's identity maintenance.[85] Rather than a form of abusive, exploitative psychological manipulation predicated upon threat of eschatological violence (cf. p. 95 n. 22 below), and/or hollow promise of eschatological reward, the impact of his future-oriented rhetoric lies in its personal and group affirmation of the choice to follow Jesus Christ despite the present difficulties.[86]

---

82. Ibid., 233.

83. Ibid., 229.

84. For further discussion on the import of self-esteem as provided by group memberships, see ch. 4 below.

85. Cinnirella, "Temporal Aspects," 239.

86. Cf. esp. here the discussion of the relationship between Paul's apocalyptic discourse and his paraenesis, as it further relates to the identity of Christ allegiants, in his letter to the Thessalonian Christ community in Wanamaker, "Apocalyptic Discourse," 131–45. Wanamaker explains: "Paul makes the crucial connection between ethics and eschatological judgment, between apocalyptic discourse and Christian moral development, preparing the way for [1 Thess] 4:1—5:22. The underlying cultural logic of this connection is important to note. The goal of increasing and abounding in love (3:12), the ethical component of the dyad, is to establish the Thessalonian Christians' hearts as 'blameless in holiness before God' at the coming of the Lord Jesus with all of his holy ones. Thus the exercise of the fundamental Christian virtue of love is motivated by what is to happen at the parousia of Christ, but its effect is to establish group solidarity. . . . At stake for the Thessalonian Christians was their very ability to maintain their Christian identity in the face of the hostile society in which they lived" (136–37).

Implications of the Seemingly Minimal Jewish Presence in First-century Philippi

Notwithstanding the analysis above, there is little to suggest in the letter that the warning Paul poses in Phil 3, if indeed expressing, at least in part, a concern over proselyte conversion to normative Judaism, reflects an *existing* problem for the Philippian *ekklēsia* on a similar scale with that of the Galatian Christ community. As pointed out, the Jewish population of Philippi was likely quite small. However, the lack of a large Jewish population in close proximity to their community may account for the distinct treatment of this issue here, as compared to Paul's letters to the other churches he founded in Galatia, where he is thoroughly preoccupied with it, and Thessalonica, where such a discourse is entirely absent (the latter letter being the only other of Paul's outside of Philippians that deals significantly with social opposition towards Christ allegiants beyond Paul and the apostles; cf. 1 Thess 1:6; 2:14—3:7[87]). Unlike in these other communities with ostensibly larger Jewish populations,[88] whereby some level of contact between Jewish groups at large and Christ allegiants would have been far more prevalent—whether in terms of dependence and/or points of conflict (as possibly the case in Thessalonica; cf. Acts 17:1–9)—the Philippians were not exposed to the same level of external influence from these groups, and thus had not up to this point experienced the same degree of real testing on this matter.[89]

---

87. The arguments put forward to date for the interpolation of 1 Thess 2:14–16 are in my view unpersuasive. I find little reason to believe that this section is not part of the original letter; for a defense of this view, see, e.g., Donfried, *Early Christianity*, 198–205; see also Zoccali, "'All Israel,'" which demonstrates that the supposed irreconcilability of this passage with Rom 11, a central argument for its lack of authenticity, is misguided.

88. For a pessimistic view regarding the actuality of a significant presence of Jews residing anywhere in Macedonia in the first century, see Ascough, *Associations*, 191–212. I am much more inclined to tentatively trust Luke's account that there were relatively sizable Jewish populations living in this region and, on the basis of Acts 16 in particular, at least a small Jewish community in Philippi. For strong and extensive argumentation on the general historicity of Acts, and thus the presence of Jewish communities in this region at the time of Paul, see Keener, *Acts 1:1—2:47*; see also here Nebreda, *Christ Identity*, 171–83.

89. The Galatians did not hold up well to mounting pressures to proselytize, and thus Paul's letter to them consists of an explicit and extensive rebuke. In contrast, his letter to the Thessalonians suggests that they had in fact been holding firm to the gospel, which therefore did not require of him any such discussion of the problem of circumcision for gentiles in Christ (cf. 1 Thess 3:5–6). I would emphasize here that I am in no way

In this light, Phil 3:1–9 might be best understood as a cautious, preventative measure. It is probably *not* to warn of an impending visit from Jewish Christ-allegiant missionaries, and certainly *not* to present Jews (whether missionaries or otherwise) as a negative object lesson, but perhaps, at least in part, to dissuade gentile Christ allegiants from what Paul understands as a *de facto* departure from the Christ movement, proselyte conversion to normative Judaism, which for him is no better than a reversion to paganism (cf. Gal 4:8–11). It would be in effect to deny the faithfulness of God, and to posit one's self outside of the sphere of salvation that God has made possible (cf. Gal 3:10–14). In other words, for gentiles to pursue proselyte conversion (or for them to be inspired to do so) is to live as though nothing had in fact happened in Christ—that Israel's restoration had not been inaugurated, and the nations qua nations are not now being brought into the people of God.[90] As such, it may very well be that he seeks to undermine the potential justifications for such a move before a

---

attempting to portray potential "influence" from Jewish groups as intentionally harmful to Paul's gentile gospel converts, and/or even *necessarily* negative from Paul's perspective (quite the contrary). It is strictly the matter of proselytism that Paul finds problematic, not "Jewish influence" of any sort, which is, indeed, what his own mission in itself represented to his congregations.

90. In my view, this is the fundamental premise of Paul's letter to the Galatians; see esp. here Zoccali, "What's the Problem with the Law?" (cf. p. 106 n. 54 below). Though coming to the same basic conclusion that Paul opposes proselyte conversion to normative Judaism for gentiles, and that this is, e.g., central to his argument in that letter, Thiessen, *Gentile Problem*, argues that the reason for this is not eschatological, but that Paul had come to believe that Jewish and gentile identity, respectively, were God-ordained (i.e., essential/primordial), and thus that the gentiles *could not* become Jews, regardless of whether they completed the prescribed course of proselyte conversion and were circumcised, and that they were, therefore, hopelessly lost outside of Christ. Thiessen notes the irony of his reading in that contemporary scholars have frequently understood Paul to be critiquing Judaism's supposed exclusivity, when he suggests that any critique of Jewish groups by Paul would be on the basis of their inappropriate inclusivity, as per the prospect of proselyte conversion. Thiessen explains: "While Paul may have formerly believed that gentile adoption of works of the law solved the problem, and his opponents continued to hold this view, the death and resurrection of God's son demonstrated to Paul that the gentile problem ran much deeper than he previously thought. Now he believes that gentiles are irremediably gentiles and no amount of Jewish law observance can alter this fact" (14). In my understanding, *Paul recognizes a problem affecting all human beings—Jew and gentile alike, namely, sin and death.* This was a problem that, for Paul, God had always planned would be ultimately dealt with through Israel's Christ, in fulfillment of the covenant promises to Israel, and thus for the benefit of the entire the world (cf. Rom 11:25–27; 15:8–12; p. 48 n. 69 above).

similar exigency as evidenced in Galatians could ever possibly materialize in Philippi, regardless of the level of actual plausibility.[91]

I suggest, then, that the fiercely antagonistic discourse against all things Jewish frequently observed in Phil 3 is far more apparent than real. Paul's rhetoric must be read, rather, in the context of a larger intra-Jewish debate, which involved very real theological commitments, as well as precarious sociopolitical and economic factors for all parties involved, as Paul well understood. While the question of the place of the other nations vis-à-vis Israel in God's redemptive purposes was answered in various ways in late Second Temple Judaism, with no real consensus view, the understanding that Paul had come to embrace was that with the coming of the Christ and dawn of the new age Jews *qua Jews* and gentiles *qua gentiles* were joining together into a single, and necessarily unified community of the redeemed. The prospect of suffering notwithstanding, it was crucial that gentiles in Christ hold fast to the full implications of this gospel that they had received from Paul, free from anxiety (Phil 4:6–7), and even rejoicing in the midst of such circumstances (Phil 1:18, 25; 2:17–18; 3:1; 4:4).

More to the Story?

But while persons influencing the Philippian Christ community toward the path of proselyte conversion may lie behind Paul's concern in Phil 3, as briefly mentioned above (p. 73), this is not the only possible agenda in view, and may represent only one-side of the potential exigency giving cause for Paul's rhetoric in this section of the letter. In the following chapter I will continue to examine Phil 3 in order to provide a fuller picture of Paul's concern for the community. Moreover, interacting with the observations I made in chapter 2 above, I will look more closely at Paul's assertions

91. Cinnirella, "Temporal Aspects," 238–39, points out that "[w]hen individuals or subgroups attempt to gain a new, desired social identity, and perhaps to abandon an old social identity at the same time, it is often the case that a degree of anticipatory identification will take place. . . . [I]ndividuals might come to endorse the norms and stereotypes of a desired social identity prior to adopting that identity." He further hypothesizes that "[t]he degree of anticipatory identification manifested by an individual is contingent on the endorsement and availability of desired possible social identities which suggest that attainment of the group membership is both possible and desirable." If Paul perceived that this dynamic was in some way at play, which, given his past experience with the Galatian exigency, is quite possible, then the rhetorical function of Paul's autobiographical discourse pointing to the supremacy of "in Christ" identity over every other in Phil 3:4–9 becomes increasingly understandable as the counterpart of his warning in 3:2.

pertaining to his own Jewish identity, the function of Torah, the meaning of "righteousness," the role of "faithfulness" (πίστις | *pistis*), and how all of this relates for him to Jesus Christ, and, ultimately, the Philippian Christ community's own identity and praxis.

4

"Rejoice, O Gentiles, with His People"
Paul's Intra-Jewish Rhetoric in Philippians 3, Part II

IN THE LAST CHAPTER I explored the implications of the Philippian Christ community's place within the Judaism of Paul's time, and how this relationship, regardless of the lack of a sizable presence of Jews in Philippi, should be the starting point for understanding Paul's exhortation to the community to remain unified and steadfast in their commitment to the gospel of Jesus Christ. If Paul is concerned that the community might be swayed by influences suggesting a move towards proselyte conversion to normative Judaism, then Paul is combating such influences not from outside of Judaism, but from the perspective of a different orientation within it. Thus, what Paul finds problematic is not Judaism in itself, but the Philippians failure to understand their appropriate role within the Jewish symbolic universe, namely, as representatives of the nations who have turned to the God of Israel through the risen Christ, and who thus stand alongside Jews qua Jews in the (re)new(ed) covenant and creation community.

The retention of "gentile" status is of utmost importance to Paul, because if certain members of the community might be tempted to take on Jewish proselyte status, then that would represent an implicit denial of God's faithfulness in fulfillment of the promises to the ancestors (cf. Rom 15:8–9). It would indicate that the new age has *not* dawned, and that God is *not* now through Jesus Christ restoring Israel, and gathering the other nations qua nations into the holy people of God—the multiethnic family promised to Abraham (cf. Rom 4:13, 17–21), the "household of faithfulness" (οἰκείους τῆς πίστεως) (Gal 6:10; cf. Phil 1:27), the citizenry of God's kingdom (cf. Phil 3:20; 1 Cor 15:50–58; see also Gal 5:16–21; 1 Cor 6:9–11).

The other side to this conviction is that the Philippians are no longer pagan idolaters (cf. 1 Thess 1:9–10). As Paul suggests in 1 Thess 4:5; 1 Cor 5:1, 9–13; 6; 10; and 12:2, Christ allegiants from the nations have ceased being members of the nations estranged from the God of Israel, and separated from God's covenant people (cf. Gal 2:15; see also Eph 2:11–22; p. 52 n. 81 above). Their praxis must uncompromisingly reflect this new covenantal and creational status, regardless of any conflict that might result; conflict that would be inevitable in light of the fact that, though inaugurated, the eschatological age is not yet fully consummated (cf. pp. 29–35 above). The present order must still be negotiated, and this will lead to God's people having to confront opposition, with the prospect, then, of suffering. In this chapter, I will offer a further suggestion as to whom Paul's warning in the opening of the chapter has in view. I will then highlight key interpretive points in the remainder of the chapter in order to demonstrate that rather than the foil to "Christian identity," Judaism remains the operative foundation and context for all of which Paul expects from the Philippian converts to his gospel.

Are You with "Us" Or "Them"?

Following his exhortation to "rejoice" in Phil 3:1, Paul launches into the warning to the Philippian *ekklēsia* regarding persons that would in some way pose a threat to the community. As pointed out in the previous chapter, it is my contention that the individuals or groups referred to here, in distinction from the oppositional forces alluded to elsewhere in the letter (cf. p. 55 n. 3 above),[1] represent a potential "danger from within." It should initially be observed that precise referent(s) to the first two epithets, "dogs" (κύνας) and "evil workers" (κακοὺς ἐργάτας) are not *prima facie* warranted. The language could readily apply to any individuals or groups whom from Paul's perspective *should* properly stand outside of the Philippian Christ community—that is, persons who have not authentically given allegiance to Jesus Christ as Lord, do not fully conform to the praxis of the Christ

---

1. While there is clearly commonality in that those referenced in Phil 1:15, 17, 28; 2:21 pose a threat to the Christ community like those suggested in Phil 3:2, the opposition mentioned in Phil 1 and 2 are, in my view, any combination of civic authorities and/or members of the greater Philippian community (e.g., fellow guild members, or other contacts) who present the prospect of civil and/or economic distress due to the ideological commitments of Christ community members, as discussed in ch. 3 above.

movement (cf. esp. Rev 22:15), and may in Paul's view pose some element of harm for the *ekklēsia*.[2]

Nanos has demonstrated that the virtually unanimous scholarly assumption that "dogs" was a common Jewish invective towards gentiles is without merit.[3] It is, then, highly unlikely that Paul is simply reversing this invective in condemnation of Jews. The literary evidence from the period demonstrates it to be, rather, a general slur. It is also commonly supposed that the reference to "evil workers" points to so-called "Judaizers," as ἐργάται ("workers") is a term frequently used for missionaries (e.g., Matt 9:37–38; Luke 10:2, 7; 2 Cor 11:13; 1 Tim 5:18;[4] 2 Tim 2:15; Did. 13:2). However, the term likely refers here more generally to the actions of particular individuals or groups. In Phil 2:12–13 Paul tells the Philippians to "work out (κατεργάζεσθε) [their] own salvation," and that "God is the one working (ἐνεργῶν) in [them]," so that they can "work (ἐνεργεῖν) for his good pleasure." And in Phil 1:6 Paul asserts that God will complete the "good work" (ἔργον ἀγαθὸν) he began in them. In this light, it seems to me that "evil workers" (κακοὺς ἐργάτας) simply refer to those whose actions are the antithesis of that which should characterize the Christ community (at least as far as Paul is concerned), i.e., those who do evil (cf. Luke 13:27). In keeping with this observation, Steven E. Fowl points out that Paul may have in mind the phrase frequently employed in the Psalter, "workers of iniquity" (e.g., LXX Pss 5:5; 6:8; 13:4; 35:12; 52:4; 58:2, 5; 91:7, 9; 93:4, 16; 118:3; 124:5; 140:4, 9).[5]

The first two invectives, even if perhaps not strictly referring to the same group in synonymous fashion, at minimum overlap with the referent of the third epithet, "the mutilation" (τὴν κατατομήν).[6] Though drawing

---

2. Thus, if Paul is directing his rhetoric here towards internal influences, this language would represent an ironic rebuke—that is, he is claiming that some who are presently on the "inside" are, by virtue of their agenda, really "outsiders." See further on this point below.

3. Nanos, "Paul's Reversal," 448–92.

4. As de Vos, *Conflicts*, 270 n. 129, points out, 1 Tim 5:18, generally cited in support of the conclusion that ἐργάτας refers to missionaries, is actually in reference to church elders.

5. Fowl, *Philippians*, 145; Fee, *Philippians*, 296 n. 47. See also de Vos, *Conflicts*, 270–71; he adds 1 Macc 3:6, in which "apostate Jews are called οἱ ἐργάται τῆς ἀνομίας" ("lawbreakers") (270).

6. Paul's seems to be making a play on words (paronomasia), contrasting the κατατομήν (*katatomē*) and the περιτομή (*peritomē*), the latter being the authentic members of the Philippian *ekklēsia*, and by extension all Christ allegiants, *both* Jewish and

problematic, if not altogether erroneous, implications from Paul's rhetoric here, there is good reason why scholars have almost uniformly understood Judaism to be in view. That Paul would evoke "circumcision" (περιτομή) (Phil 3:3), followed by a resume of his Jewish heritage (Phil 3:5; cf. Rom 11:1–2; 2 Cor 11:22), including his zeal for the traditions (Phil 3:6a; cf. Gal 1:13–14; see also Acts 8:1–3; and esp. Rom 10:2),[7] blamelessness under To-rah (Phil 3:6b), and thus reason to be "confidence in the flesh" (Phil 3:4) ostensibly points to such a conclusion.

Yet, at the same time, it should not be at all surprising that Paul would reference his own Jewish identity as an obvious, however hypothetical, ba-sis for claiming honor among Christ allegiants (cf. Rom 3:27–30), since, again, theses gentiles find their identity "in Christ" as it is within the Jew-ish symbolic universe (cf. Rom 9:1–5), and thereby follow a largely Jewish praxis (though remaining non-Jews in normative terms), as members of a Jewish movement. Thus, Paul's reference to his Jewish heritage would not necessarily have to indicate opposition to specifically Jewish influences, or an agenda that pertains in some way to Jewish identity. It is possible that Paul is simply conducting a *qal wahomer* style of argumentation, in which his willingness to relativize his own Pharisaic-Jewish identity[8] in favor of

---

gentile (cf. Rom 2:25–29; Col 2:11–13).

7. Paul refers here to a form of Pharisaic Judaism (cf. Acts 22:3–5; 26:4–5) char-acterized by violent zeal in the traditions of Phinehas, Elijah, and the Maccabees (cf. Num 25:6–18; 1 Kgs 18:40; 19:10; Sir. 45:23–24; 48:2; 1 Macc 2:15–28, 54, 58; 4 Macc 18:12; see also esp. Ps 106:30–31). This zealotry was ostensibly directed at Jews within the Christ communities throughout the Diaspora for a perceived laxity of the Torah-based boundary markers, and thus the equal participation of gentiles among them. These mixed assemblies would naturally have been viewed by many Jews as a serious threat to the Jewish community at large (cf. 1 Thess 2:16; p. 81 n. 87 above). However, accord-ing to Acts 8, the original persecution of which Paul took part preceded the mission to non-Jews, which suggests that at its core this persecution was motivated by the Christ movement's conviction that allegiance to Jesus Christ as Lord and Savior rather than full Torah submission was the means to righteous status/covenant membership, and thus the means to "life" (cf. Gal 2:15–16; 3:10–14). It should be observed that "zeal" itself is not considered problematic by Paul (Bockmeuhl, *Philippians*, 199, notes the positive use of the term in 1 Cor 12:31; 14:1, 39; 2 Cor 9:2; 11:2; cf. Titus 2:14; 1 Pet 3:1); it is, rather, an uninformed "zeal" that does not recognize the culmination of God's faithfulness to God's people in the Christ event that is the problem he identifies (cf. Rom 9:30—10:4).

8. It is important to point out that Paul would *not* be relativizing Jewish identity in the broad sense, since, for him, Judaism in general terms is a reflection of appropriate hu-man identity, which is thus fundamental to *all* people. Interrelated, as pointed out above, Christ-movement identity was no less an orientation of Judaism, despite the fact that it was (a) an *ethnically inclusive* identity category, allowing for subordinate identity salience,

"in Christ" identity,[9] and suffer in the process, is *all the more reason* for the Philippian Christ allegiants to rate their own prior social identity as "loss" (ζημίαν)—indeed, counting it as "crap" (σκύβαλα)—*in comparison to* the superordinate identity they now possess in Christ, even if this means enduring similar suffering as to that which Paul himself experienced.

In light of Paul's claim that the Philippian Christ community represents "the circumcision," which points to their membership in the (re) new(ed) covenant community—those who "worship/serve by the Spirit of God" (οἱ πνεύματι θεοῦ λατρεύοντες), it is quite possible that "the mutilation," as with the other two epithets, represents any potential entrants into the covenant community who would join under false pretenses, and/or internal influences of some sort that would likewise misrepresent or otherwise skew the implications of "in Christ" identity.[10] That is, as far as Paul is concerned, they are (or would be), once again, individuals who have *not* authentically given allegiance to Jesus Christ, and whose praxis does *not* ultimately accord with that which should characterize the Christ community (and thus the first two epithets). *Because they place trust in their own devices and/or relative status vis-à-vis the larger Greco-Roman world rather than in God's act in Christ, such individuals represent a distortion of the true covenant people, and are therefore representatives of "the mutilation" rather than "the circumcision."*

In keeping with such a reading, Fowl makes the interesting observation "that in Lev 21:5 those sons of Aaron who have 'mutilated' themselves are barred from performing service in the Temple."[11] I would additionally

---

and thus varied, culturally-informed manifestations of it, and, further, (b) understood by Paul to ultimately be the *only* appropriate interpretation of the Jewish tradition.

9. In other words, since Paul's Pharisaic-Jewish identity is much closer in origin and form with his "in Christ" identity (cf. Rom 9:1–5; 11:13–24), how much more should the Philippians regard their former "pagan" identity as worthless in comparison to what they have become in Jesus Christ? This would represent a classic *qal wahomer* argument, that is, an extrapolation from a minor premise to a major one.

10. It could also, then, more plausibly point to other Jewish Christ-allegiant missionaries who proclaim a different gospel from Paul's, since the issue of compelling gentiles to take on normative Jewish identity would not have to be the content of their message, and thus their hypothetical presence would be more in keeping with the only explicit evidence we have for such individuals found in 2 Corinthians. However, even if Paul may have such "external" influences somewhere in mind, I suggest that his primary concern is, nevertheless, with *internal* ones—that is, individuals that either presently or might potentially participate in the Philippian *ekklēsia*.

11. Fowl, *Philippians*, 148.

note here Deut 23:1 LXX, which forbids anyone with mutilated genitals to enter the *ekklēsia* of the Lord.[12] In this light, Paul may not be (strictly) using "mutilation" in an ironic sense indicative of the rite of physical circumcision, as per the process of proselyte conversion to normative Judaism, or, for that matter, in a literal sense, as per the practices of local pagan cults. He may instead be employing the epithet more generally, as metaphorically representative of those who should be excluded from the (re)new(ed) covenant and creation multiethnic worshiping/serving assembly, to the extent that they remain committed to a mindset and course of action that prove to be fundamentally out of step with the teaching the community has received from Paul, and thus failing in themselves to embody the will of God, as per, e.g., his admonition in Rom 12:1–2:

> I appeal to you therefore, brothers and sisters, by the compassions of God, to present your bodies as a living sacrifice [cf. Phil 2:17], holy and acceptable to God, which is your spiritual worship/service [cf. Phil 3:3]. Do not be conformed to this world, but be transformed by the renewing of your minds [cf. Phil 2:1–2], so that you may discern what is the will of God—what is good and acceptable and perfect [cf. Phil 1:8–11; 3:15].

Luke portrays a similar warning as found in Phil 3:2, 18 on the part of Paul to the Ephesian *ekklēsia* leadership. Regardless of the historicity of this meeting, there is very little reason to believe that such a warning did not represent an actual, perennial concern of Paul for the communities he founded:

> I know that after I have gone, savage wolves will come in among you, not sparing the flock. Some even from your own group will come distorting the truth in order to entice them. Therefore be alert, remembering that for three years I did not cease night or day to warn everyone with tears. And now I commend you to God and to the message of his grace, a message that is able to build you up and to give you the inheritance among all who are sanctified. (Acts 20:29–32)

12. Interestingly, the terms "dogs," "evil workers," and "mutilation," are also found in 1 Kgs 18:1—22:40, where these terms appear in the context of Elijah's battle with the prophets of Baal, and the condemnation of the house of Ahab and Jezebel for their idolatry leading Israel astray from their covenant with God. Paul explicitly refers to the same text in Rom 11:2–4, in which he seemingly aligns himself with Elijah, and the body of Jewish Christ allegiants with the faithful Israelites of Elijah's time.

That Paul would feel the need to warn the Philippians "with tears" (Phil 3:18) of such potentially divisive influences is even more understandable given the possible turnover within the community due to the probably significant numbers of migrant workers engaged in specialized service occupations.[13]

The earlier chapters of the letter might hint in the direction of such a concern on Paul's part for the community, as being grounded in his own personal experience. In 1:14–17 Paul states,

> [A]nd most of the brothers and sisters, having been made confident in the Lord by my imprisonment, dare to speak the word with greater boldness and without fear. *Some proclaim Christ from envy* [φθόνον] *and strife* [ἔριν], but others from goodwill. These proclaim Christ out of love, knowing that I have been put here for the defense of the gospel; *the others proclaim Christ out of selfish ambition, not sincerely but intending to increase my suffering in my imprisonment.*

Although Paul does not seem to discount here that the individuals to whom he refers are genuine Christ allegiants, in chapter 2, following his admonition to the Philippians in vv. 3–4 to "do nothing according to rivalry or empty conceit," and to "look not to your own interests, but to the interests of others," his rhetoric in reference to the same group intensifies: "I have no one like [Timothy] who will be genuinely concerned for your welfare. *All of them are seeking their own interests, not those of Jesus Christ*" (Phil 2:21). In Phil 3:18–20, Paul's rhetoric intensifies still further:

> For many live as enemies of the cross of Christ; I have often told you of them, and now I tell you even with tears. Their end is destruction; their god is the belly; and their glory is in their shame; their minds are set on earthly things.

As Fowl points out, *"envy"* (φθόνον) and *"strife"* (ἔριν) both occur in the vice lists of Gal 5:20–21 and Rom 1:29. A matter that Fowl does not take up is that they are explicitly connected in Galatians with the desires of the "flesh."[14] The specific acts of the flesh delineated in his letter to the Gala-

---

13. Damico and Chavez, "Determining What Is Best," 267; Oakes, *Philippians*, 35.

14. Fowl, *Philippians*, 40. Garlington, "Role Reversal," 93, correctly notes: "'Flesh', in this place, by way of contrast with 'Spirit', is not 'the sinful nature' or 'human effort' (as per NIV); it is, rather, the *era* of the flesh, that is, the old covenant/creation." Yet, Garlington continues by incorrectly suggesting that Paul equates the former era with the "flesh," because the Torah ministered largely to this dimension of human nature (cf. p.

tians—in contrast to the "fruit of the Spirit," that is, the Torah-based ethics he prescribes in Gal 5:22–25 (cf. esp. Phil 1:11)—are portrayed by Paul as being fundamentally rooted in self-interest at the expense of the other (cf. Gal 5:13–15), and as disqualifiers for entrance into God's kingdom (cf. Gal 5:21; Phil 3:20).[15]

It would not seem extraordinary, then, that drawing from his own recent experience Paul would warn the Philippians of similar individuals who (from Paul's perspective) might demonstrate a pretense of commitment to the gospel, but who in fact were seeking their own interests or gain (cf. Phil 3:7), as generally consistent with the social values of the greater Greco-Roman world, but in contradistinction to the implications of covenant and creation renewal. In doing so they would invariably be placing confidence in the "flesh," attempting to manipulate circumstances according to their own power, sensibilities, and personal advantage (as indicative of the present/old order; cf. Phil 3:19; Gal 1:4), rather than placing complete trust in and reliance upon God's act in Christ and the concomitant empowering of the Spirit (as indicative of the dawning eschatological age; cf. Phil 3:20; 2 Cor 4:16–18), regardless of the consequences (i.e., "the sharing of [Christ's] sufferings" [Phil 3:10]; cf. 2 Cor 4:7–11; 1 Cor 4:8–13; see similarly Mark 13:9–13). As J. B. Tyson aptly suggests, Paul makes an implicit comparison between "two groups"; they "differ in that one has confidence in the flesh, and the other expects transformation of the flesh."[16] Paul warns the Roman Christ community of these same sorts of persons in Rom 16:17–18:

> I urge you, brothers and sisters, to keep an eye on those who cause dissensions and offenses, in opposition to the teaching that you have learned; avoid them. For such people do not serve our Lord Christ, but their own belly, and by smooth speech and praise they deceive the hearts of the simple-minded. (cf. Phil 1:9–11; 3:15)

Thus, it is quite possible that in his letter to the Philippians Paul may have at least partially in mind those advocating a compromised disposition towards the greater civic community, including preeminently a more

106 n. 53 below). In my view, as in Galatians so also in Philippians, this term has nothing to do with a dichotomy between the "external" and "internal" facets of human nature. Rather, I suggest that while "flesh" does not directly equate to the "sinful nature" it points to humanity's *vulnerability* to the power of sin and death, which was characteristic of the former dispensation in contradistinction to the new era of the Spirit.

15. Paul concludes this section of his letter to the Galatians by asserting, "Let us not become conceited, provoking one another, envying one another" (5:26).

16. Tyson, "Opponents," 93.

lax position on idolatry. Those proposing such a course of action might include individuals possessing a higher socioeconomic status relative to the majority of the Philippian Christ community, and/or were imperial slaves, *liberti*, or even Roman citizens who may have had some level of influence to mitigate any sort of civic or socioeconomic oppression community members were facing, though not without some alteration of community praxis.

Somewhat similarly, Noelle Damico and Gerardo Reyes Chavez propose the interesting hypothesis that, perhaps having been informed about the situation by Epaphroditus, Paul may be directing his rhetoric at persons who have infiltrated the Philippian Christ community for the purpose of undermining it. They explain:

> Paul had been jailed for his activities, which leads us to believe that he and his message were viewed as a threat (or at least opposed) to Roman control. Would local Roman magistrates in Philippi have worried enough about a fledgling Jesus-following assembly to infiltrate it? Or would people variously attracted or even partially attached to the assembly have a range of views of the empire or local imperial authorities (complacent, complicit, sympathetic, aligned, or even employed)? While it is impossible to answer definitively, we immediately noticed Paul's use of hyperbole, because it is one tactic for misdirecting those who represent powerful interests. Paul opens his letter with brash statements calculated to illustrate that he is not in any way intimidated by his opponents and to imply that neither should the Philippian assembly (Phil 1:12 14). Not only is the whole imperial guard hearing the gospel, but most of the brothers and sisters (presumably within and without of jail) are emboldened. Such an opening salvo in the first person sends a strong message while keeping focus off the Philippian assembly itself. Through hyperbole, he is deftly irritating any imperially aligned or affiliated hearers who may be within the assembly, while not endangering any of the other Philippian assembly members. That this blustery pronouncement comes with the first twelve verses is also significant. He may also be warning the Philippian assembly that infiltrators (or those with competing loyalties) may be present, if they do not already suspect as much.[17]

They continue to point out that the veiled epithets in the warning of Phil 3:2 might lead any infiltrators to perceive that they have been exposed upon the letter's reading to the community, and either then reveal themselves, or

---

17. Damico and Chavez, "Determining What Is Best," 269–70.

exit the community. But because Paul avoids "naming names," he would not be placing the Christ community's leadership in danger.[18]

While I would not exclude this possibility out of hand, I am not especially convinced that Paul self-consciously has in view "infiltrators" functioning as guised imperial agents seeking to gain more information about and ultimately undermine the community. He simply may appreciate in a more general sense the ever-possibility that there will be persons within the community that will negatively influence it—which, in turn, would prove that such individuals may not be authentic allegiants—and who would thereby jeopardize the stability of the entire community.[19]

Research drawing together insights from SIT/SCT has demonstrated that prototypical group members tend to demonstrate greater loyalty to the group when it is under significant threat, whereas peripheral members are far more unpredictable in their response[20]—a social psychological reality

---

18 Ibid., 271.

19. Cf. esp. 2 Cor 13:5–7. Since one's "faith" has no meaning outside of what one does, and what one does is inextricably linked with who one is, Paul exhorts his gospel converts to test and prove themselves to determine whether they truly possess "in Christ" identity, and do then what is good, in keeping with his gospel.

20. Cf. Jetten et al., "Distinctiveness Threat and Prototypicality," 635–57. The two studies conducted conclude the following: "In accordance with social identity theory and with previous research (Allen & Wilder, 1975; Brown & Abrams, 1986; Diehl, 1988; Mummendey & Schreiber, 1984; Roccas & Schwartz, 1993; Turner, 1978), high threat to distinctiveness led to enhanced levels of ingroup bias. Furthermore, in Study 1, a similar pattern was found in ingroup and outgroup stereotyping, indicating that prototypical group members under distinctiveness-threatening conditions stereotype their own group more (see also Spears et al.,1997), which presumably leads to greater ingroup bias and other strategies used to enhance group distinctiveness and to achieve a positive identity. Moreover, Study 2 provided support for the prediction that ingroup bias among prototypical (but not peripheral) group members would be a positive linear function of distinctiveness threat. The question of who is most likely to express the most ingroup bias can be answered in the following terms: prototypical group members show this bias but only (Study 1) or especially (Study 2) when their group distinctiveness is threatened. This demonstrates that prototypical and peripheral group members have different perceptions of their group and adopt different identity management strategies when their group distinctiveness is threatened (cf. Doosje et al., 1995). The more central position of prototypical group members makes them more strongly linked to the group, which implies that a group-distinctiveness threat affects their own identity and the self-esteem that they derive from this group membership to a larger extent, compared to peripheral group members. Prototypical group members cope with this distinctiveness threat by means of a group-centred strategy. Peripheral group members, on the other hand, are less inclined to display ingroup bias when group distinctiveness is threatened (pp. 654–55)."

that Paul surely understood intuitively.[21] While he may have had much more confidence that the core members of the Philippian *ekklēsia* would ultimately "stand firm/in one spirit" (Phil 1:27; 4:1) amidst pressures to conform their identity and praxis in ways that would contradict the implications of the gospel,[22] he likely would have had far less certainty about new entrants, whose negative influence could then spread to the whole community, placing it at risk. Cinnirella explains,

> When an individual's sense of social identity is not entrenched, there is low commitment to the group . . . , and [when] group boundaries are perceived to be permeable, then perception of a feared possible social identity may lead [him/her] to focus on other social identities in their repertoire . . . , attempt to "pass" as a member of another group . . . , or even leave the group in order to join a more satisfying one.[23]

As Paul points out to the Corinthian and Galatian Christ communities, "a little yeast leavens the whole batch" (Gal 5:9; 1 Cor 5:6). Perhaps it was his own lens of suspicion regarding such peripheral members that compelled him to warn the entire community in this passage. As suggested

21. Cf. Tucker, *You Belong To Christ*, 38–40: "If the discipline of social psychology is universal in scope, then the significance of time is mitigated with regard to understanding aspects of the human condition that are consistent over time. . . . [I]t is legitimate to interpret that which is intrinsic to humankind and to delve into the world associated with the text by means of social psychological categories . . . . This approach . . . has been employed by social-scientific biblical scholars with convincing results. Thus, the field of social psychology provides language to better explain the exegetical findings for passages that deal with social relationships and group memberships" (40).

22. Contra Marchal, *Hierarchy*, 144, 161, 164, 177–78; Marchal, *Philippians*, 53, 62, 71, 77, 105, 149 n. 73, I do not find Paul to be making a veiled violent threat in Phil 3:15. The context for Paul's assertion here is that those who would be "perfect" should perceive the pursuit of "Christ-likeness" as the driving force behind all of life. He suggests that if certain members of the community who otherwise desire "perfection" (which is clearly a good thing) do not share this understanding, God will nevertheless reveal it to them. Rather than appealing to some form of divine retribution for thinking differently than Paul does, it seems to me that Paul is expressing his confidence that community members who are truly intent on reaching full maturity in Christ (ultimately accomplished in the general resurrection) will eventually come to understand, as Paul has, what this maturation process that God utilizes actually entails—namely, enduring suffering as a result of one's commitment to the gospel (cf. Rom 5:1–5). Paul is not wishing hardship and suffering on the Philippian Christ community, nor suggesting that this is in itself a good thing (cf. p. 72 n. 59 above), but is hoping that the Philippians will properly interpret, learn, and grow from it in their life in Christ (cf. Phil 1:9, 29–30; 4:12–13).

23. Cinnirella, "Temporal Aspects," 241.

above, then, Phil 3:2 may not point to precise individuals that could be named by Paul, or even perhaps by the Philippians themselves. Rather, it may point more generally to a *potential* group (however actual in terms of the larger Christ movement; cf. Phil 3:18) serving as the foil for Paul's rhetorical goal of *inhibiting* as many as might ultimately fall into this category of "out-group" threat (i.e., "the mutilation") by simultaneously *promoting* a common in-group identity (i.e., "the circumcision"), and thereby encouraging peripheral members towards the center (cf. Phil 1:27).[24]

Throughout the letter, Paul utilizes stereotyping to draw a sharp contrast between the character of the Christ community and that of the greater Philippian/Greco-Roman society. Out-group stereotypes include: the "crooked and perverse,"[25] "dogs," "evil workers," "the mutilation," those who "glory in their shame," whose "God is their belly,"[26] and who are "enemies of the cross." In-group stereotypes include: the "blameless and innocent,"[27] "children of God without blemish,"[28] those "shining like stars in the world,"[29]

24. Though I do not follow his line of thought entirely, see similarly deSilva, "No Confidence," 29–30, 52. However, it is also quite possible that even if Paul was not aware of specific individuals within the community who had violated the appropriate communal norms, at least certain members of the community may have been able to readily identify those others to whom Paul's warning would apply.

25. Cf. Deut 32:5. A passage very familiar to Paul (cf. p. 33 n. 31 above), he applies the language of the Song of Moses, which warns of Israel's coming unfaithfulness (in contrast to God's persistent faithfulness), to the greater Philippian civic community, while simultaneously presenting the Christ community as the *renewed* covenant community, who by virtue of God's faithfulness manifest in the Christ event (cf. Phil 2:6–11) have *now* been empowered via the Spirit to be faithful to God, culminating in the general resurrection (cf. Phil 1:6, 10–11; 2:13; 3:3, 10–14; n. 29 below).

26. For a through exploration of the belly-*topos* in the relevant literature, see Sandnes, *Belly and Body*. He concludes: "Body and character do belong together, not in the sense that the depths of human character can be inferred from outward appearance of the body, but in the sense that lifestyle, which also includes matters of food, drinking and sex, represents a yardstick by which the spiritual life may be measured, judged or corrected. Faith was to Paul not merely a matter of the heart, invisible to all but God. Faith worked itself out also in body and stomach. . . . Sharing in Christ's suffering implies not only bodily decay, which applies to all human beings, but taking his unselfish suffering as an example. The self-pleasing attitude which marks belly-worship is, therefore, tantamount to enmity to Christ's death. Furthermore, participation with Christ means sharing in his glorious body through the indwelling Spirit. . . . Believers must not be involved in bodily conduct which is inappropriate for a body destined to be fully transformed" (269–71); cf. esp. 1 Cor 6; n. 30 below.

27. Cf. Gen 17 LXX (esp. v. 1); Wis 10:15.

28. Cf. Ps 14 LXX (esp. v. 2); Wis 2:22.

29. Particularly in light of the fact that Phil 2:14–16 in total reflects the story of Israel

"who worship/serve by the Spirit of God," "claim honor in Christ Jesus," "have no confidence in the flesh," whose "citizenship is in heaven,"[30] who are destined for a glorified body, and are "the circumcision."

(cf. Exod 16; Num 14; n. 25 above; and esp. Ps 106), the echoes here of Gen 15:5; 22:17; 26:4; Exod 32:13; Deut 1:10; 10:22; Sir 44:21 (cf. Jer 33:22) in combination with Dan 12:3 are, in my view, unmistakable, and point to Paul's thoroughly eschatological understanding of the Christ community as *already* representing in the present order—on the basis of Christ's resurrection and exaltation (cf. Phil 2:9–11; 3:10)—God's redeemed and renewed humanity. That is, they are the multiethnic children of Abraham (cf. esp. Rom 4:13; 9:7–8, 23–26), who will be fully realized as such in the general resurrection from the dead (cf. Phil 3:11), upon Christ's return and the establishment of God's kingdom on earth (cf. Phil 1:6, 10–11; 2:16; 3:20–21; 1 Cor 15:50–58; see also Zoccali, *Whom God Has Called*, 158–70). Cf. Fowl, *Philippians*, 126: "Paul's allusions to Israel in the desert provide a negative example for the Philippians. Attention to the ways in which Israel misapprehended the movements of God's economy and, as a result, fell to grumbling and foolish reasoning can serve as a cautionary warning to the Philippians. Paul here presumes some sort of analogy between Israel's sojourn in the desert, somewhere between slavery and the Promised Land, and the Philippians' situation. Life in the desert calls for a particular practical wisdom. The same wisdom will enable sojourners in Philippi to manifest a common life worthy of the gospel by attending to the *telos* toward which God is directing them."

30. Regarding the contrast between a preoccupation with "earthly things," and Christ allegiants' "citizenship in heaven," Paul is not engaging in a Platonic dualism between lower and higher categories, with the material or "earthly" occupying the former category over against the immaterial, disembodied, and thus "heavenly" occupying the latter category. Such a view grossly misinterprets Paul's worldview, which is predicated instead upon a dualism of *ages:* the new age, as characterized by God's perfect will currently carried out in the heavenly realm, eventually becoming a full reality on earth, and thus supplanting "the present evil age" from which God has rescued his people (Gal 1:4; cf. Phil 2:15). Indeed, bodily (and therefore, I submit, gendered and ethnically-differentiated) human existence endures for Paul into the new age (cf. Rom 8:23; 1 Cor 6:12–20). Thus, rather than a refutation of earthly existence in itself, he has in view here the coming kingdom of God (cf. 1 Cor 15:50–58; see similarly Matt 6:10; also esp. p. 31 n. 29 above) with its king, Jesus Christ, who will "make *all things* subject to himself" (Phil 3:20–21; cf. Col 1:15–20; as made explicit in Colossians, clearly, in this context, "all things" includes heaven *and* earth). Thus, to set one's mind on "earthly things" is to remain ignorant of and aloof to what God has done, and still has left to do, in Christ via the Spirit—that is, covenant and creation renewal. It is ultimately to live, therefore, as if the *present* order is final and fully normative. See similarly 1 Cor 2:6–10: "Yet among the mature we do speak wisdom, though it is not a wisdom of this age or of the rulers of this age, who are doomed to perish. But we speak God's wisdom, secret and hidden, which God decreed before the ages for our glory. None of the rulers of this age understood this; for if they had, they would not have crucified the Lord of glory. But, as it is written, 'What no eye has seen, nor ear heard, nor the human heart conceived, what God has prepared for those who love him'—these things God has revealed to us through the Spirit; for the Spirit searches everything, even the depths of God."

| Philippians 2:14; 3:2, 17–21 ||
Out-Group	In-Group
Crooked and perverse	Blameless and innocent
Dogs	Children of God without blemish
Evil workers	Shining like stars in the world
The mutilation	The circumcision
Glory in their shame	Who worship by the Spirit of God
Enemies of the cross	Claim honor in Christ Jesus
God is their belly	No confidence in the flesh
Minds set on earthly things	Citizenship is in heaven
End is destruction	Will experience a transformation into glory

Paul's rhetoric here may be understood, then, as negotiating the underlying sociocognitive processes of social categorization and social comparison that serve to strengthen *intergroup boundaries,* and provide for self-evaluation and self-enhancement of group members in the assumption "that people have a basic need to see themselves in a positive light in relation to relevant others (i.e., to have an evaluatively positive self-concept), and that self-enhancement can be achieved in groups by making comparisons between the in-group and relevant out-groups in ways that favor the in-group."[31] Michael A. Hogg, Dominic Abrams, Sabine Otten, and Steve Hinkle explain this social psychological dynamic accordingly:

> Prototype-based perception of out-group members is more commonly called stereotyping: You view "them" as being similar to one another and all having outgroup attributes. When you categorize yourself, exactly the same depersonalization process applies to self: You view yourself in terms of the attributes of the in-group (self-stereotyping), and because prototypes also describe and prescribe group-appropriate ways to feel and behave, you feel and behave normatively. In this way, self-categorization also produces, within a group, conformity and patterns of in-group liking, trust, and solidarity.[32]

31. Hogg et al., "Tale of Two Theories," 260.

32. Hogg et al., "Social Identity Perspective," 254. Note that as Hogg et al., "Tale of Two Theories," 261, explains: "Depersonalization of self is the basic process underlying group phenomena—for example, social stereotyping, group cohesion and ethnocentrism, cooperation and altruism, emotional contagion and empathy, collective behavior, shared norms, and the mutual influence process. It has none of the negative implications

Philippians 3:2–3 would seem to function, therefore, as a means of clarifying for the *ekklēsia* who *genuinely* represents "us" over against "them," with the purpose of instigating conformity to the implications of his gospel among group members, particularly those on the periphery, against pressures working to distort this shared identity (cf. Phil 2:15). Rather than primarily understood as a warning against a *specific* group of outsiders, e.g., "Judaizers," the passage read purely in terms of Paul's concerns over the Philippians' sense of intra-group solidarity, and his attempt to make the Philippians' "in Christ" identity more salient over against either their prior (non-Jewish) social identities, or perhaps the prospect of Jewish proselyte status, finds more immediate correspondence with several of his appeals to the community throughout the letter:

> 1:27: standing firm in one spirit, with one accord contending for the faithfulness of the gospel.

> 2:5: Have this way of thinking among you, which is yours in Christ Jesus.[33]

> 3:15: Let those of us who are mature think this way, and if you think differently about anything, this too God will reveal to you.

This understanding also directly comports with Paul's emphasis on observing and emulating in-group exemplars (cf. Phil 3:17; 4:9). As Hoggs explains, "Within a salient group then, people who are perceived to occupy the most prototypical position are perceived to best embody the behaviors to which other, less prototypical members are conforming."[34] Likewise sharing this goal of in-group conformity to the implications of the gospel is Paul's appeal to the common eschatological orientation of the Christ community, in which they are *presently* citizens of God's coming kingdom. James C. Miller remarks,

> [I]n ascribing citizenship to his auditors in a realm other [than] Rome and in positing a κύριος ["Lord"] other than the emperor, [Paul] subverts central commonplace experiences and images,

---

of terms such as 'dehumanization' or 'deindividuation'; it simply refers to a contextual change in the level of identity (from unique individual to group member), not to a loss of identity."

33. "τοῦτο φρονεῖτε ἐν ὑμῖν ὃ καὶ ἐν Χριστῷ Ἰησοῦ." For a similar translation, see Brawley, "Reflex," 138.

34. Hogg, "Leadership," 189.

and the stories they embody, with their world. In other words, he exploits central vehicles used to construct and maintain Roman identity in order to create an alternative identity rooted in a different story with another empire ruled by a κύριος before whom all will bow.[35]

As is also well-established in social psychological research, affective states influence social cognition. Positive affective states have shown to signal familiarity,[36] as well as reduce racial bias,[37] indicating that collective emotional positivity is vital for improving the perception of a common social identity among group members, and the attainment, then, of intra-group unity. Particularly given Paul's awareness of the community's precarious circumstances, his prohibitions against "grumblings and arguments" (Phil 2:14) and "anxiety" (Phil 4:6), emphasis on positive thinking (cf. Phil 4:8), and frequent exhortations to "rejoice" in the midst of, and (in a certain sense) as a response to, opposition and suffering (cf. Phil 2:17–18; 3:1; 4:4; see similarly Matt 5:11–12) can similarly be understood as a concerted attempt by him at influencing social cohesion among the Philippian Christ allegiants.

Moreover, Paul's assertions regarding the surety of God's sovereign purposes being accomplished in and through the community (Phil 1:5–6), and the provision of divine empowerment (Phil 2:13), in combination with his *koinōnia* language regarding the community's sharing in the gospel (Phil 1:5), God's grace (Phil 1:7), the activity of the Spirit (Phil 2:1), and especially (by extension) the sufferings of Christ (Phil 3:10; cf. 1:29–30),[38]

35. Miller, "Communal Identity," 20. De Vos, *Conflicts*, 274–75, suggests along these lines that "in [Phil] 3:20 there is an unambiguous contrast drawn between Christ and the Emperor. In fact, Christ is described as both σωτήρ and κύριος, something that is unique among Paul's writings. Structurally, this contrast is presented as Paul's direct response to the temptation of the cults. Hence, it is likely that Paul is deliberately warning them not to join *collegia* that offered worship to the Emperor."

36. T. Garcia-Marques et al., "Positivity," 585–93.

37. Ito et al., "Facial Feedback," 256–61.

38. Hansen, *Philippians*, 245, remarks: "Paul's development of the concept of *participation* (*koinōnia*) places the human partnership for the sake of the common venture of advancing the gospel (1:5) within the divine-human communion with the Spirit (2:1) and sufferings of Christ (3:10). The *partnership in the gospel* resulting from *common sharing in the Spirit* leads to *participation* in the sufferings of Christ. Just as human partnership in the gospel requires active participation of the partners, so sharing in the Spirit and participation in the sufferings of Christ involve deliberate decisions as well. The term *participation* (*koinōnia*) points to the solidarity of all believers who have chosen to participate in the sufferings of Christ. Paul is not presenting his participation as an

represent no less his aim to strengthen in-group identity salience and soli-darity through sheer discursive power.[39] In all, Paul was a seeming realist who understood well the challenges inherent to intra- and inter-group dynamics, and made every effort to ensure the continued viability of the Christ community, especially in light of what was in this case a community experiencing intense external pressures, and also very probably internal ones as a result.[40]

Thus, putting together the interpretive conclusions of the previous and present chapter, I would conclude here that Paul primarily has in mind *potential* influences from *within* the community[41] that would seek to initiate in their own mind a more viable, honorable way forward for the Philippian Christ community, i.e., one free(er) from social death, and/or persecution. This agenda might have consisted of a move towards proselyte conversion to normative Judaism, and/or a more compromised disposition in relation to the gentile Philippians' prior non-Jewish social identity. But all such maneuvering is for Paul a betrayal of the ostensible allegiance they had of-

---

individualistic enterprise reserved only for martyrs. This participation in the sufferings of Christ cannot happen in isolation from others. According to Paul, all believers are called to share in the sufferings of Christ. . . . By their experience in community of *participation in his sufferings*, believers grow in their knowledge of Christ. The longing to know *participation in his sufferings* is a longing for a *community* experience. By suffering together for the sake of Christ, believers are drawn together in Christ" (italics original).

Though it does not, in any case, detract from my overall thesis here, I would note that I remain unconvinced that Paul's *koinōnia* language points strictly (or even primarily) to the economic partnership between Paul and the community. For a recent argument along these lines, see Ogereau, *Koinonia*.

39. For a succinct and informative summary of the various theories regarding the discursive nature of identity, and Paul's negotiation of it, cf. Tucker, *You Belong to Christ*, 55–58.

40. As Esler, *Galatians*, 216–17, has pointed out, "there is a close relationship between the position of a group with respect to outsiders and its internal conditions." The "uneasy relationship" of a community with other competing groups, is often "reflected in tensions among the membership." It is inappropriate, then, to draw a "sharp distinction between the outer and inner aspects of a community." Successful incorporation of community members is necessarily dependent upon "their developing a distinctive identity" rather than "simply acquiring a new status or a different set of ethical norms."

In 1 Thessalonians it seems clear that the Christ allegiants in Thessalonica have held up quite well in Paul's estimation to counter-pressures. It does not seem, however, that Paul understands the Philippians to have yet proven their fidelity to Christ to the same degree—that is, they have not yet demonstrated the same level of prototypicality that Paul desires from every community he has founded.

41. Of course, such potential internal influences would themselves be influenced from external factors, both directly oppositional in nature, and perhaps "friendly."

fered to Jesus Christ as Lord and Savior, and fundamentally contrary to the normative values of the Christ community—values grounded upon Jesus' own self-sacrificial use of power, and willingness to suffer for the benefit of the other. It is thereby an affront to the unity of God's people, an impediment to the gospel mission (cf. Phil 2:16), and a cause for shame (cf. Phil 3:19). It renders such persons "evil workers," "dogs," "the mutilation" (Phil 3:2), and "enemies of the cross" (Phil 3:18). Those who would ultimately choose to follow this path should be seen, therefore, as *ipso facto* outside of the covenant community (cf. esp. 1 Cor 5:9–13; Gal 4:30).

Now that the eschatological age has dawned, the nations qua nations are joining Israel qua Israel in worship of the God of Israel through the risen Christ—the chief prototype and ruling citizen of God's coming kingdom (Phil 2:6–11). As citizens of this kingdom (Phil 3:20), the Philippians must "stand firm in the Lord" (Phil 4:1). As far as Paul is concerned, regardless of the motivation on their part, the Christ community's compromise vis-à-vis reliance on the "flesh" is simply not an option, lest they forfeit their place in God's gracious future (Phil 2:15–16; Gal 5:16–21; 1 Cor 6:9–12). In this respect, the Torah's command that "the mutilated are *not* to be admitted into the *ekklēsia* of the Lord," indeed, stands firm (Deut 23:1 LXX).[42]

Christ is Most Important . . . But What Does That Mean for Identity and Praxis?

Given that Paul has offered a resume of his past achievement in Judaism to only then declare it to be "crap" (Phil 3:8) it is important for any post-supersessionist reading to explain the way in which Paul could maintain the importance and abiding salience of his Jewish identity, while also regarding his "in Christ" identity to be exceedingly more important. Often, scholars will affirm that Paul is not claiming in this passage (and/or elsewhere) that he departed from Judaism. However, as explained in chapter 1, the implications of their respective readings make it nevertheless difficult to understand how Paul could have maintained the saliency of his Jewish identity in any meaningful sense. A central matter here concerns the

---

42. As pointed out in p. 25 n. 12 above, a literal reading of this passage is overturned in Isa 56, and, clearly, Paul and the Pauline mission represented the inclusive vision of Isaiah, in which those from outside of Israel would be welcomed into the people of God to the extent that they are willing to keep the covenant. That Paul, no less than modern interpreters, could appropriate Scripture in multivalent ways should not be surprising.

question of "righteousness" as it further relates to Torah, God, and πίστεως Χριστοῦ *(pisteōs Christou)*.[43] Drawing on the analysis in chapter 2 of Paul's theological premises according to which he interprets the Christ event and consequent formation of the *ekklēsia*, in the following I will examine Paul's specific assertions in Phil 3:4–9 in the attempt to demonstrate how Paul understands "in Christ" identity, its relationship to normative Jewish identity, and the way in which it relatives all prior social identities (though itself being a form of Jewish identity) without obliterating them.

A Jew's Jew: Paul as a Jewish Archetype[44]

It has been proposed that Paul's self-description as an archetypal Jew serves as a rhetorical mechanism, in which he ascribes to himself the highest authority within Judaism to only then denounce Judaism and Jewish identity,[45] in favor of a "Christian" identity—a reading that goes back at least as far John Chrysostom.[46] Integral to this reading is the assumption that Judaism is an inherently flawed religion, which, at least as came to be practiced by the late Second Temple period, precipitated a collective attitude among Jews of self-righteousness and presumption towards God.

As suggested in chapters 1 and 2 above, immediately problematic with this view is that it fundamentally mischaracterizes Judaism as a religion of "work-righteousness" (in direct contrast to Christianity), rather than an ethnicity whose religious elements were predicated firstly upon God's merciful and gracious activity on behalf of Israel. The gracious and merciful actions of God included the giving of Torah in order to guide the praxis of God's people, and the covenantal requirement to live faithfully, as the only appropriate response to God's faithfulness shown them, and part and parcel of the very deliverance God provided. Since Paul's teaching to the Philippians (as well as to the other Christ communities he addresses in his

43. See my translation of this highly debated phrase in Phil 3:9 below.

44. I have borrowed this phraseology from Jacob, "A Jew's Jew," 258–86.

45. 2 Cor 11:22 is often seen as a clear parallel, whereby Paul compares his Jewish credentials with other Jewish teachers that have come to the Corinthian Christ community, whom he sarcastically refers to as "super-apostles" (11:5), and whom he believes are leading the Corinthians astray from his gospel.

46. John Chrysostom, *St. Paul's Epistle to the Philippians*, homily 10. For an excellent discussion on Chrysostom's treatment of this passage, see Jacob, "A Jew's Jew," 267–86. Of course, contemporary scholars who may read the passage along these lines would not draw the same explicitly anti-Jewish conclusions as did Chrysostom.

extant letters) presupposes this same covenantal dynamic, which was operative in at least most strands of late Second Temple Judaism, it is difficult to believe that Paul could be suggesting that there was something problematic with Jewish identity in and of itself. Though misleadingly casting the early Christ movement as something distinct from, rather than embedded within, first-century Judaism, in this very *limited* sense, E. P. Sanders' assertion that what Paul finds wrong with Judaism is that it is not Christianity is essentially correct.[47] That is, Paul's contention with non-Christ-allegiant Judaism is fundamentally centered on the question of the identity of Jesus of Nazareth—whether he is the Christ, and therefore Lord and Savior.[48]

Thus, the intra-Jewish debate in which Paul was involved had first and foremost to do with his conviction concerning Jesus—that he is the ultimate means of reconciliation and right standing with God, and, by virtue of his resurrection from the dead, that the new age has *now* dawned, resulting in the ingathering of gentiles qua gentiles into the people of God on the singular basis of their allegiance to Israel's Christ. In light of this conviction, I suggest that what is found in Paul's autobiographical account is *not* the *abandoning* but rather the *subordination* and *alteration* of his Pharisaic-Jewish identity to the new superordinate identity he has attained "in Christ," and this precisely in the context of the culmination of salvation history, according to which the promises to the Jewish ancestors are now being fulfilled (cf. Rom 11:25–28; 15:8–12).[49]

---

47. Sanders, *Palestinian Judaism*, 552.

48. A derivative of this question is that of the place of gentiles among God's people, which received different answers even from Jews within the Christ movement (and from gentiles in Christ as well; cf. Rom 11:13–24). However, while there did not exist a uniform understanding of the significance of Jesus Christ among Jews (or gentiles) *within* the Christ community, as I have argued in Zoccali, *Whom God Has Called*, the classic thesis of F. C. Baur predicated upon the supposed conflict between Petrine (i.e., "Jewish") and Pauline (i.e., "Torah-free") Christianity (as per his dialectical concept of historical criticism) misrepresents the Pauline mission vis-à-vis the larger Christ movement, overstating (or perhaps better, fabricating) the supposed antithesis between Paul's vision of the *ekklēsia* and that of the Jerusalem apostles.

49. In my view, Paul's self-understanding was that he remained not only a Jew but also a Pharisee, though this identity was transformed upon his encounter with the risen Christ, and reception of his apostolic call among the nations; a view that Luke's portrait of Paul confirms (cf. Acts 23:6). As far as the question regarding which school of Pharisaic Judaism Paul originally belonged to, I am presently uncommitted to any of the various proposals put forward to date. For a brief overview of the options, see Reumann, *Philippians*, 513–14 n. 30.

As Campbell has convincingly argued, Paul is engaged here in the rhetoric of comparison.[50] Elsewhere, Paul is quite clear that Jewish identity and praxis are of much value. The question is raised by his imaginary interlocutor in Romans: "What advantage, then, is there in being a Jew, or what value is there in circumcision?" It is answered, "Much in every way!" (Rom 3:1). What Paul is suggesting in Phil 3, then, is that *in comparison to knowing Christ even the most highly regarded things infinitely pale in significance.*[51]

I have already stated above that the rhetorical strength of the argument in Phil 3 necessarily rests upon an ordinarily high value placed upon Jewish identity, which would be shared by both Paul and his audience. It would certainly not make much sense for Paul to demonstrate that knowing Christ is superior to something that is already thought to be intrinsically deficient, lest he was unconcerned to impress upon his audience why their "in Christ" identity is of paramount importance. Of course, scholars have generally argued that even if the Philippians may have been persuadable of the value of Judaism, or at least the import of circumcision (and perhaps other Jewish rites), Paul desires to show them that they are wrong in this evaluation; that Judaism and its narrow focus on Torah observance as the basis of righteousness is the antithesis of what it means to be a "Christian." However, nothing in any of his extant letters, let alone Philippians, suggests that Paul believed normative Jewish identity has become obsolete now that the Christ has come. Quite the contrary, Paul assumes—even commands in 1 Cor 7:17–20—that Jews in Christ should continue to live as Jews, and, further, that what ultimately matters for both Jews and gentiles alike is keeping the commandments of God (cf. esp. Rom 2:6–29).[52]

50. Campbell, *Unity and Diversity*; see also on this point Reumann, *Philippians*, 511.

51. Cf. Campbell, *Unity and Diversity*, 213: "The present tense of the verb ἥγημαι ['consider'] points to the fact that this is a continuing process of evaluation, not limited to his previous life in Judaism (see Gal 1:13). Thus, as Paul makes clear, it is not just his Jewish privileges that are re-evaluated but everything else in life, even in his life after his Damascus road experience."

52. See similarly, Rudolph, "Paul's Rule." Paul affirms in Rom 11:11–24 that rather than standing in tension with "in Christ" identity, normative Jewish identity more naturally corresponds to it. Whereas gentiles are brought into the covenant people of God wholly new, Jews in Paul's historical context are *confirmed* in the covenant in which they *already* stand through their embrace of his gospel (cf. Rom 4:12, 16). While Gal 3:28 says there is neither Jew nor Greek for all are one in Christ, Paul does not intend here to negate difference wholesale. Ethnic differences are part of God's good creation, and in continuity, then, with the (re)new(ed) creation inaugurated in Christ (cf. Gal 6:15–16). Paul is calling, rather, for the unity and equality of the various groups who belong to the greater Christ community (cf. Col 3:10–14). This, in turn, argues against the need for

Where I believe a great deal of scholarship has gone wrong on this issue is confusing the salvation-historical contrast[53] that Paul presupposes (especially in his letter to the Galatians) between the dispensations before and after Christ, particularly in terms of the implications for gentiles (i.e., his adamant rejection of proselyte conversion to normative Judaism), and how the Torah itself may continue to function in the dispensation of Christ.[54]

---

gentiles to become Jews, or for Jews to become like gentiles.

The allowance for ethnic difference is also precisely what Paul affirms in Rom 2:11; 3:22; and 10:12. God shows no partiality for, or discrimination against, either Jews or gentiles. It is this seminal conviction of Paul regarding the unity and equality of God's multiethnic people that was violated by Peter and the other Jews in the narrative of Gal 2:11–14. It was violated *not* because they observed kashrut (which undoubtedly could have been facilitated in an ethnically-mixed Christ community), but because they withdrew from table fellowship with gentile Christ allegiants. Commenting on 1 Cor 7:19 (cf. Gal 6:15), the remarks of Thiselton, *Corinthians*, 50–51, bear mentioning: "to remain Jewish or non-Jewish does not spring forth from general indifference, but from its salvific irrelevance. As in the case of gender, such distinctions are not abrogated wholesale. . . . The new creation *transforms* and *relativizes* such distinctions, but they have a place."

53. In 2 Cor 3 Paul highlights the comparatively greater glory of the dispensation of Christ/the (re)new(ed) covenant and creation over against the *still glorious* dispensation of Torah/old covenant and creation (cf. 2 Cor 5:16–21). While the fulfillment of God's redemptive program is surely more important than what precedes it, such "fulfillment" would be utterly meaningless outside of the larger story of God's purposes in both the original act of creation, and the calling of Israel as the bearer of the "oracles of God" (Rom 3:2). Hafemann, "'Temple,'" 38, points out in his comments on 2 Cor 3:6: "The problem with the Sinai covenant is not with the law itself, but, as Ezekiel and Jeremiah testify, with the people whose hearts remain hardened under it. . . . [T]he letter/Spirit contrast is not a contrast between the law and the gospel as two distinct ways of relating to God. Nor is it a contrast between two distinct ways God relates to us (i.e., externally in the old covenant and internally in the new), since what distinguishes the ministry of the new covenant in Jeremiah 31:31–34 is that the law itself is now kept as a result of a transformed heart. As the expression of the abiding will of God, it is not the law *per se* that kills but the law without the Spirit, i.e., the law as 'letter.'"

54. As I have argued in Zoccali, "What's the Problem with the Law?" Paul's concern in Galatians is entirely the prospect of gentile Christ allegiants taking on Jewish proselyte status. His contrasting synecdoches in 3:10–12, "Torah" and "faithfulness," have to do with the basis of covenant identity now that the new age has dawned—that is, is covenant identity defined in terms of normative Jewish identity (i.e., [works of the] Torah) or Christ (i.e., "faithfulness"; cf. Gal 3:23–25)? As also argued here, for Paul, the only way that Jews or gentiles can ultimately persevere in Torah, and thereby "live," is by being "in Christ," and being in Christ is irreconcilable, *not* with Judaism generally, but with gentiles seeking proselyte conversion to normative Judaism. Neither Jews nor gentiles in Christ are under the dispensation of Torah (Gal 5:18; cf. Rom 6:14; p. 45 n. 58 above), which means they are free from the Torah's sentence of death (Gal 5:1; cf. n. 56 below), but that also precisely means that they are enabled to actually *do* the Torah

In brief summary of the findings of chapter 2 above, being in Christ means that Jews and gentiles are no longer under the *dispensation of Torah* (cf. Gal 3:23–29; 5:18; Rom 6:14), but that does *not* mean that the Torah ceases altogether to play an important role for Jews in particular, and the Christ community collectively (cf. pp. 49–52, esp. n. 80 above). Paul is otherwise unambiguous that his gospel *confirms* the Torah, and does not overthrow it (cf. esp. Rom 3:31; see also Gal 4:21). Despite the popularity of the claim in scholarly and lay circles, he simply knows nothing of a "Law-free" gospel in any sort of absolute sense of that phrase.

The idea that normative Jewish identity, as well as the Torah's role in revealing God's will for *both* Israel and all creation, are suddenly rendered obsolete because the promises have been fulfilled in Christ rests upon a precarious notion that fulfillment indicates obsolescence. But the content of God's promises, as found in, e.g., Deut 30, Jer 31, and Ezek 36, is in terms of Torah being once and for all *faithfully kept* by God's people. While Paul does indeed advance the significance of Christ's death in terms of both expiation and propitiation, the consequence of the Christ event is not only the atonement for sins (e.g., Rom 3:25; 4:25; 5:9, 16; 8:3a; 1 Cor 15:3; 2 Cor 5:19–21), but *the total defeat of sin and death, and concomitant enabling of obedience via the Spirit* (e.g., Rom 5:10, 17; 6; 8:1–17; Gal 3:12–14; 5:5, 16–25). It logically follows, then, that perfect obedience by virtue of God's special intervention in Christ is integral to the "mechanism" by which the Torah's sentence of death is obviated, and resurrection (or eternal) life is realized (cf. pp. 33–35, 49–51 above).

In other words, since "eternal life" is unquestionably for Paul a qualitative existence inseparable from obedience to God (cf. Phil 1:9–11; 2:12), the enabling of Torah obedience (cf. Phil 2:13) is presupposed in his conviction that God's people in Christ are free from "condemnation" (Rom 8:1–2). Thus, in accepting Jesus Christ as risen Lord and Savior—i.e., the "obedient allegiance [to Christ]" (ὑπακοὴν πίστεως) (Rom 1:5; 16:26)[55]—the

---

(Gal 3:12; 5:13–26; see also esp. Rom 2:25–29) in the dispensation of Christ, either in terms of a full submission for Jews, or a "limited" submission for gentiles; the latter being the equivalent of "Christ's Torah" (Gal 6:2; 1 Cor 9:21), or "Torah of faithfulness" (Rom 3:27) (cf. pp. 49–52 above). Moo, *Galatians*, 204, seems, then, to miss the point when he asserts that "the law provides no basis for the blessing because it involves 'doing': a 'doing' that humans find to be impossible." Rather, the "doing" of the law, and the blessing that results, *is* humanly possible—but only so "in Christ," and realized in full in the general resurrection.

55. This Pauline phrase clearly resonates with Paul's discourse in Rom 10:14–18 concerning "hearing" (ἀκοή) the gospel message. The notion of "hearing" in the Hebrew

Torah has reached its (intended) "telos" (Rom 10:4), which precisely means freedom from sin and death, but clearly *not from the Torah itself* (cf. esp. Rom 7:11–20; 8:4, 7–11);[56] a reality that will be consummated at the general resurrection from the dead (cf. Phil 3:10–14; 1 Cor 15:20–28, 50–58; Rom 6:4–5; see also p. 33 n. 32; p. 52 n. 80 above). Understanding Paul's underlying convictions regarding the relationship of Christ and Torah provides the proper context for interpreting Paul's autobiography in Phil 3:4–9.

Torah, Christ, and Righteousness

Throughout his letters Paul's focus on the present implications of the new age, vis-à-vis the contingent matters of each community he addresses, means that he does not provide a full exposition regarding his understand of Israel's covenantal status in the previous dispensation. In light of this ambiguity, I suggest that there is a strong hermeneutical warrant to assume basic harmony with the larger traditions in which Paul, as a first-century Jew, was grounded, unless there is sufficiently powerful reason to hold that he has moved outside of, reinterprets, and/or otherwise contradicts the basic tenets of late Second Temple Judaism, tenets shared in varying degree by most Jewish communities.

Accordingly, it should initially be observed that though Israel's failure to abide by the covenant is portrayed as fully anticipated by God (cf. Deut

---

Bible (שמע/*shema*) denotes obedience/submission to—and not mere sensory perception or even intellectual comprehension of—the message in question (cf. Deut 6:4–6; Isa 6:9–10; 53:1–2).

56. The "yoke of slavery" that Paul evokes in Gal 5:1 points *not* to the Torah in itself, but to *sin* and the Torah's condemnation of it (cf. esp. Rom 8:1–2). All mention of "freedom" for Paul is freedom in Christ from the power and penalty of *sin* (cf. esp. Rom 6:6–7, 22–23), especially indicated for gentiles by their repentance from idolatry (cf. Gal 4:8–9; 1 Thess 1:9–10; see also Rom 1:18–23), as per the renewal of the covenant (cf. esp. Gal 4:24–26; Rom 11:27), and all creation (cf. esp. Gal 6:15; Rom 8:21). This freedom from sin and death lies behind Paul's admonition in Gal 5:13 that the Galatians should not (paradoxically) use such liberty as a pretext to live as though the new age of the Spirit had not been inaugurated (cf. Rom 6:14–15). Paul exhorts the Philippians much in the same way in Phil 2:3–16. Similarly, when Paul refers in Gal 2:4–5 to the "false brothers" that sought to "spy out on the freedom we have in Christ Jesus, so that they might enslave us," the issue is whether God's people are still to be demarcated by the terms of the former dispensation, *as if* God's faithfulness in fulfillment of the promises—as particularly signaled by the ingathering of the nations (cf. Gal 3:8, 14)—had not in fact been inaugurated, that redemption had not been accomplished, and therefore that the enslaving power of sin and condemnation of death are still in force (cf. esp. Gal 4:25, 30–31).

30:1; 31:16–22), there is no hint anywhere in the Torah or prophets that God's standard of obedience is an impossible one. Rather, in the Hebrew Bible obedience to God is consistently portrayed as humanly achievable (e.g., Deut 12:12–21; 30:11–14; Mic 6:8; Isa 1:10–20; 5:7; 56:1; Jer 7:3–7, 21–26; Amos 5:14–15, 21–27; Hos 6:6–7; see also Gen 6:9; Job 1:1; Tob 1:3), and this perception is generally presupposed in the relevant extrabiblical Jewish literature of the period.[57] Thus, when Paul reflects upon his life in Judaism here, and claims to have been "blameless" under the Torah (v. 6), he is almost certainly claiming that he was faithful to the stipulations of God's merciful and gracious election of Israel, including his appropriate participation in the temple cult and active repentance from sin, according to which his covenant standing was sustained (cf. Pss 32; 51).[58] But what,

57. Das, *Galatians*, 314–15, points out that the relevant Jewish literature demonstrates: (a) at least some Jews, such as the Qumran community, lamented over the inability of human beings to completely abstain from sin until the eschaton (e.g., 1QS 3.21–23; 4.18–22; 11.14–15; 1QH 7–8); and (b) only a small number of "exception individuals," such as Noah (Jub. 5:19), Abraham (Jub. 23:10), and Moses (Philo, *Moses* 2.8–11) were conceived of as being in some sense "perfect." Though Das supposes on the basis of these examples that the impossibility of doing the Torah was considered by Jews to be an existential problem, I would argue that they fail to support any conclusion in which it was believed that the Torah was unfulfillable in the present order. The examples from Jubilees and Philo actually suggest, if anything, the opposite conclusion. The Qumran community, as with other Jewish groups of the late Second Temple period generally, possessed a keen sense of the reality and pervasiveness of sin, and sought to avoid it in the obvious conviction that sin was detrimental to relationship with God and others. However, no such groups believed that a lack of moral perfection indicated that they were ultimately not in right standing with God. Thus, the idealized reflections on the patriarchs in Jubilees and Philo notwithstanding, living a Torah-faithful life simply did not mean the complete absence of sin for any significant known Jewish group prior to 70 CE. It is clearly not what the Torah or any part of the Hebrew Bible itself puts forward as the necessary grounds for a proper relationship with YHWH in the present order; indeed, the Torah is given to Israel *because* of the reality of human sinfulness, Israel included, *not* in spite of it (cf. Rom 5:12–14; 1 Kgs 8:46; Eccl 7:20; see also, e.g., Sir 25:24; 4 Ezra 3:7–27; 7:116–26; Apoc. Ab. 23:12–14). Even though the Torah (sometimes conceived as being trans-temporal; cf. n. 60 below) was generally interpreted to be the very answer to the problem of sin, that the Torah could eliminate it altogether is—with the possible exception of a very few select individuals in Israel's history—unattested in the relevant literature, and, moreover, defied by the sacrificial system contained within the Torah. Similarly, neither Paul nor any part of the New Testament (cf. esp. 1 John 1:8–10) suggests that a "sin-free" life prior to the general resurrection is practically attainable, though it remains the goal to which Christ allegiants should strive, as did Paul himself, in light of its future realization for all those in Christ (Phil 3:10–14; 1 Cor 9:24–27; cf. esp. Matt 5:48).

58. I am not convinced by attempts to read Paul's affirmation of blamelessness under the dispensation of Torah in less than a straightforward way, as suggested by, e.g.,

then, could he be indicating in Phil 3:9: "and be found in him, not having a righteousness of my own—the one from the Torah"?

I suggest that Paul came to believe that righteous status under the terms of the former dispensation of Torah was always intended by God to be merely provisional, and requiring all along confirmation through a fresh act of divine intervention in fulfillment of the promises (cf. 2 Cor 3:7–11). Likewise, prior to the giving of the Torah Paul quite likely believed that individuals could be deemed righteous (such as Noah; cf. Gen 6:9; Sir 44:17; Jub. 5:19) *relative to the divine economy in which they lived.*[59] The basis of this "proto-righteousness" would be, then, the appropriate relational response to God's grace and mercy—that is, trust in God and God's promises, along with concomitant obedient actions as the leaning of one's life.[60]

Though "righteousness" indicates in the first place *doing* or *having done* what is right/just, in the Hebrew Bible this is *always* understood in terms of God's proper expectations for humankind in creation and election, and vice-versa. As A. A. Anderson correctly points out, "Righteousness (*ṣĕdāqâ*) is a term of relationships, denoting the kind of conduct which serves to maintain established ties. . . . In a covenant context 'righteousness'

Westerholm, *Israel's Law*, 161; Thompson, "Blameless," 5–12. Those arguing that Paul's is merely reflecting his "pre-conversion" attitude, which was overturned upon his acceptance of Jesus as the Christ, in my view, simply misunderstand the nature of first-century Judaism as a religion of "works-righteousness," as well as the Pauline antithesis on faith and works, which has nothing to do with "believing" over against "doing" as distinct ways of salvation, but of how the covenant people are demarcated now that the Christ has come—that is, by allegiance to Jesus Christ ("*pistis*") rather than normative Jewish identity ("works [of the Torah]"). Further, contra Reumann, *Philippians*, 516, Paul's claim to have been "blameless" does not contradict the notion that at least many Jews of Paul's time were awaiting the fulfillment of the prophetic promises of national restoration. Here, an immediate distinction needs to be made between individual Jews and the fate of the nation collectively. That is, Paul, and other Jews like him, could have simultaneously believed himself/themselves to be blameless, while at the same time understanding Israel as a whole to have not yet been (fully) delivered from the experience of "exile"—though having returned to the land of promise in the sixth century BCE, they were still under the oppressive control of foreign nations, presently Rome. Cf. Zoccali, *Whom God Has Called*, 150–70.

59. This is made explicit by Philo concerning Noah in *Abr.* 7.36–39. Highlighting Gen 7:1, he points out that Noah "was perfect in his generation," that is, "in comparison with others who lived at that time."

60. This understanding of righteousness would be no less the case for Paul's in-group exemplar of it, Abraham. Though in the relevant Jewish literature Abraham is portrayed as someone already obeying Torah (cf. 2 Bar. 57:1–2; Jub. 24:11; Sir 44:20; CD 3.2), Paul clearly does not adopt such an idea.

signifies faithfulness to the obligations stipulated by the Covenant."[61] For Paul, the primary import of human righteousness is an eschatological status obtained "in Christ," which is synonymous with participation in the (re)new(ed) covenant and creation. This covenantal status is therefore indicative of those, both Jews and gentiles, who have been confirmed or brought anew in a positive relationship with God (cf. Gal 1:6; Rom 9:23–24), and receive the eschatological life that this relationship promises.[62] To

61. Anderson, *Psalms*, 262. I would briefly note here that I am not persuaded by recent counter-arguments for separating Paul's δικαιο (righteousness)-language from the covenant relationship between God and God's people. Westerholm, *Perspectives*, 286–96, argues for this separation particularly through (a) an appeal to the wisdom literature of the Hebrew Bible, which he suggests does not connect the idea of "righteousness" with that of "covenant" (however, see Hubbard, "Wisdom"; Schultz, "Unity"; Grant, "Wisdom"; see also Middleton, *New Heaven and a New Earth*, 96–103), and (b) his claim that explicit mention of διαθήκη (covenant) is rare in Paul's letters. Westerholm's argument, in my view, misses the point of why Paul's δικαιο-language is decidedly covenantal. It is not that δικαιοσύνη—whether with respect to humans or God—automatically means "covenant membership" or "covenant faithfulness," respectively. As asserted above, I would basically agree that on a more strict lexical level "righteousness" means simply doing or having done rightly/justly—though clearly in the Hebrew Bible this is always understood in relational terms, even if only implicit, between God (the law- and promise-giver) and people (those expected to be faithful to God's laws and promises, and who can properly expect God to do right according to both; e.g., Pss 7, 33, 97; and esp. Isa 45:23–24 [cf. Phil 2:10–11]). The point is that in Paul's theology the matter of "righteousness" simply cannot be abstracted from the salvation-historical context according to which God relates to God's people, and according to which the Christ event gains significance; cf. esp. here the collection of essays by Hafemann, *Covenant Context*, which explicate various aspects of this covenantal/salvation-historical framework to Paul's theology.

Moreover, Westerholm's argument concerning the paucity of explicit mention of "covenant" in Paul confuses "word" and "concept." The presence of the latter is *not* dependent on that of the former, especially when the concept exists on the level of fundamental conviction for an author, and may thus remain only *implicit* in any relatable discourse. This is even more likely the case when the term in itself would generally carry little resonance with the addressees, though the idea(s) the term represents is basic to the author, which, with few exceptions, is precisely the situation here for Paul and his largely gentile auditors.

62. The correspondence between covenant and righteousness explicitly surfaces in Paul's discussion of Abraham in Rom 4:11, where Paul's rewording of Gen 17:11 LXX, replacing διαθήκη (covenant) with δικαιοσύνη (righteousness), speaks to the virtually synonymous nature of righteous status and covenant membership in his understanding (cf. Wright, *Romans*, 494–95). The status of righteousness or covenant membership is therefore central to "in Christ" identity (cf. Esler, *Conflict*, 167–68). Importantly, though the status of righteousness is conferred upon the offering of one's allegiance to the risen Christ as Lord and Savior, its full significance for Paul will not be realized until the general resurrection of the dead and final judgment, when vindication and moral perfection/

speak of this relationship (e.g., Gal 3:26—4:7; Rom 8:14–17) is to simultaneously point to a particular way of life in accordance with God's will for God's people, as revealed in the Torah. In other words, covenant members who are faithful to God by virtue of their membership are "righteous ones." This human faithfulness on the basis of God's grace shown to the Philippians is what Paul affirms in Phil 1:7–11.

Thus, in Phil 3:4–9 Paul is making clear that one's covenant membership and right standing with God *cannot* be secured by any other means than Christ and the Spirit, as a consequence of the new age having been inaugurated through Christ's death and resurrection (cf. Rom 8:7–9; pp. 29–35 above). Any such attempt has become merely a "righteous status" of one's own estimation (i.e., of the "flesh," or *old order* of things), rather than the single means to righteousness that God has *now* made possible (cf. esp. Rom 9:30—10:4). It is therefore ineffectual.[63]

Verses 4–9 are decidedly *not*, then, a denunciation of human achievement and desire to merit favor with God, as per the traditional Protestant/ Old Perspective view.[64] Indeed, Paul instructs the Philippians (as he does

---

glorification is obtained for all those in Christ (cf. Phil 1:6, 10–11; 3:10–14; see also esp. Gal 5:5; Rom 8:18–19, 28–30; 2 Cor 3:18). At no time prior to the general resurrection does righteous status indicate for Paul moral perfection, because of his understanding of the uncompromising reality of human sinfulness. Of course, central to Paul's theology is the conviction that sin's defeat has been inaugurated in Christ's death and resurrection, and thus, ultimately, only the righteousness that comes to God's people/Abraham's descendants through Christ and the Spirit brings with it the eschatological life that was promised (cf. Gal 3:21–22; 5:5; Rom 7:24–25).

63. In this light, Rom 3:19–20; 10:3–4; and Gal 3:10–11 should be understood in terms of an eschatological pronouncement (cf. 1 Cor 10:11)—*now* that God has acted once and for all in Christ there is no other means of righteousness available (cf. esp. Rom 8:1–14). Thus, while it is evident that Paul believed Christ's death and resurrection to be the ultimate means through which all people of any time could be saved, he presumably understood that those who lived and died prior to the eschatological age were secured in what God would eventually do in Christ by virtue of their allegiance to God relative to the divine economy in which they lived. In this respect, Paul's thinking would be in line with the author of Hebrews (cf. Heb 11; Gal 5:5; Rom 8:24–25).

64 Contra O'Brien, *Philippians*, 395–96, who states: "[A]gainst Sanders [cf. Sanders, *Jewish People*, 43–45, 139–41] the expression ἐμὴν δικαιοσύνην τὴν ἐκ νόμου is about 'attitudinal self-righteousness'. Several writers, including R. H. Gundry, have pointed out that although Paul begins his discussion of Phil 3:2–11 by recounting privileges of his Jewish inheritance (v. 5), he moves on to describe his personal accomplishments (vv. 5–6), in which he had place his confidence (v. 4). There is a shift in dispensations, and clearly salvation history does play a part, But 'Salvation history does not account for all Paul says, much less for the passion with which he says it; we are dealing with an autobiographical as well as dispensational shift' [Gundry, "Grace," 13]. The three

every Christ community he addresses in his letters) to strive for greater faithfulness to God, as manifest in their obedient actions (cf. Phil 1:6–11; 2:12–13; cf. pp. 49–51, esp. nn. 70–71 above), and appeals to his own striving for resurrection life in the present time as an example to be emulated by community (cf. Phil 3:10–14; see also 1 Cor 9:24–27).[65] Nor is Paul likely expressing here a rejection of "automatic national privilege," as suggested in Wright's approach, and similarly put forward by Markus Bockmuehl.[66] Rather, these verses are exactly an affirmation of *God's faithfulness* in once and for all redeeming Israel and all creation—that is, the (apocalyptic)

κατὰ-['according to'] expressions of v. 6 point to individual performances alongside Jewish status. A zeal for the law was good; but not the self-righteousness that resulted."

Though I do not ultimately follow his reading of the passage, Campbell, *Deliverance*, 901, citing O'Brien, Gundry et al., rightly asserts: "It need hardly be said that these statements are all additions to what Paul actually says, and moreover, they tend to override what he says—that what was previously gain for him is now loss in comparison with Christ, and only therefore in comparison with Christ."

65. As pointed out in ch. 2 above, Paul shows no hesitancy in demanding rigorous obedience from gentile converts to his gospel, as *inextricable from their salvation*. As explicitly demonstrated in Rom 6–8, Paul's communal ethics are likewise inextricable from his eschatology (cf. esp. vv. 4–5; see also Rom 13:11–14). I find little reason, then, to understand Paul to be admonishing the community of an attitude of "perfectionism" in 3:12–16. To the contrary, Paul is encouraging the community toward *greater* faithfulness to Christ in light of their future resurrection. The passage is thus a warning against the sort of complacency that may leave the community more vulnerable to compromising their "in Christ" identity amidst oppressive, counter-pressures (cf. esp. 1 Cor 9:24–27).

66. For Wright, *Climax*, 239–41, in the similar passage in Rom 10:3, and presumably here as well, a "righteousness of my own" means for Jews and Jews alone on the basis of their historical election, in contradistinction to the non-Jewish world (cf. pp. 115–16 below). Bockmuehl, *Philippians*, 203, similarly remarks on Phil 3:6, "the following verses suggest that this type of externally measured and nationalistically appropriated righteousness in the Law turned out to be wholly inadequate. This was not because Paul had been wrong to observe it and excel in it . . . . Instead, he has rejected the Jewish nationalism of his 'earlier life' (Gal. 1:13–14) precisely because in his encounter with Christ he discovered that the way of narrow national exclusiveness is not the one that God has chosen in Christ." He further comments on Phil 3:9: "This former self-righteousness is derived from the Torah. Paul does not reject here faithful Torah observance but rather the attitude which finds in the observance of the 'works of the Law' grounds both for self-confidence before God and for the exclusion of others. It is this attitude which was once his own, as verse 6 showed; it now appears to characterize the Judaizers, who 'put their confidence in the flesh' (v. 3f.) and who exclude others, calling them 'dogs' . . . . In contrast to this self-made righteousness derived from the Torah is another kind of righteousness . . . . Where the former state of righteousness was attained by human achievement, this one is the gift of God" (209–10).

culmination of salvation history in God's act in Christ (cf. Phil 3:12b).[67] I translate all of v. 9 accordingly:

> And be found in him, not having a righteousness of my own—the one from the Torah—but the one through faithfulness realized in Jesus Christ,[68] which is the righteousness from God, based on faithfulness.[69]

For Paul, the gospel of Jesus Christ *is* "the righteousness from God" that is "*apart from the Torah, but testified to by the Torah and the prophets*" (Rom 3:21; cf. 1 Cor 1:30). "Torah" and "gospel" are not in a fundamentally antithetical relationship, as is often assumed to be Paul's view, but a *chronological* one, with the former depending on the advent of the latter for its ultimate fulfillment (cf. Matt 5:17–18). This expression of God's righteousness is,

---

67. The inseparability of divine and human faithfulness in Paul's thought is rightly observed by Campbell, *Deliverance*, 905: "[I]t is worth emphasizing that the apostle's account of life in Christ oscillates constantly throughout this argument as it develops (i.e., 3:12–21) between present realization and future fulfillment, and between divine and human agency [cf. n. 65 above]. Paul emphasizes strongly in what follows the human agent's striving for this goal (thereby also denoting its future aspect), in one of his most concentrated deployments of ἀγών material—imagery that emphasizes human agency emphatically. But he also qualifies this account in v. 12b with an assertion of God's agency within the contest as well (and in a way that disrupts his deployment of the athletic imagery)—διώκω δὲ εἰ καὶ καταλάβω, ἐφ' ᾧ καὶ κατελήμφθην ὑπὸ Χριστοῦ (and see 1:3–6; 2:12–13)." See further on this point below.

68. I translate πίστεως [Ἰησοῦ] Χριστοῦ (e.g., Gal 2:16; 3:22; Rom 3:26) such that it is essentially synonymous with the gospel, that is, God's faithful eschatological act of redemption/reconciliation/restoration through Jesus Christ, which calls for and enables the human response of fidelity to God (cf. Gal 3:13; 4:4–5; see similarly Martyn, *Galatians*, 314). For a recent analysis of πίστις χριστοῦ (*pistis Christou*) as an "eschatological event" (a so-called "third view" that moves beyond the subjective or objective genitive debate), see Schliesser, "'Christ-Faith,'" 277–300. For a similar interpretation here, cf. also Bockmuehl, *Philippians*, 211; Fowl, *Philippians*, 154. See additionally on this matter below.

69. In Rom 1:16–17 Paul equates the gospel with the revelation of God's righteousness, adding that such righteousness is revealed from faithfulness to faithfulness, which, in my view, points to the intersection of divine and human faithfulness, as likewise here in Phil 3:9. This intersection of faithfulness is also suggested by Paul's modified citation of Hab 2:4. As I have argued in Zoccali, "What's the Problem with the Law?" 402, regarding the quotation of this prophetic passage in Gal 3:11, "Paul's ambiguity with regard to whose faithfulness is in view is due to the fact that πίστις functions as a synecdoche for the gospel of Jesus Christ. . . . All possible readings of the Hebrew text [God, the righteous one, or the vision itself as the subject of this faithfulness] are thus simultaneously fulfilled by the gospel" (cf. p. 118 n. 73 below).

for him, what Isaiah had prophesied would come (cf. Rom 1:1–2). In Phil 2:10–11, he points to a key passage:

> Turn to me, and you will be saved, those from the ends of the earth! I am God, and there is no other. By myself I swear, most certainly, righteousness will proceed from my mouth; my word will not be diverted: that to me every knee will bow, and every tongue will confess to God, saying, righteousness and glory will come to him, and all who exclude themselves will be put to shame. By the Lord they will be made righteous, and in God all the offspring of the children of Israel will be glorified (Isa 45:22–25 LXX; cf. 1 Thess 2:13; 2 Cor 5:18–21; Rom 8:30).

Excursus: God's Righteousness vs. A Righteousness of Their/My Own (Philippians 3:9 and Romans 10:3): What is the Nature of Paul's Argument?

> For being ignorant of the righteousness of God, and seeking to establish a righteousness of their own, they did not submit to the righteousness of God. (Rom 10:3)

Philippians 3:9 and Rom 10:3 convey the same basic meaning. There is, in my view, little reason to believe that the respective genitive constructs of the two passages—a genitive of origin in the former (τὴν ἐκ θεοῦ δικαιοσύνην/"the righteousness from God"), and a subjective genitive in the latter (τὴν τοῦ θεοῦ δικαιοσύνην/"the righteousness of God")—indicate any fundamental difference, as each of these senses are inextricably connected. In both cases, God's righteousness refers squarely to the gospel of Jesus Christ as the eschatological fulfillment of God's *ḥesed* to Israel and the other nations, and according to which God will judge the world (cf. Rom 2:5–16; 3:19–26). As portrayed especially in Isaiah, *the eschatological coming of God's righteousness secures the righteous status of God's people* (cf. (cf. Isa 45:21–25; 46:12–13; 51:5–8; 56:1; see also esp. Rom 3:26).

Thus, Paul is casting a straightforward contrast between Christ and *any* other basis of righteousness. Because an anachronistic understanding of Torah-based righteousness (i.e., viewing the Torah from the perspective of the former dispensation)—rather than, e.g., the wholesale rejection of Torah/Torah obedience—is strictly in view in each passage, reading into his argument either (a) a "works vs. faith," or (b) an "exclusive vs. inclusive" dichotomy seems to me to be completely unnecessary, and quite misguided.

With respect to dichotomy (a), Paul utilizes the phrase ἔργων νόμου (works of the Torah) as the equivalent of normative Jewish identity, and thus basis of covenant identity in the previous dispensation,[70] and πίστις/ *pistis* (faithfulness) as the equivalent of Christ allegiance, which for him is the new basis of covenant identity.[71] He *nowhere* employs a contrast between doing good deeds to merit salvation over against receiving salvation from God through intellectual assent alone, and/or a disposition abstracted from action; this is an utterly foreign concept to Paul.

Dichotomy (b) is merely a secondary inference from Paul's main point. Especially since proselytism was a live option in first-century Judaism, and, further, that there existed the concept of the "righteous gentile" (even if not in terms of such non-Jews participating in the covenant between God and Israel), he was almost certainly *not* troubled by the need for full Torah submission and normative Jewish identity in order to be named among God's covenant people prior to God's act in Christ. The exclusion of gentiles qua gentiles from the community of righteous ones becomes problematic for him precisely in light of the fact that the Christ has now come, and, as Scripture had prophesied, the gentiles are being gathered in among them (cf. Gal 5:11; see also esp. Rom 3:27–30). It is unlikely, then, that Paul would attack as a first-order criticism a conviction among Jews that only they may possess righteous status as God's people. In all, my understanding of Phil 3:9 and Rom 10:3 as a reference to Jesus Christ and concomitant eschatological reality as the final manifestation of God's *ḥesed* fully comports with every mention of God's righteousness throughout his letter to the Romans (cf. Rom 1:17; 3:5, 22, 25, 26; see also 4:13; p. 32 n. 30 above).

Fowl similarly observes of Phil 3:9: "There is concern not with Jewish pride or exclusiveness but with a fundamental misperception of the *telos* of the Law."[72] Whereas in the previous dispensation normative Jewish identity and thus full Torah submission was the equivalent of covenant identity, in the present dispensation covenant identity is found in Christ for Jews and gentiles alike (cf. p. 106 n. 54 above). *Any deviation from the implications of*

70. Cf. Rom 3:20; 3:27; 4:2; 9:12; 11:5; Gal 2:16; 3:2, 5, 10.
71. Cf. esp. Rom 1:16–17; 3:21–26; Gal 3:21–29.
72. Fowl, *Philippians*, 154.

"in Christ" identity is therefore irreconcilable with participation among God's people, leaving one vulnerable to death/destruction.

However, to emphasize: this new (though always anticipated) basis of covenant identity does *not* replace Jewish identity, or in any way suggest normative Jewish praxis should not continue as before. It means strictly that Jews qua Jews along with gentiles qua gentiles find their necessary superordinate identity in Christ and Christ alone. As suggested above, it is crucial to recognize that Paul's use of *pistis* as a synecdoche for the Christ event/"in Christ" identity, which he contrasts with "works (of the Torah)," does *not* mean that Jews (before/outside of Christ) did not and/or do not exercise faithfulness to God, or, again, that Christ allegiants need not obey the Torah as inseparable from there salvation (even if done so differently by Jews and gentiles, respectively). Rather, *pistis* points to the intersection of divine and human faithfulness in light of the eschatological fulfillment of God's promises in Christ. Thus, "faith" or "faithfulness" as integral to relationship with God is not a Pauline innovation or polemic, as if this was generally lacking or lost among the Jews of Paul's day. It is specifically *faithfulness vis-à-vis God's act in Christ* that is at stake for him, and is the heart of his theology.

Paul's "Autobiography" as a Challenge to the Philippians

There is simply no middle ground as far as Paul is concerned. The Philippians, as (largely) members of the nations, who, like the Thessalonians, have "turned to God from idols, to serve a living and true God, and to wait for his Son from heaven" (1 Thess 1:9–10), must remain true to the superordinate identity they now possess as members of the Christ community, i.e., as God's holy ones. This means that any compromising move towards idolatry *or* Jewish proselytism is not acceptable; it is a *de facto* departure from the *ekklēsia*. Paul has already made it clear in Phil 2:6–8 that Jesus Christ himself refused any maneuvering predicated upon the status that was rightfully his in order to circumvent the prospect of suffering. Instead, he remained faithful to God and God's purposes. So too for the Philippians; there can be no loyalty to Christ without a similar commitment on their part.

Importantly, with this commitment comes the promise that just as Christ was vindicated by God, God will, in turn, deliver and vindicate the community. When Jesus returns as Lord and Savior, the Philippians will undergo a glorious transformation unto Christ-likeness. This transformation will make possible the full implications of the righteous status that they already now possess, having then become incorruptible—morally perfected, and thereby forever free from the Torah's sentence of death as the inevitable consequence of sin (cf. Rom 5:12–21; 1 Cor 15:50–58; Gal 3:10–14)—a sentence that will not be escaped by the oppressive actors outside the greater Christ community. God's faithfulness in bringing about the fulfillment of the promises, securing redemption for both Israel and the nations, is to be answered, then, by the Philippians' continued faithfulness to God vis-à-vis the gospel of the Jesus Christ. As with the similarly programmatic phrase appearing in Phil 1:27, this eschatological and covenantal dynamic is likewise fully summarized in the phrase appearing in Phil 3:9, πίστεως Χριστοῦ: "faithfulness realized in Christ"—that is, *God's faithfulness, that calls for and enables the faithfulness of God's people* (cf. Phil 2:12–13; 3:12; see also Rom 3:27).[73]

The phenomenon of faithfulness, both human and divine, is thus central to and ultimately inseparable from the question of identity for the Philippians. To illustrate the point, Paul utilizes the interrelated examples of himself and of Jesus Christ. Paul's explanation regarding his own genuinely prized Jewish status that he counts as worthless in comparison to the "prize" of knowing Christ (Phil 3:14; cf. 1 Cor 13:8–12) is patterned after Christ's similar disregard for the attendant rights of his divine status. There was nothing inherently wrong with the identity of the pre-incarnate Christ as "being in the form of God" (Phil 2:6), or the identity of the pre-apostolic Paul as being a "Hebrew of Hebrews" (Phil 3:5). Nevertheless, they each voluntarily subordinated this respective identity to another, which resulted in their native identity having undergone a (radical) transformation, *but not, in any way, a negation*. That is, neither Jesus Christ nor the apostle Paul fundamentally ceased being what they once were.[74] However, both Jesus

---

73. Of course, the divine and human faithfulness in view are mediated through Christ's own faithfulness to God's redemptive program (cf. Phil 2:6–11).

74. Nebreda, *Christ Identity*, 302, translates Phil 2:6–7a: "who being in the form of God did not consider an advantage to be equal with God, instead he emptied himself taking the form of a slave" (ὃς ἐν μορφῇ θεοῦ ὑπάρχων οὐχ ἁρπαγμὸν ἡγήσατο τὸ εἶναι ἴσα θεῷ, ἀλλ ἀ ἑαυτὸν ἐκένωσεν μορφὴν δούλου λαβών). He remarks: "My translation reflects an active sense which stresses Jesus already possessed what he was willing to refrain from using for his own advantage. Jesus did not give up being equal to God all along; he merely did not use this privilege in order to advance, but sought the interest of the *other* in complete submission, totally abased." He explains further: "Christ's self-humiliation is never opposed to 'being equal to God'. Jesus Christ never lost this privilege . . . but willingly renounced using it for his own advantage, even when it cost him his own life on the

and Paul placed God's purposes above the rights, privileges, and immediate self-interests that were properly their own (cf. 2 Cor 8:9; Rom 15:3; 1 Cor 4:9–13; 2 Cor 4:8–12; 11:23—12:10).[75] Having become a Jewish peasant ultimately crucified by the Empire, Jesus chose not to exploit his identity as being "equal with God."[76] For Paul, the subordination of his Pharisaic-Jewish identity to that which he now possessed in Christ meant that, not only as a Christ allegiant but also an apostle, he was now suffering in prison as a result. But, like Christ's wrongful execution on the cross, even this was interpreted by Paul as ultimately serving God's good purposes on behalf of all creation, including both Israel and the other nations (cf. Phil 1:12–14).[77]

---

cross. . . . This understanding is crucial. It implies that there was no exchange in Christ of the form of God for the form of a slave, 'instead, he *manifested* the form of God in the form of a slave' [O'Brien, *Philippians*, 134]. Thus, the core message of the passage [Phil 2:6–11] is not simply a new view about Jesus, but a new understanding of God" (305).

Accordingly, that Jesus' identity as "being in the form of God" is, by virtue of the incarnation, never compromised nor diminished, but also forever *transformed* seems evident to me. For Paul, the resurrected and exalted Jesus has become the prototypical true human—the "first fruits" of the general resurrection of the dead, the "last Adam," and "life-giving spirit" whose image Christ allegiants will bear (cf. 1 Cor 15:23, 45–49; Rom 5:12–21; see also esp. Col 1:15–20). As Paul asserts in Rom 8:1–4: "There is therefore now no condemnation for those who are in Christ Jesus. For the Torah of the Spirit of life in Christ Jesus has freed you from the Torah of sin and death. For what the Torah was powerless to do because it was weakened by the flesh, God did by sending his own Son in the likeness of sinful flesh to be a sin offering. And so he condemned sin in the flesh, in order that the righteous requirements of the Torah might be fulfilled in us, who do not live according to the flesh but according to the Spirit."

75. I suggest that "self-interest" is not *intrinsically* problematic for Paul. The problem occurs when a person or group's concern for their own well-being works to the detriment of others, whether through omission or commission. Thus, it is not the concern for "self" that is wrong, but the failure to properly situate that concern within the larger context of God's good purposes for the whole world, which may necessitate the need for self-sacrifice, but never to the extent that a person or group is ultimately lost in the pursuit of what is best for all. Such a totalizing self-denial would subvert the very promise of salvation, which serves as the primary motivation for being and doing what a person or group ought.

76. As suggested in n. 74 above, I take the two phrases in Phil 2:6, "being in the form of God" (ἐν μορφῇ θεοῦ ὑπάρχων), and "equality with God" (τὸ εἶναι ἴσα θεῷ), such that the latter phrase is the natural corollary of the former, and that they are in this respect parallel in meaning, each pointing to Christ's divine identity—that is, by being in the form of God, Jesus was also equal to God. Of course, it is only in the incarnation that Jesus Christ becomes as such, i.e., a historically-embodied person.

77. As parallel to the revelation of God's true identity in the incarnate, crucified, and exalted Jesus in Phil 2:6–11, it may very well be that Paul's autobiography in Phil 3:5–14 similarly implies that being found in Christ (v. 9) represents the ultimate expression of

Paul's autobiography, shaped here by the story of Jesus Christ, provides, in turn, precedence, pattern, and motivation for the Philippian Christ allegiants to live true to the identity that they now possess as members of the *ekklēsia*, no matter what the cost. This does *not* mean that they should abandon wholesale their prior social identities. In fact, to the extent that a desire to proselytize to normative Judaism is in view here, the implications of Paul's discourse is that his gentile auditors should *not* abandon their status as members of the nations. But this also means that as gentiles who have turned to the God of Israel through the risen Christ (i.e., as righteous gentiles) they must refrain from any praxis that conflicts with the full implications of the gospel. They are no longer pagan idolaters, but have been brought into God's covenant people alongside Israel,[78] and must live and act accordingly, even if this will mean further marginalization, social death, economic loss, civic persecution, and/or suffering of any sort. Such is the immensely difficult challenge posed by Paul to the Philippian Christ community (cf. pp. 73–75 above; see similarly Matt 16:24–28; Mark 8:34–38; Luke 9:23–27). Though he hopes that his own willingness to sacrifice everything for the cause of the gospel, along with that of the other exemplars to which he points (Timothy, Epaphroditus) will encourage the whole community to stand firm in their allegiance to Jesus Christ, the chief exemplar of a cruciform life in service to the other.[79]

---

what it means to be a Jew, in as much as the Jewish people represent the historical chosen people of God, the bearers of the promises (cf. Rom 2:28—3:2; 9:4–8; 11:1–5, 15–32).

78. As pointed out in p. 63 n. 30 above, Paul can conceive of the covenant people of God as both Israel and the nations together, as well as, in a certain sense, "Israel," in so much as this is the historic title for God's (holy) people, the children of Abraham.

79. Hawthorne, "Imitation," 178, importantly observes: "[T]he call to imitate Christ Jesus is made possible by the power of the living, exalted Christ, who is present and at work within the lives of believers through the work of his Holy Spirit."

5

Concluding Reflections

Paul's Call to the Philippian Christ Community and Beyond

WHAT IMPORT DOES A post-supersessionist reading of Paul's letter to the Philippians possess, not only for understanding Paul's teaching in its historical context, but also for the contemporary church and world at large? At the risk of seemingly overstating my case, I would like to propose that some form of post-supersessionism is critical to the coherence, and, ultimately, the value of not only the letter's message, but that of Christianity itself. In making this claim I have in mind two primary and interrelated ideas. The first is that the Christian notion of "salvation," as it is presupposed in Philippians and throughout the Pauline corpus, necessarily implies that within the Christ community there is *both* continuity and discontinuity with previous social identities—not least that of Jewish identity. The second is that supersessionist understandings of Pauline/Christian doctrine, asserting the obsolescence of such prior social identities, cannot survive the charge that this teaching is inherently imperialistic and oppressive, thereby disqualifying Christianity as a liberating and ethical metanarrative,[1] according to which one may find his/her identity.

1. Simply stated, the term "metanarrative" refers to a master story that functions as the fundamental grounding for normative beliefs, praxis, etc., for *all* people. It generally seeks to answer basic worldview questions, such as: (1) Who are we—what does it mean to be a human being (individually, collectively)? (2) Where and when are we—what is the nature of the world in which we live, and when do we find ourselves in the course of time? (3) What's the problem—what is the nature of the brokenness that all people experience in some fashion? (4) What's the solution—how can people move through this brokenness and find wholeness? It is my conviction that such a universal storyline according to which people may understand themselves and the rest of the world is

Saved or Switched?

In the following, I will offer two broad sketches of the intent and meaning that lay behind Paul's apostolic work among the Philippians through appeal to explicit passages in his letter to them.

Sketch #1

- Phil 2:6–11: The apostle Paul was convinced that the creator God, the God of Israel, had acted in history through the death, resurrection, and exaltation of Jesus Christ—the true and only Lord and Savior of the world.

- Phil 3:20–21: To borrow a phrase from Wright, God was now "putting the world to rights."[2] It was time that not only Israel but the other nations as well offer allegiance to God's Christ, in anticipation of the final judgment and establishment of God's kingdom, in which Jesus' rule, to which the Philippians have already yielded, would become entirely manifest to the whole world.

- Phil 1:28: God's act in Christ will deliver the Philippian Christ community from all opposition (cf. Phil 3:19), while condemning such opposition to destruction for their failure to recognized and submit to what God has done, is doing, and will fully accomplish in the imminent future through Jesus Christ.

---

inextricable to the human condition. Indeed, even the postmodern critique that metanarratives are inherently illegitimate (e.g., prone to violence and oppression), and should therefore be replaced by localized narratives that do not seek to make absolute, universalizing claims, betrays its own master narrative, which is the very thing it wishes to subvert. A totalizing rejection of metanarratives is therefore necessarily self-contradictory. The appropriate question, then, is not whether a universal story exists, but rather which one sufficiently evidences truth. Of course, the truthfulness of a metanarrative can never be legitimately claimed in any sort of objective, *a priori* fashion. Thus, the basis for judgment is invariably a subjective one, to which appeal may be made on the grounds of its explanatory power (intellectually, emotionally, experientially, socially, etc.), predicated upon the givenness and fundamental commonality of human existence. For an argument that Christianity represents an authentically ethical and liberating metanarrative, see Middleton and Walsh, *Truth Is Stranger*. My observations here would serve to supplement and strengthen their conclusions.

2. Wright, "New Perspectives," 264.

- Phil 1:6, 10; 2:12–16: "The day of Christ" is the telos towards which all of history is moving, and is the fundamental motivation for Paul's apostolic ministry, and thus his teaching and exhortation to the Philippian Christ community, who must remain faithful to that end.

Sketch #2

- Phil 1:27; 2:12–13: The apostle Paul was convinced that it was his duty to effect the reordering of the lives of the Philippians by means of the gospel message and its implications (cf. Phil 1:22–26). His work would serve the establishment of a new, predominately (if not entirely) non-Jewish community whose collective lifestyle would largely correspond to the superior moral values found in first-century Judaism.

- Phil 2:14–16: Though they would remain as they are in terms of their ethnic status and social location within the larger Greco-Roman world (that is, as gentiles according to the standard bifurcated view of humankind in late Second Temple Jewish thought), the praxis of such gentiles would be in most every other respect "Jewish" (cf. Phil 3:3)—that is, in accordance with God's desire for all humanity, as per a Jewish worldview.

- Phil 1:9–11; 2:1–8: Paul's desire was that through their exercising of the preeminent Jewish virtues of love of God and love of neighbor vis-à-vis their allegiance to Jesus Christ—who exemplifies what it means to be truly human through his own self-sacrificial use of power on behalf of the other—this community would authentically represent the justice and righteousness (cf. p. 52 n. 79 above) indicative of God's desire for the entirety of creation (cf. Phil 3:10–14).

- Phil 2:16; 4:10–18: The Philippians themselves are tasked by Paul with "holding forth the word of life" to those outside of the community, and their financial support of Paul symbolized their solidarity with him, and active participation in his gospel ministry. The Philippians thus sought the establishment of other communities as their own, so that the world would better reflect God's purpose for it (cf. Phil 2:13).

Negotiating Concepts of "Salvation"

Neither of these sketches, in my view, is fundamentally incorrect. The first sketch rightly emphasizes the radical, global, and eschatological import of Paul's worldview that he passed on to the communities he founded, especially in terms of final judgment. The second rightly emphasizes the practical consequences of Paul's work, as manifest in the daily lived experience of those same communities. Yet, each sketch by itself portrays an insufficient picture of Paul's apostolic work and teaching. Thus, given the generalities of these depictions, it is not terribly difficult to understand why his agenda in the first could be characterized as a totalizing critique of the Greco-Roman world, in which nothing of the old survives, and in the second a purely social (Jewish) reform movement that seeks to make the secular world a better place. However, such (mis)characterizations fail in light of the very notion of "salvation" itself that pervades Paul's letters, and is unquestionably understood by him to be the purpose of his gospel proclamation (cf. Rom 1:16).

Paul's discourse regarding salvation, as discerned throughout his letters, contains important threads of (a) discontinuity and continuity, (b) universalism and particularism, and (c) finality and continuation. I submit that, in dialectical fashion, each of these pairings represents aspects of Pauline soteriology that depend upon one another for their full significance to be completely realized. I would categorize the first aspect of each pairing—discontinuity, universalism, and finality—as especially indicative of the climactic quality of "salvation."

Salvation as Climactic

The eschatological consummation of God's salvific program envisaged by Paul is a radical terminus of the present age (cf. Phil 3:19–21; Gal 1:4; 2 Cor 4:4). Sin and every vestige of evil will be completely eliminated (cf. 1 Cor 15:25–26). And it is not simply the ethical dimension that evinces such a discontinuous state of affairs. The coming terminus he poses includes the total "corruptibility" of the human condition, including death itself, and even "flesh and blood" existence (1 Cor 15:50–58). The scope of this eschatological consummation includes "all things" (Phil 3:21; cf. Col 1:15–20). While Christ allegiants will experience a positive transformation such that they are remade into conformity with the resurrected Christ, those who remain disobedient will experience "destruction" instead (Phil 1:28; 3:19).

Accordingly, upon his return from heaven, in "the day of Christ" (Phil 1:6, 10; 2:16; 1 Cor 1:8; 2 Cor 1:14; see also 1 Thess 5:2ff.), Jesus will judge the world—including both Christ allegiants and those outside of the Christ community—on the basis of what they have done (cf. p. 33 n. 32 above); all people will be made subject to his authority (Phil 2:9–11). When this time comes, so Paul hopes, he will be able to claim an "honor" (καύχημα) for his personal sacrifice on behalf of the Philippians (Phil 2:16; cf. 1:18–20, 26). That is, by the community remaining faithful to God to the very end, vis-à-vis the traditions they received from Paul, his apostolic work would thereby receive validation (Phil 2:16–17).

In order for the gospel of Jesus Christ to adequately serve as the ultimate hope for all of creation, nothing short of such a transformative event will achieve the end to which it promises, namely, the deliverance of God's people, and the establishment of true justice in the world. But if the climactic dimension of salvation, as I have articulated it above, is allowed to completely dominate Paul's notion of salvation, then any concern for ethnic differentiation (or, for that matter, gender differentiation) is called into question. Indeed, if, following the final judgment, those in Christ will experience so radical a transition into a new form of existence by which they cease to live according to recognizable patterns of human activity and inter-personal/group relationships, would not any kind of identity-shaping praxis simply function as a means to an end, and thus be ultimately expendable? What would it matter for Paul, or the contemporary church, for Jewish identity—or *any* ethnic identity—to continue in any meaningful sense if salvation precludes the continuation in some sense of the original order of things, including the diversity of people groups, their culture, customs, language, geographic origins, etc.? In short, is there still a place for "blood, soil, race, and tribe" in salvation?[3]

---

3. Wright, *Saint Paul*, 162. Of course, I am in no way attempting to advocate for the ideology of "blood and soil," particularly as it became associated with extreme nationalism, and eventually Nazism. The point is that ethnic identity is not something that Paul envisions as being abandoned or dissolved in Christ or in the resurrection age, as if the total transcendence of ethnicity, and even modest nationalism represents a morally and socially superiority state of being. However, so as not to unfairly critique or misrepresent Wright's view, it should be pointed out that he has argued forcefully for a "this-worldly" biblical soteriology, as preeminently evidenced in the phenomenon of resurrection itself; cf. N. T. Wright, *Resurrection*; and on the popular level: *Surprised by Hope*. However, I would press Wright's thesis here to better account for the abiding value of difference among God's people in the context of both unity and equality, which I believe is significantly lacking in his articulation of Pauline/biblical soteriology.

Salvation as Mundane[4]

Terence E. Fretheim has pointed out that "salvation is deliverance from anything inimical to true life, issuing in well-being and a trustworthy world in which there is space to live."[5] This characterization of salvation is clearly relevant to Philippians, which is a letter written to those experiencing concrete oppression and suffering (cf. Phil 1:27–30; see also with respect to Paul himself Phil 1:12–19)—much like the experience of Israel in Egypt in the story of the exodus, which came to function as the paradigm for salvation in the Hebrew Bible.[6] I suggest along these lines that Paul's conception of salvation accords with the basic meaning found in the Jewish Scriptures of deliverance from/preservation through/restoration following times of evil, distress, and/or acts of faithlessness, and is thus similarly concerned with the state of *embodied* existence and corresponding praxis *within* the world. Pauline salvation concerns, therefore, lived experience, and not merely the gracious and merciful extension of divine approval vis-à-vis final judgment, as is commonly understood.[7]

---

4. For an excellent treatment of biblical eschatology understood in terms of holistic, earthly redemption, in addition to the work of Wright noted above, see esp. Middleton, *New Heaven and a New Earth*.

5. Fretheim, "Salvation in the Bible," 364. Pointing first to the verbs ישע and σώζειν (both: "to save"), Fretheim continues by explaining that "[s]alvation language is wide-ranging and occurs across all types of literature from every period. Other words include *nāṣal, pādāh, gāʾal* (deliver, redeem); *ṣedeqāh* (righteousness). U. Mauser (*The Gospel of Peace* . . .) shows peace/well-being (*šālôm; eirēnē*) has a comparable range of meaning ('the healing of the sick, the feeding of the hungry, the care of the neglected and despised, and the forgiveness of sins are all aspects of the restoration of God's peace. . . . [If recognized] christological and soteriological thought will then be opened up to the material side of human existence,' 188)" (364–65).

6. For example, the motif of a "second exodus" for God's people following the judgment of exile permeates Isa 40–66; cf. 4:2–6; 10:24–26; 11:11, 15–16; 35:5–10; 40:3–5; 41:17–20; 42:14–16; 43:1–3, 14–21; 48:20–21; 49:8–12; 51:9–10; 52:11–12; 55:12–13; 58:8; 60:2, 19; 63; see also Hos 2:14–23; 12.9; Mic 7:14–20; and further below.

7. I am pointing here to a view of divine approval and final judgment as representing a singular, punctiliar event. Representing a holistic understanding of salvation in the Hebrew Bible, cf. Gen 45:5–7; Exod 3:7–10; Deut 30:1–5; Judg 10:10–16; 2 Sam 22:3–4; 2 Kgs 19:34; 1 Chr 16:19–23, 35–36; 2 Chr 20:9; Pss 6; 7:1–2; 17:13; 22:19–21; 28; 31; 40:9–13; 54:1; 59:2; 60:5; 69:35–36; 71:2–4; 72:4, 13–14; 76:9; 86:1–2; 106:47; 108:6; 109:21–31; 116:4–8; 118:25; 119:146; 120:1–2; 138:7; Isa 35:4; 46:12–13; 49:25–26; 52:7–12; 59:1; Jer 15:19–21; 30:10–11; 42:11–12; Ezek 13:21–23; 34:22; 37:23; Hos 1:7; Zech 8:7–8, 13.

Because of this understanding of salvation, he is able to portray the consequences of God's act in Christ in terms of a "new exodus" for all creation, which "will be set free from its bondage to decay and will obtain the freedom of the glory of the children of God" (Rom 8:21).[8] Human existence is, for Paul, presently corrupted; victimized by sin, death, and decay, and this is precisely why God has acted in Christ: *to set right that which has gone wrong in creation.*[9] Notwithstanding the significant discontinuity brought about in the coming redemption when Jesus returns from heaven to earth, if this is Paul's basic conception of salvation, then one must contend with a larger *continuity* of divine purpose, which includes the calling of Israel as a particular people (cf. Exod 19:4–6),[10] the ordering of the other nations (cf. Gen 10; see also Acts 17:26), the giving of Torah, and the call to obedience, all of which are part and parcel of the human flourishing that God always intended.[11]

In this light, Paul's salvation discourse in Philippians and elsewhere cannot be taken to mean a *wholly* new state, completely dissociated from the present reality—a reality that includes important, *God-ordained differences* among humankind,[12] and therefore varied cultural praxis within the

8. Cf. Keesmaat, "Exodus," 29–56; Keesmaat, *Paul and His Story.*

9. As Jesus communicated to John the Baptist: "The blind receive their sight, the lame walk, the lepers are cleansed, the deaf hear, the dead are raised, and the poor have good news brought to them. And blessed is anyone who takes no offense at me" (Matt 11:5).

10. It would seem from the narrative in the Torah that the calling of Abraham/Israel is a direct response to the corruption of creation, and thus that Israel's identity is bound up in the redemptive call to bring blessing to the other nations. If Paul understood that this vocation is ultimately fulfilled by Jesus Christ, this does *not* then indicate that historical Israel loses its significance (anymore than Paul's claim in 1 Cor 12:27 that the *ekklēsia* is the body of Christ means that the *ekklēsia* replaces Christ). Rather, as a good creation of God (and despite the real evolution of its ethnic demarcations), it surely continues for Paul as a salient social identity, alongside the nations, in perpetuity.

11. Middleton, *New Heaven and a New Earth,* 87–88, points out from the Exodus narrative: "[O]bedience to the Torah is not simply the appropriate response to God's prior deliverance; in a fundamental sense, obedience completes the salvation begun in the exodus. The exodus was only the beginning of the process of Israel's salvation. Deliverance from bondage must now be matched by conformity to the creator's will, which will require substantial changes in the way of life of God's people. Salvation thus cannot be limited to deliverance from external circumstances; it must include what we might call 'sanctification.' The Torah given at Sinai constitutes God's instructions for holy living, meant to direct the life of the redeemed community toward justice and righteousness, that they might be restored to flourishing."

12. This observation does not necessitate an essentialist view of ethnicity, but points

context of God's overarching purposes for all humanity, as revealed in the Torah and prophets. Rather, it necessarily includes a *continuation* of (a) what God has already set in motion in the original act of creation and historical election of Israel, and (consequently) (b) that which is to be *presently* manifested in and through the multiethnic Christ community.[13]

But if the continuation of God's original (good) purposes in creation and election are ignored or obscured, then "salvation" risks being emptied of its fundamental meaning; the world would not be "saved" as such, but switched for something else. Rather than an authentic source of hope in terms of restoration and the experience of wholeness, and thus a pattern and directive for present life (cf. esp. Phil 3:10–14; see also, e.g., 1 Cor 6:1–3), salvific language would arguably be reduced to little more than a vague instrument of manipulation.[14] In addition to finding this theologically unsatisfying, I do not believe that such a view represents an historically accurate construction of Paul's message to the Philippians, or his other auditors throughout his writings where such salvific discourse likewise appears.

---

only to the importance and necessity of ethnic *diversification* in God's sovereign purposes as I believe Paul understood it.

13. Of course, this does not mean that there are certain things that the Christ community would no longer do in the resurrection as an obvious result of the cessation of sin, death, and suffering (e.g., Phil 2:25–30). If, for example, the sacrifice of one's own well-being for the benefit of others is a central component of Christ-community identity (cf. Phil 3:10), and such sacrifice would no longer be necessary in the resurrection due to lack of need, then it could be argued that a necessary change as this points in the direction of a more radical discontinuity of identity in the kingdom of God. Likewise, it might be supposed that many conceivable forms of identity in the present age are at least partially predicated upon the "fallenness" of the created order. However, it is not my argument to deny the significant transformation that Paul indicates in the coming age when Jesus returns, but to point out that the resurrection does not represent for him something fundamentally severed from the present order of things; e.g., it does *not* represent the end of space-time, or the end of humanity's role on the earth, as set forward in the Torah. Rather, it is Paul's conviction that, regardless of how exactly it takes shape, "in Christ" identity *as it now is*—which necessarily entails the continued saliency of Jewish and gentile subordinate identities—will be *perfected* in the resurrection (cf. Phil 3:11–14). That is, the resurrected Christ allegiant is made *truly* human, and human existence necessarily includes ethnic variation, as per God's purposes in creation and election.

14. In other words, the concept of salvation can only bear so much discontinuity until it ceases to actually represent "salvation" in any proper sense of the term. And if the concept no longer carries the basic meaning of the term, then it seems to me that it can only really function as a fairly vacuous counterpart to divine condemnation—something desired more because of what it is not, rather than what it positively affirms.

Salvation and Post-Supersessionism

Human beings, as an inextricable part of *this* world (cf. Gen 1:26–28), and the primary recipients of salvation,[15] must retain in some fashion, therefore, those particularities that make them who they are, including ethnicity, but in the absence of sin, death, and decay. While Paul's understanding of the resurrection suggests a spirit-body that is not "flesh and blood" (1 Cor 15:50) in a sense comparable to the present human condition,[16] it is still clearly a corporeal existence that maintains some organic connection to what it once was, as his metaphor of a seed in relation to a fully grown plant suggests (cf. 1 Cor 15:37–38; see also esp. Rom 8:23; 2 Cor 5:1–5). A pneumatic and incorruptible body does *not* in any way necessitate that the resurrection state does away with basic aspects of human identity, including ethnicity. Further, if such bodily existence and mundane praxis continues unabated in the eschaton, it is ineluctably the case that one's superordinate identity in Christ cannot be severed from its historical grounding in first-century Judaism.

I conclude that, for Paul, Israel and the nations, as distinct social categories, continue in perpetuity in the *renewal* of "all things" (Phil 3:21) in "the day of Christ" (Phil 1:6, 10; 2:16). Because he locates both social

---

15. Though I believe Paul's primary concern is clearly with the redemption of people, if indeed he is grounded in the teaching of the Torah, the role of human beings is fundamentally portrayed as stewards over the nonhuman order. Thus, the salvation of humanity—that is, the restoration of the *imago dei* in the world, precisely means that they are enabled to enact the sort of faithful dominion over the nonhuman order that God intended in creation. The priority of humans in God's redemptive program, as I believe Paul likely understood it, is never at the expense of nonhumans, but for their ultimate benefit (cf. esp. Rom 8:22–25; see also Isa 11:6–9; Ps 36:6).

16. Paul's entire rhetorical goal in 1 Cor 15 is to stress the integral "not yet" aspect of God's eschatological program begun in the resurrection of Christ (cf. esp. Paul's sardonic rebuke of the Corinthian Christ allegiants in 1 Cor 4:8–21). It will only be at the general resurrection when Christ allegiants will be made fit to reign in God's kingdom. "Flesh and blood" thus denotes the present, pre-resurrection state of Christ allegiants as compared to the new, incorruptible body that is to come; in context, the phrase in no way suggests by way of contrast a supposed non-physicality to the future state. Paul's reference in 1 Cor 15:44 (cf. v. 46) to a σῶμα ψυχικόν (soul-body) over against the σῶμα πνευματικόν (spirit-body) suggests not a physical vs. non-physical dichotomy, but rather a dichotomy of *ages* to which human beings may belong, and thereby possess the corollary characteristics (cf. 1 Cor 2; Jas 3:15; Jude 1:19; see also esp. Gal 1:4). Further, as pointed out on pp. 47–48 above, while not uniformly understood as such (e.g., Luke 24:39–40) in the ancient worldview that informed Paul's thought, "spirit" (πνεῦμα/ *pneuma*) could be conceived of as possessing an equally material quality.

categories in the context of a Jewish worldview, and determines the boundaries of appropriate praxis for each group according to the teaching of Torah, Torah obedience—as an integral component of the very meaning and import of salvation—likewise extends into eternity. Thus, Judaism/Jewish identity are not superseded in Christ. Post-supersessionist readings offer, then, a necessary corrective to much Christian theology, as well as biblical scholarship of all orientations, which has all too often supposed that the work of Christ has rendered ethnic differentiation in general, and Judaism in particular, as wholly irrelevant because of a *hyper* eschatological (a) finality (e.g., divine approval at the final judgment as salvific telos in Christ), and/or (b) discontinuity (e.g., celestial existence as the post-judgment eternal state for Christ allegiants) thought to be inherent to Paul's understanding of God's redemptive program, and therefore to "in Christ"/Christian identity (cf. p. 31 n. 29 above).

Moreover, particularly in the light of the overarching theme of unity in the letter to the Philippians, as well as the corresponding value of equality implicit throughout much of Paul's writings, post-supersessionist sensibilities also challenge the fallacious notion that this unity for which Paul calls requires unqualified "sameness."[17]

17. Of course, both "equality" and "sameness" are highly contextual concepts. There is a sense in which equality, and thus "sameness" in terms of fundamental value, being a creation of God's love, being affected by sin (however in varying degrees), and being a eligible for salvation, is crucial to Paul's vision of God's people in God's redemptive program, and there are other senses that are foreign, irrelevant, or even contrary to his thought. I will not provide a thorough analysis of each concept, but will only presuppose their most basic sense as I understand them. With respect to "equality" in particular, I interpret this concept as being fundamentally positive and life-affirming. Specifically, my view entails that human beings should understand and relate to one another as engaged in a cooperative task of negotiating the world in ways that offer the highest good, possessing inherent equal value before God, and being afforded, then, equal opportunity in the world to fulfill their true potential. The conclusion reached here is that these values properly obtain without the supposition that they require unmitigated "sameness," and, further, that they obtain in Paul's teaching, rightly understood.

There has been in the contemporary era, in particular, a growing awareness that equality can and should co-exist in the context of difference, though not without a great deal of confusion and debate about how this properly works out in real society. Nevertheless, there is a still quite popular sentiment in the modern Western world that difference should be overlooked if equality is to be achieved. In contemporary America, for example, the notion of "color blindness" as an idealized absolute value in the pursuit of social justice has been and continues to be heralded. While I do not deny the positive intention behind the use of such language, or that the notion possesses a certain contextual legitimacy, e.g., equal protection under the law, it nevertheless often betrays an understanding of difference (in this case, racial difference) as something to be ignored or

Paul's Gospel, Liberation, and the Problem of "Sameness"

We must cut out all that is different like a cancerous growth! It is essential in this society that we not only have a norm but that we conform to that norm. Differences weaken us. Variations destroy us. An incredible permissiveness to deviation from this norm is what has ended nations and brought them to their knees. Conformity we must worship and hold all sacred. Conformity is the key to survival.[18]

On Difference

"Difference" can be threatening, especially to those in positions of relative power. Unfortunately, the apprehension, consciously or otherwise, of that which is different than the perceived norm, and thus the desire for either the unmitigated assimilation or suppression of the "other," is not uncommonly manifest in the real world.[19] In keeping with this concern—which is especially critical when considered in the context of the calls to unity, likemindedness, and imitation in Philippians—it is my contention that nothing of any normative theological or ethical value can if fact come from readings that find as their conclusion Paul's rejection of prior social identities whole-

---

overcome, rather than something to be embraced and celebrated.

18. *The Twilight Zone*, "The Eye of the Beholder." This quote is taken from a televised speech given by an apparent totalitarian ruler in a world in which everyone must look the same in order to participate in the mainstream society. Those who look different, if they are unable to be successfully altered by surgical means, are forced to live in internment communities with others like them. The ironic twist in the episode is that the acceptable appearance is deformed, while the outcasts are contrastively attractive according to mainstream contemporary American standards.

19. Illustrative, the history of Christian mission, particularly as undertaken by colonial Western Empires from the late fifteenth century forward, includes examples of missionary efforts that extended beyond the proclamation of the gospel, and the provision of material need to the effecting of the abandonment of native peoples' cultural particularities in favor of the cultural norms of the missionary nations in question. A full discussion of the relationship between colonialism and Christian missionary efforts is beyond the scope of the present work. I would note, however, that there has been, in my estimation, a problematic counter-impulse in some postcolonial studies to indiscriminately color the entire missionary enterprise of the West as almost exclusively an exercise of imperialism. It will suffice to note here that I do not follow such a stark assessment, though I recognize—and believe it is crucial to recognize—the very real abuses, even if intended to be otherwise, that have occurred and may continue to occur. For a balanced treatment on this issue, see, e.g., Andrews, "Christian Missions," 663–91.

sale in favor of "in Christ" identity.[20] Some form of post-supersessionism, therefore, is necessary for Christianity to authentically represent a liberating and ethical worldview.

The eschatological implications I outlined above aside, there is one fundamental reason why I have come to such a conclusion. Namely, "in Christ"/Christian identity, though a form of Judaism, is simply *not* practically viable as one that can replace existing ethnicities, and does *not*, in Paul's view, intend to be, despite this ostensible claim made by some early Christians, and also proposed in the interpretation of Paul by the majority of contemporary New Testament scholars.[21] I certainly do not discount that modes of "ethnic reasoning" lay behind much of the construction of "in Christ"/Christian identity, including in Paul's letters, as has been argued by Denise Kimber Buell.[22] There is an important sense in which Christ allegiants/Christians are themselves a distinct people, as I have pointed out throughout this study. However, for Paul (if not the entire New Testament), the peoplehood of the Christ community remains on the level of the superordinate, which not only allows for subordinate social identities, but depends on these for its material expression. *Christianity will always thus be incarnated in the culture of the particular Christian group(s)/person(s) in question*; a reality that I suggest Paul himself presupposed, and which is empirically demonstrable.[23]

20. Certainly, readings of Paul that come to supersessionist conclusions may otherwise evidence fruitful theological or ethical implications, but this would be *in spite of* the supersessionist findings, not because of them.

21. As a form of Jewish identity that nevertheless allows for the equal participation of gentiles qua gentiles, there is simply no sense in which "in Christ"/Christian identity could properly represent an alternative to existing ethnicities; that would be a category error.

22. Cf. Kimber Buell, "Relevance of Race," 449–76; Kimber Buell, *Why This New Race.*

23. Cf. esp. Rom 14:1—15:12. The point being made here needs to be clearly differentiated from assertions I have made throughout this study, concerning the Philippians' superordinate identity in Christ, as well as, e.g., the interpretive conclusions drawn from Paul's first letter to the Corinthians by Tucker, *You Belong to Christ* and *Remain in Your Calling.* Tucker asserts that Paul perceives a lack of "in Christ" identity salience in favor of Roman civic identity within the Corinthian Christ community, which, in my view, makes good sense of the letter. As argued above, a similar situation may very well be at play in Philippians. Accordingly, I am in no way suggesting that "in Christ" identity is not a discernible social identity distinct from others, but that "in Christ" identity itself appropriately manifests differently, and necessarily so, among different Christ allegiant groups. I would additionally point out that this view is not a form of identity hybridity, as per the model proposed by postcolonial scholar, Homi Bhobda (cf. Bhobda, *Location*

The recognition of the legitimacy of other forms of Christian identity, in critical awareness of natural ethnocentric tendencies, may serve to ward off the prospect of marginalization, or even demonization of certain Christian groups over against more dominant ones; a recognition that has perhaps gained strength in the contemporary world. Yet, the problem of imposing one's own cultural particularities as universally normative in the context of appropriate Christian expression is a perennial one. It is exactly what happened as Christianity became increasingly dominated by non-Jews, leading to increasing vitriol against Jews and all things Jewish in much of the early Christian literature.[24] And it is an undeniable and sobering reality for those of us living in the post-Shoah world that such anti-Judaism sadly endures, with appalling consequences.

Within his own historical location, Paul demonstrates a clear awareness of ethnocentric tendencies in both directions—a danger that predominately gentile expressions of "in Christ" identity would marginalize more thoroughly Jewish forms, as evidenced in his letter to the Romans (cf. esp. Rom 11, 14), and a danger that non-Jews might be denied equal participation in the greater Christ community, as reflected in his letter to the Galatians.[25]

If there is an implicit oppressive threat lurking behind the impulse to deny or reject difference in the Western theological and philosophical traditions, as postmodernism has claimed,[26] I submit that Paul's writings examined afresh provide a resource to counter this oppressive tendency by demonstrating how difference is critical to Pauline theology, and inte-

---

of Culture), but of the intrinsic incarnational quality of "in Christ"/Christian existence.

24. Cf. esp. John Chrysostom, *Adv Jud. (Against the Jews)*.

25. As I have attempted to demonstrate in this study, since "in Christ" identity falls within the spectrum of first-century Judaism, there is really no such thing for Paul as "non-Jewish" forms of Christ community identity in a strict sense. Rather, what I mean here is that there is a proper mode of Christ-community identity taken on by non-Jews (normatively defined), in which their praxis is thereby informed by non-Jewish cultural patterns, but within the boundaries of what is appropriate for the Christ allegiant regardless of ethnic affiliation.

Further, while I do not hold to "ethnocentrism" as representing the cornerstone of Paul's critique of Judaism, as per the standard New Perspective view, it seems nevertheless evident that Paul was keenly aware of the potential of such an attitude among Jews, in as much as with any other ethnic group (cf. esp. Gal 2:1–14).

26. See especially here the recent analysis of theoretical and hermeneutical perspectives on "difference" in interaction with postmodern, postcolonial, and feminist criticism in Lee, *Politics of Difference*, 29–69.

gral to the Christian worldview.[27] Paul himself did not depart from Judaism, and his gospel demands that Christ allegiants retain in some sense the fundamental cultural identity they possessed upon entrance into the Christ community, whether Jewish, or, in the case of the majority of his addressees in Philippi, Greek and Roman.[28] Rather than replacing existing ethnicities, "in Christ" identity represents, therefore, a superordinate identity that significantly *reorients* the worldview and praxis of both Jews and gentiles (especially gentiles), but it does not eradicate who they were prior to entering the Christ community.

On Conformity

Notwithstanding the above, the transformation of prior social identities—especially gentile identity—is no less crucial to Paul's theological and missionary vision. *The unity and equality found in the Christ community is only made possible because of the common story and redemption into which Christ allegiants have been brought* (cf. Rom 3:30). For Paul, the God of Israel's sovereign activity through history, revealed in the Hebrew Bible, and culminating in the Christ event, is the nonnegotiable truth for the whole world. Recognition of this truth demands a particular praxis. That is, though broad and allowing for a great deal of variant cultural and personal expression, the basic pattern of life prescribed in Scripture is nevertheless required as the *only* appropriate response of human beings to God—indeed, it is the very definition of what it means to be human. Thus, membership in the covenant community—"the circumcision, who worship/serve by the Spirit of God" (Phil 3:3)—does require one to conform, yet this conformity positively includes respect for the various subordinate identities, and corresponding variations of praxis that properly accord with communal norms.

27. In addition to Rom 14:1—15:12, the importance and significance of "difference" is explicitly expressed by Paul in 1 Cor 12:12–27, in the context of differing roles taken by Christ allegiants within the greater Christ community or "body of Christ." Much of what Paul asserts in the passage would almost certainly carry over for him in any reflection on the sort of difference being discussed here.

28. As pointed out by de Vos, *Conflict*, 240–44, Oakes, *Philippians*, 71–76, and Marchal, *Hierarchy*, 106–8, there was a good deal of ethnic diversity in Philippi. However, it does not seem that many, if any, Thracians were part of the Philippian *ekklēsia*, as they predominately inhabited rural territory, while Paul's gospel converts were largely drawn from the town (Bockmeuhl, *Philippians*, 18). Further, Thasians, Macedonians, and later immigrants from the Greek East may have shared much of a common Greek social identity at the time of Paul.

To the extent, then, that Paul compels the Philippians to conform, *it is clearly not to him in any sort of absolute sense.* Rather, it is to those qualities that reflect God's desire for all humanity, as embodied especially in Jesus Christ. If Paul fashions himself as a community prototype, it is for the *express purpose of effecting the Philippian Christ allegiants to become equally so*, though they should remain properly different from Paul in a number of other ways, including his ethnicity. Ultimately, only such an outcome— unity and equality in the context of abiding difference—would provide Paul with the honor and approval from God that he seeks as an apostle of Jesus Christ.

While absolute, universal claims as these may strike postmodern ears as incredulous, even perhaps as offensive, one should note that the stark relativism of the postmodern worldview is nothing more or less than a competing universal claim. There is simply no escape from a master narrative; a story that claims truth as applicable to all human beings, and which will invariably call, then, for some manner of conformity from those who situate themselves within it.

The Philippians had decided that Paul's gospel of Jesus Christ represented truth; a story of the world and their place in it that was superior to that put forward by the Empire. Adherence to this story—*Israel's story*— meant that they were now experiencing suffering, with all the disorientation that such suffering involves. Yet, it was Paul's hope that they would "stand firm" (Phil 4:1) as members of the nations who have now joined God's historical covenant people, Jews qua Jews in Christ, as God's holy ones (Phil 1:1), destined for a glorious transformation when their Lord and Savior, Jesus Christ, returns from heaven to "make all things subject to himself" (Phil 3:21).

Conclusion

I have argued that Paul's letter to the Philippians is best understood through a post-supersessionist lens, in which Paul's gospel of Jesus Christ in no way represents the supersession of Jewish identity, Torah-shaped praxis, or, further still, any ethnic identity upon entrance into the Christ community. Though Phil 3 has been commonly read as an invective against Judaism, which has now been replaced by "Christianity," it has been suggested here that the passage is best understood as an exhortation to the Philippians to remain as they are, that is, members of the nations who have given allegiance to Jesus Christ. This phenomenon was understood by Paul to be in fulfillment of the prophetic hope of the inclusion of the nations among God's people following Israel's restoration, as per God's faithfulness to the promises of covenant and creation renewal. Thus, together with the faithful among Israel, they are the "holy ones" who will receive the kingdom as foreseen in the book of Daniel, and, as such, have become part of a decidedly Jewish movement embedded within the spectrum of views contained within first-century Judaism. Finally, it was pointed out that the very notion of salvation that the gospel promises *requires* that previous ethnic identities retain their fundamental salience in perpetuity. Furthermore, this interpretation of Paul is required if Christian faith is to truly represent a liberating and ethical metanarrative.

Bibliography

Abrahamsen, Valerie. "Priestesses and Other Female Cult Leaders at Philippi in the Early Christian Era." In *The People Besides Paul: The Philippian Assembly and History from Below*, edited by Joseph A. Marchal, 25–62. Atlanta: SBL, 2015.

Anderson, A. A. *Psalms*, NCB. London: Marshall, Morgan & Scott, 1972.

Andrews, Edward E. "Christian Missions and Colonial Empires Reconsidered: A Black Evangelist in West Africa, 1766–1816." *Journal of Church and State* 51.4 (2009) 663–91.

Ascough, Richard S. *Paul's Macedonian Associations*, WUNT 161. Tübingen: Mohr Siebeck, 2003.

———. "Response: Broadening the Context at Philippi." In *The People Besides Paul: The Philippian Assembly and History from Below*, edited by Joseph A. Marchal, 99–106. Atlanta: SBL, 2015.

Barclay, John M. G. *Jews in the Mediterranean Diaspora: From Alexander to Trajan (323 BCE–117 CE)*. Edinburgh: T. & T. Clark, 1996.

———. "Mirror-Reading a Polemical Letter: Galatians as a Test Case." *JSNT* 31 (1987) 73–93.

Barclay, John M. G., and Simon J. Gathercole, eds. *Divine and Human Agency in Paul and His Cultural Environment*. LNTS. London: T & T Clark, 2006.

Beale, G. K. "Peace and Mercy upon the Israel of God: The Old Testament Background of Galatians 6,16b." *Bib* 80 (1999) 204–23.

Beker, J. Christiaan. *Paul the Apostle: The Triumph of God in Life and Thought*. Philadelphia: Fortress, 1980.

Betz, Hans Dieter. *Studies in Paul's Letter to the Philippians*. WUNT 343. Tübingen: Mohr Siebeck, 2015.

Bhobda, Homi. *The Location of Culture*. London: Routledge, 1994.

Bockmuehl, Marcus. *The Epistle to the Philippians*. BNTC 11. Peabody, MA: Hendrickson, 1998.

Bormann, Lukas. *Philippi: Stadt und Christengemeinde zur Zeit des Paulus*. NovTSup. Leiden: Brill, 1994.

Brawley, Robert L. "From Reflex to Reflection? Identity in Philippians 2.6–11 and Its Context." In *Reading Paul in Context: Explorations in Identity Formation: Essays in Honor of William S. Campbell*, edited by Kathy Ehrensperger and J. Brian Tucker, 128–46. LNTS 428. London: T. & T. Clark, 2010.

Brooten, Bernadette. *Women Leaders in the Ancient Synagogue: Inscriptional Evidence and Background Issues*. Chico, CA: Scholars, 1982.

Brown, Rupert. *Group Processes: Dynamics within and between Groups*. 2nd ed. Oxford: Blackwell, 2000.

Buell, Denise Kimber. "Rethinking the Relevance of Race for Early Christian Self-Definition." *HTR* 94.4 (2001) 449–76.

———. *Why This New Race: Ethnic Reasoning in Early Christianity*. New York: Columbia University Press, 2005.

Burnett, David A. "'So Shall Your Seed Be': Paul's Use of Genesis 15 in Romans 4:18 in Light of Early Jewish Deification Traditions." *JSPL* 5.2 (2015) 211–36.

Caird, George Bradford. *Paul's Letters from Prison*. NCB. Oxford: Oxford University Press, 1976.

Campbell, Douglas A. *The Deliverance of God: An Apocalyptic Rereading of Justification in Paul*. Grand Rapids: Eerdmans, 2009.

———. *The Quest for Paul's Gospel: A Suggested Strategy*. London: T. & T. Clark, 2005.

Campbell, William S. *Paul and the Creation of Christian Identity*. London: T. & T. Clark, 2006.

———. *Unity & Diversity in Christ: Interpreting Paul in Context*. Eugene, OR: Cascade, 2013.

Carson, D. A. "Mirror-Reading with Paul and against Paul: Galatians 2:12–14 as a Test Case." In *Studies in the Pauline Epistles: Essays in Honor of Douglas J. Moo*, edited by Matthew S. Harmon and Jay E. Smith, 99–112. Grand Rapids: Zondervan, 2014.

Carson, D. A., Peter T. O'Brien, and Mark A. Seifred, eds. *Justification and Variegated Nomism*. Grand Rapids: Baker Academic, 2004.

Castelli, Elizabeth A. *Imitating Paul: Discourse of Power*. LCBI. Westminster John Knox, 1991.

Cinnerella, Marco. "Exploring Temporal Aspects of Social Identity: The Concept of Possible Social Identities." *EJSP* 28 (1998) 228–48.

Cohen, Shaye. *The Beginnings of Jewishness: Boundaries, Varieties, Uncertainties*. Berkeley: University of California Press, 1999.

Damico, Noelle, and Gerardo Reyes Chavez. "Determining What Is Best: The Campaign for Fair Food and the Nascent Assembly in Philippi." In *The People Besides Paul: The Philippian Assembly and History from Below*, edited by Joseph A. Marchal, 247–84. Atlanta: SBL, 2015.

Das, Andrew A. *Galatians*. St Louis: Concordia, 2014.

———. "Paul and Works of Obedience in Second Temple Judaism: Romans 4:4–5 as a 'New Perspective' Case Study." *CBQ* 71 (2009) 795–812.

———. *Solving the Romans Debate*. Minneapolis: Fortress, 2007.

Davies, W. D. *Paul and Rabbinic Judaism*. London: SPCK, 1948.

de Boer, Martinus C. *The Defeat of Death: Apocalyptic Eschatology in 1 Corinthians 15 and Romans 5*. Sheffield, UK: Sheffield Academic, 1988.

deSilva, David A. "No Confidence in the Flesh: The Meaning and Function of Philippians 3:2–21." *TJ* 15NS (1994) 27–54.

de Vos, Craig Steven. *Church and Community Conflicts: The Relationship of the Thessalonian, Corinthian, and Philippian Churches with Their Wider Civic Communities*. SBLDS 168. Atlanta: Scholars, 1999.

Donaldson, Terence L. "The Curse of the Law and the Inclusion of the Gentiles: Galatians 3.13–14." *NTS* 32 (1986) 94–112.

———. *Judaism and the Gentiles: Jewish Patterns of Universalism (to 135 CE)*. Waco, TX: Baylor University Press, 2007.

———. *Paul and the Gentiles: Remapping the Apostle's Convictional World*. Minneapolis: Fortress, 1997.

———. "Paul within Judaism: A Critical Evaluation from a 'New Perspective.'" In *Paul within Judaism: Restoring the First-Century Context for the Apostle*, edited by Mark D. Nanos and Magnus Zetterholm, 277–302. Minneapolis: Fortress, 2015.

Donfried, Karl Paul. *Paul, Thessalonica, and Early Christianity*. London: T. & T. Clark, 2002.

Dunn, James D. G. "How New Was Paul's Gospel? The Problem of Continuity and Discontinuity." In *Gospel in Paul: Studies on Corinthians, Galatians and Romans for Richard N. Longenecker*, edited by L. Ann Jervis and Peter Richardson, 367–88. JSNTSup 108. Sheffield, UK: Sheffield Academic, 1994.

———. "What's Right about the Old Perspective on Paul." In *Studies in the Pauline Epistles: Essays in Honor of Douglas J. Moo*, edited by Matthew S. Harmon and Jay E. Smith, 214–29. Grand Rapids: Zondervan, 2014.

Ehrensperger, Kathy. "Be Imitators of Me as I am of Christ: A Hidden Discourse of Power and Domination in Paul?" *LTQ* 38 (2003) 241–61.

———. "'Called to be Saints'"—The Identity-Shaping Dimension of Paul's Priestly Discourse in Romans." In *Reading Paul in Context: Explorations in Identity Formation: Essays in Honour of William S. Campbell*, edited by Kathy Ehrensperger and J. Brian Tucker, 90–109. LNTS 428. London: T. & T. Clark, 2010.

———. "The Question of Gender: Relocating Paul in Relation to Judaism." In *Paul within Judaism: Restoring the First-Century Context of the Apostle*, edited by Mark D. Nanos and Magnus Zetterholm, 245–76. Minneapolis: Fortress, 2015.

Elliot, Neil. *The Arrogance of the Nations: Reading Romans in the Shadow of the Empire*. Minneapolis: Fortress, 2008.

Elliot, Susan. *Cutting Too Close for Comfort: Paul's Letter to the Galatians in Its Anatolian Cultic Context*. JSNTSup 248. London: T. & T. Clark, 2003.

Ellis, E. Earle. "Paul and His Opponents: Trends in Research." In *Christianity, Judaism and Other Greco-Roman Cults: Studies for Morton Smith at Sixty*, edited by Jacob Neusner 264–98. Leiden: Brill, 1975.

Esler, Phillip F. *Conflict and Identity in Romans: The Social Setting of Paul's Letter*. Minneapolis: Fortress, 2003.

———. *Galatians*. London: Routledge, 1998.

Fee, Gordon. *Paul's Letter to the Philippians*. NICNT. Grand Rapids: Eerdmans, 1995.

Fowl, Steven E. *Philippians*. Grand Rapids: Eerdmans, 2005.

Fredriksen, Paula. "Why Should a Law-Free Mission Mean a 'Law-Free' Apostle?" *JBL* 134 (2015) 637–50.

Fretheim, Terence E. "Salvation in the Bible vs. Salvation in the Church." *Word & World* 3.4 (1993) 363–72.

Fuller, Michael E. *The Restoration of Israel: Israel's Re-gathering and the Fate of the Nations in Early Jewish Literature and Luke-Acts*. BZNW 138. New York: de Gruyter, 2006.

Gager, John G. "Paul, the Apostle of Judaism." In *Jesus, Judaism, and Christian Anti-Judaism: Reading the New Testament after the Holocaust*, edited by Paula Fredriksen and Adele Reinhartz, 56–76. Louisville: Westminster John Knox, 2000.

———. *Reinventing Paul*. New York: Oxford University Press, 2000.

Garcia-Marques, Teresa, Diane M. Mackie, Heather M. Claypool, and Leonel Garcia-Marques. "Positivity Can Cue Familiarity." *PSPB* 30.5 (2004) 585–93.

Garland, David E. "The Composition and Unity of Philippians: Some Neglected Literary Factors." *NovT* 27 (1985) 141–73.

Garlington, Don. "Role Reversal and Paul's Use of Scripture in Galatians 3.10–12." *JSNT* 65 (1997) 85–121.

Gaston, Lloyd. *Paul and the Torah.* Vancouver: University of British Columbia Press, 1987.

Gaventa, Beverly Roberts, ed. *Apocalyptic Paul: Cosmos and Anthropos in Romans 5–8.* Waco, TX: Baylor University Press, 2013.

Gorman, Michael J. *Becoming the Gospel: Paul, Participation, and Mission.* Grand Rapids: Eerdmans, 2015.

Grant, Jamie A. "Wisdom and Covenant: Revisiting Zimmerli." *EuroJTh* 12.2 (2003) 103–13.

Grayston, Kenneth. "The Opponents in Philippians 3." *ExpTim* 97 (1986) 170–72.

Gundry, Robert H. "Grace, Works, and Staying Saved in Paul." *Bib* 66 (1985) 1–38.

Gunther, John J. *St. Paul's Opponents and Their Background. A Study of Apocalyptic and Jewish Sectarian Teachings.* NovTSup 35. Leiden: Brill, 1973.

Hafemann, Scott J. *Paul's Message and Ministry in Covenant Context: Selected Essays.* Eugene, OR: Cascade, 2015.

———. "The 'Temple of the Spirit' as the Inaugural Fulfillment of the New Covenant within the Corinthian Correspondence." *ExAud* 12 (1996) 29–42.

Hansen, Walter G. *The Letter to the Philippians.* PNTC. Grand Rapids: Eerdmans, 2009.

Hanson, Paul D. *Isaiah 40–66.* IBC. Louisville: John Knox, 1995.

Hardin, Justin K. "Galatians without a Mirror: Reflections on Paul's Conflict with the Agitators." *TynBul* 65 (2014) 275–303.

———. *Galatians and the Imperial Cult.* WUNT 237. Tübingen: Mohr Siebeck, 2008.

Harink, Douglas. *Paul among the Postliberals: Pauline Theology beyond Christendom and Modernity.* Grand Rapids: Brazos, 2003.

Harland, Philip A. *Associations, Synagogues, and Congregations: Claiming a Place in Ancient Mediterranean Society.* Minneapolis: Fortress, 2003.

Hawthorne, Gerald F. "The Imitation of Christ: Discipleship in Philippians." In *Patterns of Discipleship in the New Testament*, edited by Richard N. Longenecker, 163–79. Grand Rapids: Eerdmans, 1996.

———. *Philippians.* WBC 43. Waco, TX: Word, 1983.

Hays, Richard B. *The Conversion of the Imagination: Paul as Interpreter of Israel's Scriptures.* Grand Rapids: Eerdmans, 2005.

———. *Echoes of Scriptures in the Letters of Paul.* New Haven: Yale University Press, 1989.

Heinsch, Ryan "Reassessing Mirror Reading in Galatians: The Identity of Paul's Opponents as a Test Case." Paper presented at SBL Midwest Annual Meeting, Bourbonnais, IL, 2015.

Heitanen, Mika. *Paul's Argumentation in Galatians: A Pragma-Dialectical Analysis.* LNTS 344. London: T. & T. Clark, 2007.

Hellerman, Joseph H. *Reconstructing Honor in Roman Philippi: Carmen Christi as Cursus Pudorum.* SNTSMS. Cambridge: Cambridge University Press, 2005.

Hofius, Otfried. "The Fourth Servant Song in the New Testament Letters." In *The Suffering Servant: Isaiah 53 in Jewish and Christian Sources*, edited by Bernd Janowski and Peter Stuhlmacher, 175–83. Grand Rapids: Eerdmans, 2004.

Hogg, Michael A. "A Social Identity Theory of Leadership." *PSPR* 5.3 (2001) 184–200.

Hogg, Michael A., Deborah J. Terry, and Katherine M. White. "A Tale of Two Theories: A Critical Comparison of Identity Theory with Social Identity Theory." *SPQ* 58.4 (1995) 255–69.

Hogg, Michael A., Dominic Abrams, Sabine Otten, and Steve Hinkle. "The Social Identity Perspective: Intergroup Relations, Self-Conception, and Small Groups." *SGR* 35.3 (2004) 246–76.

Holladay, Carl R. "Paul's Opponents in Philippians 3." *RQ* 12.3 (1969) 77–90.

Hooker, Morna D. *Philippians*. NIB 11. Nashville: Abingdon, 2000.

Hubbard, D. A. "The Wisdom Movement and Israel's Covenant Faith." *TynBul* 17 (1996) 3–33.

Hutchinson, John, and Anthony D. Smith, eds. *Ethnicity*. Oxford: Oxford University Press, 1996.

Ito, Tiffany A., Krystal W. Chiao, Patricia G. Devine, Tyler S. Lorig, and John T. Cacioppo. "The Influence of Facial Feedback on Race Bias." *PS* 17.3 (2006) 256–61.

Jacob, Andrew S. "A Jew's Jew: Paul and the Early Christian Problem of Jewish Origins." *JR* 86.2 (2006) 258–86.

Jetten, Jolanda, Russel Spears, and Antony S. R. Manstead. "Distinctiveness Threat and Prototypicality: Combined Effects on Intergroup Discrimination and Collective Self-esteem." *EJSP* 27 (1997) 635–57.

Jewett, Robert. "Conflicting Movements in the Early Church as Reflected in Philippians." *NovT* 12 (1970) 362–90.

Johnson Hodge, Caroline. *If Sons, Then Heirs: A Study of Kinship and Ethnicity in the Letters of Paul*. New York: Oxford University Press, 2007.

Käsemann, Ernst. *New Testament Questions of Today*. London: SCM, 1969.

Keener, Craig S. *Acts: An Exegetical Commentary: Introduction and 1:1—2:47*. Grand Rapids: Baker, 2012.

———. *Acts: An Exegetical Commentary: 15:1—23:35*. Grand Rapids: Baker, 2014.

Keesmaat, Sylvia C. "Exodus and the Intertextual Transformation of Tradition in Romans 8:14–30." *JSNT* 54 (1994) 29–56.

———. *Paul and His Story: (Re)Interpreting the Exodus Tradition*. Sheffield, UK: Sheffield Academic Press, 1999.

Klijn, A. P. J. "Paul's Opponents in Philippians iii." *NovT* 7 (1965) 278–84.

Kilpatrick, George D. "ΒΛΕΠΕΤΕ, Philippians 3:2." In *In Memorium Paul Kahle*, edited by M. Black and G. Fohrer, 146–48. Berlin: Töpelmann, 1968.

Kim, Seyoon. *Paul and the New Perspective: Second Thoughts on the Origin of Paul's Gospel*. Grand Rapids: Eerdmans, 2002.

King, Justin D. "Paul, Zechariah, and the Identity of the 'Holy Ones' in 1 Thessalonians 3:13: Correcting an Un'Fee'sible Approach." *PRS* 39.1 (2012) 25–38.

Koester, Helmut. "The Purpose of the Polemic of a Pauline Fragment." *NTS* 8 (1961–62) 317–32.

Korner, Ralph John. "Before 'Church': Political, Ethno-Religious, and Theological Implications of the Collective Designation of Pauline Christ-Followers as Ekklesiai." Ph.D. Thesis, McMaster University, 2014.

Koukouli-Chrysantaki, Chaido. "Colonia Iulia Augusta Philippensis." In *Philippi at the Time of Paul and After His Death*, edited by Charalambos Bakirtzis and Helmut Koester, 5–35. Eugene, OR: Wipf & Stock, 1998.

Lee, Jae Won. *Paul and the Politics of Difference: A Contextual Study of the Jewish-Gentile Difference in Galatians and Romans*. Eugene, OR: Pickwick, 2014.

Levine, Lee I. *The Ancient Synagogue: The First Thousand Years*. Yale University Press, 1999.

Lieu, Judith M. *Christianity in the Jewish and Graeco-Roman World*. New York: Oxford University Press, USA, 2006.

Lohmeyer, Ernst. *Der Brief an die Philipper*. KEK. Göttingen: Vandenhoeck & Ruprecht, 1974.

Lyons, George. *Pauline Autobiography: Toward a New Understanding*. SBLDS. Atlanta: Scholars, 2012.

Marchal, Joseph A. *Hierarchy, Unity, and Imitation: A Feminist Rhetorical Analysis of Power Dynamics in Paul's Letter to the Philippians*. Atlanta: SBL, 2006.

———. *Hierarchy, Unity, and Imitation: The Politics of Heaven, Women, Gender, and Empire in the Study of Paul*. Minneapolis: Fortress, 2008.

———. *Philippians: Historical Problems, Hierarchical Visions, Hysterical Anxieties*. Sheffield, UK: Sheffield Phoenix, 2014.

Marshall, I. Howard. *The Epistle to the Philippians*. EC. London: Epworth, 1991.

Martin, Ralph P. "Paul on the Law, His Opponents, and the Jewish People in Philippians 3 and 2 Corinthians 11." In *Anti-Judaism in Early Christianity: Paul and the Gospels*, edited by Peter Richardson and David M. Granskou, 75–90. Waterloo, ON: Wilfrid Laurier University Press, 1986.

———. *Philippians*. NCB. London: Marshall, Morgan & Scott, 1976.

Martin, Ralph P., and Gerald F. Hawthorne. *Philippians*. 2nd ed. WBC 43. Nashville: Thomas Nelson, 2004.

Martyn, J. Louis. "Events in Galatia: Modified Covenantal Nomism versus God's Invasion of the Cosmos in the Singular Gospel: A Response to J. D. G. Dunn and B. R. Gaventa." In *Pauline Theology, volume 1: Thessalonians, Philippians, Galatians, Philemon*, edited by Jouette M. Bassler, 160–79. Minneapolis: Fortress, 1991.

———. *Galatians: A New Translation with Introduction and Commentary*. AB 33A. New York: Doubleday, 1997.

———. *Theological Issues in the Letters of Paul*. Nashville: Abingdon, 1997.

Mason, Steve. "Jews, Judaeans, Judaizing, Judaism: Problems of Categorization in Ancient History." *JSJ* 38 (2007) 457–512.

Mauser, Ulrich. *The Gospel of Peace: A Scriptural Message for Today's World*. Louisville, KY: Westminster John Knox, 1992.

Middleton, J. Richard. *A New Heaven and a New Earth: Reclaiming Biblical Eschatology*. Grand Rapids: Baker Academic, 2014.

Middleton, J. Richard, and Brian Walsh. *Truth Is Stranger Than It Used to Be: Biblical Faith in a Postmodern Age*. Downers Grove, IL: IVP, 1995.

Miller, James C. "Communal Identity in *Philippians*." *ASE* 27.2 (2010) 11–23.

Moo, Douglas J. *Galatians*. BECNT. Grand Rapids: Baker Academic, 2013.

Nanos, Mark D. "'Callused,' Not 'Hardened': Paul's Revelation of Temporary Protection Until All Israel Can Be Healed." In *Reading Paul in Context: Explorations in Identity Formation: Essays In Honour of William S. Campbell*, edited by Kathy Ehrensperger and J. Brian Tucker, 52–73. LNTS 48. London: T. & T. Clark, 2010.

———. "The Inter- and Intra-Jewish Political Contexts of Paul and the Galatians." In *The Galatians Debate: Contemporary Issues in Rhetorical and Historical Interpretation*, edited by Mark D. Nanos, 396–407. Peabody, MA: Hendrickson, 2002.

———. *The Irony of Galatians: Paul's Letter in First Century Context*. Philadelphia: Fortress, 2002.

———. "Paul and Judaism: Why Not Paul's Judaism?" In *Paul Unbound: Other Perspectives on the Apostle*, edited by Mark Given, 117–60. Peabody, MA: Hendrickson, 2009.

Reprinted in Mark D. Nanos, *Reading Paul within Judaism: Collected Essays of Mark D. Nanos, vol. 1*. Eugene, OR: Cascade, forthcoming 2017.

———. "Paul's Non-Jews Do Not Become 'Jews,' But Do They Become 'Jewish'? Reading Romans 2:25–29 within Judaism, Alongside Josephus." *JJMJS* 1 (2014) 26–53.

———. "Paul's Reversal of Jews Calling Gentiles 'Dogs' (Philippians 3.2): 1600 Years of an Ideological Tale Wagging an Exegetical Dog?" *BibInt* 17 (2009) 448–92. Reprinted in Mark D. Nanos, *Reading Corinthians and Philippians within Judaism: Collected Essays of Mark D. Nanos, vol. 4*. Eugene, OR: Cascade, forthcoming 2017.

———. "Out Howling the Cynics." In *The People Besides Paul: The Philippian Assembly and History from Below*, edited by Joseph A. Marchal, 183–222. Atlanta: SBL, 2015.

Nebreda, Sergio Rosell. *Christ Identity: A Social-Scientific Reading Philippians of 2:5–11*. FRLANT. Oakville, CT: Vandemhoeck & Ruprecht, 2011.

Oakes, Peter. *Philippians: From People to Letter*. SNTSMS. Cambridge: Cambridge University Press, 2007.

O'Brien, Peter T. *The Epistle to the Philippians*. NIGTC. Grand Rapids: Eerdmans, 1991.

Ogereau, Julien. *Paul's Koinonia with the Philippians: A Sociohistorical Investigation of a Pauline Economic Partnership*. WUNT 2/377. Tübingen: Mohr Siebeck, 2014.

Orepeza, B. J. *Jews, Gentiles, and the Opponents of Paul: The Pauline Letters*. Apostasy in the New Testament Communities 2. Eugene, OR: Cascade, 2011.

Park, M. Sydney. *Submission in the Godhead and the Church in the Epistle to the Philippians*. LNTS. London: T. & T. Clark, 2007.

Potter, David S. *Literary Texts and the Roman Historian*. London: Routledge, 1999.

Räisänen, Heikki. *Paul and the Law*. Philadelphia: Fortress, 1986.

Rajak, Tessa. "Jewish Rights in the Greek Cities under Roman Rule: A New Approach." In *Studies in Judaism and Its Greco-Roman Context*, edited by William Scott Green, 19–35. AAJ 5. Atlanta: Scholars, 1985.

———. "Was There a Roman Charter for the Jews?" *JRS* 74 (1984) 107–23.

Routledge, Robin. "Ḥesed as Obligation: A Re-Examination." *TynBul* 46 (1995) 179–96.

Rudolph, David J. "Paul's 'Rule in All the Churches' (1 Cor 7:17–24) and Torah-Defined Ecclesiological Variegation." *SCJR* 5 (2010) 1–24.

Reumann, John. *Philippians: A New Translation with Introduction and Commentary*. AB 33B. New Haven: Yale University Press, 2008.

Runesson, Anders. "The Question of Terminology: The Architecture of Contemporary Discussions on Paul." In *Paul within Judaism: Restoring the First-Century Context to the Apostle*, edited by Mark D. Nanos and Magnus Zetterholm, 53–78. Minneapolis: Fortress, 2015.

Safrai, Hannah. "Women and the Ancient Synagogue." In *Daughters of the King: Women and the Synagogue*, edited by Susan Grossman and Rivka Haut, 39–50. Philadelphia: Jewish Publication Society, 1992.

Sanders, E. P. *Paul, the Law, and the Jewish People*. Minneapolis: Augsburg Fortress, 1983.

———. *Paul and Palestinian Judaism: A Comparison of Patterns of Religions*. Philadelphia: Fortress, 1977.

Sandnes, Karl Olav. *Belly and Body in the Pauline Epistles*. SNTSMS 120. Cambridge: Cambridge University Press, 2002.

Schliesser, Benjamin. "'Christ-Faith' as an Eschatological Event (Galatians 3.23–26): A 'Third View' on Πίστις Χριστοῦ." *JSNT* 38 (2016) 277–300.

Schultz, Richard L. "Unity or Diversity in Wisdom Tradition? A Canonical and Covenantal Perspective." *TynBul* 48.2 (1997) 271–306.

Schüssler Firoenza, Elizabeth. "Paul and the Politics of Interpretation." In *Paul and Politics: Ekklesia, Israel, Imperium, Interpretation: Essays in Honor of Krister Stendahl*, edited by Richard A. Horsley, 40–57. Harrisburg, PA: Trinity, 2000.

Seitz, Christopher R. *Isaiah 40–66*. NIB 6. Nashville: Abingdon, 2001.

Silva, Moisés. *Epistle to the Philippians*. NIGTC. Grand Rapids: Eerdmans, 2005.

Spigel, Chad. "Reconsidering the Question of Separate Seating in Ancient Synagogues." *JJS* 63.1 (2012) 62–83.

Stone, Catriona H., and Richard J. Crisp. "Superordinate and Subgroup Identification as Predictors of Intergroup Evaluation in Common Ingroup Contexts." *CPIR* 10.4 (2007) 493–513.

Stowers, Stanley K. "Friends and Enemies in the Politics of Heaven: Reading Theology in Philippians." In *Pauline Theology, vol. 1: Thessalonians, Philippians, Galatians, Philemon*, edited by Jouette M. Bassler, 105–21. Minneapolis: Fortress, 1991.

———. "What Is 'Pauline Participation in Christ'?" In *Redefining First-Century Jewish and Christian Identities: Essays in Honor of Ed Parish Sanders*, edited by Fabian E. Udoh, Susannah Herschel, et al., 352–71. Notre Dame, IN: University of Notre Dame Press, 2008.

Sumney, Jerry L. *Identifying Paul's Opponents*. JSNTSup 40. Sheffield, UK: Sheffield Academic, 1990.

———. *'Servants of Satan', 'False Brothers', and Other Opponents of Paul*. JSNTSup 180. Sheffield, UK. Sheffield Academic, 1999.

Tajfel, Henri. "Social Categorization, Social Identity and Social Comparison." In *Differentiation between Social Groups: Studies in the Social Psychology of Intergroup Relations*, edited by Henri Tajfel, 61–76. New York: Academic, 1978.

Tellbe, Mikael. *Paul between Synagogue and State: Christians, Jews, and Civic Authorities in 1 Thessalonians, Romans, and Philippians*. CBNTS 34. Stockholm: Almquiest & Wiksell International, 2001.

———. "The Sociological Factors Behind Philippians 3.1–11 and the Conflict at Philippi." *JSNT* 55 (1994) 97–121.

Thiessen, Matthew. *Contesting Conversion: Genealogy, Circumcision, and Identity in Ancient Judaism and Christianity*. New York: Oxford University Press, 2011.

———. *Paul and the Gentile Problem*. New York: Oxford University Press, 2016.

Thiselton, Anthony C. *The First Epistle to the Corinthians: A Commentary on the Greek Text*. NIGTC. Grand Rapids: Eerdmans, 2013.

Thompson, A. J. "Blameless before God? Philippians 3:6 in Context." *Them* 28 (2002) 5–12.

Tucker, J. Brian. *Remain in Your Calling: Paul and the Continuation of Social Identity in 1 Corinthians*. Eugene, OR: Pickwick, 2011.

———. *You Belong to Christ: Paul and the Formation of Social Identity in 1 Corinthians 1–4*. Eugene, OR: Pickwick, 2010.

Turner, John C. "A Self-categorization Theory." In *Rediscovering the Social Group: A Self-categorization Theory*, edited by John C. Turner, 42–67. Oxford: Blackwell, 1987.

Tyson, J. B. "Paul's Opponents at Philippi." *PRS* 3 (1976) 83–96.

Wagner, J. Ross. *Herald of the Good News: Isaiah and Paul in Concert in the Letter to the Romans*. Leiden: Brill, 2002.

———. "The Heralds of Isaiah and the Mission of Paul: An Investigation of Paul's Use of Isaiah 51–55 in Romans." In *Jesus and the Suffering Servant: Isaiah 53 and Christian*

Origins, edited by W. H. Bellinger and William Farmer, 193–222. Harrisburg, PA: Trinity, 1998.

Walters, James C. *Ethnic Issues in Paul's Letter to the Romans: Changing Self-Definitions in Earliest Roman Christianity.* Valley Forge, PA: Trinity, 1993.

Wanamaker, Charles A. "Apocalyptic Discourse, Paraenesis, and Identity Maintenance in 1 Thessalonians." *Neot* 36.1–2 (2002) 131–45.

Ware, James A. *Paul and the Mission of the Church: Philippians in Ancient Jewish Context.* Grand Rapids: Baker Academic, 2011.

Watson, Francis. "The Hermeneutics of Salvation: Paul, Isaiah, and the Servant." Paper presented at the *Pauline Soteriology Group* at the SBL Annual Meeting, San Diego, 2007.

————. *Paul and the Hermeneutics of Faith.* London: T. & T. Clark, 2004.

————. *Paul, Judaism, and the Gentiles: Beyond the New Perspective.* 2nd ed. Grand Rapids: Eerdmans, 2007.

Westerholm, Steven. *Israel's Law and the Church's Faith: Paul and His Recent Interpreters.* Grand Rapids: Eerdmans, 1988.

————. *Perspectives Old and New on Paul: The "Lutheran" Paul and His Critics.* Grand Rapids: Eerdmans, 2004.

Weymouth, Richard J. "The Christ-Story of Philippians 2:6–11: Narrative Shape and Paraenetic Purpose in Paul's Letter to Philippi." PhD thesis, University of Otago, 2015.

Winter Bruce W. *Divine Honours for the Caesars: The First Christians' Responses.* Grand Rapids: Eerdmans, 2015.

————. "The Imperial Cult and Early Christians in Roman Galatia (Acts Xiii 13–50 and Galatians Vi 11–18)." In *Actes Du Ier Congrès International Sur Antioche De Pisidie*, edited by T. Drew-Bear, M. Tashalan, and C. M. Thomas, 67–75. Lyon: Université Lumière-Lyon, 2002.

————. *Seek the Welfare of the City: Christians as Benefactors and Citizens.* Grand Rapids: Eerdmans, 1994.

Witherington III, Ben. *Friendship and Finances in Philippi: The Letter of Paul to the Philippians*, NTC. Valley Forge, PA: Trinity, 1990.

Woodward, Stephen. "The Provenance of the Term 'Saints': A Religionsgeschichtliche Study." *JETS* 24/2 (1981) 107–16.

Wright, N. T. *The Climax of the Covenant: Christ and the Law in Pauline Theology.* Minneapolis: Fortress, 1993.

————. *The Letter to the Romans.* NIB 10. Nashville: Abingdon, 2002.

————. "New Perspectives on Paul." In *Justification in Perspective: Historical Developments and Contemporary Challenges*, edited by Bruce L. McCormack, 243–64. Grand Rapids: Baker Academic, 2006.

————. *The Resurrection of the Son of God.* Christian Origins and the Question of God, Volume 3. Minneapolis: Fortress, 2003.

————. "Romans and the Theology of Paul." In *Pauline Theology, Volume 3: Romans*, edited by David M. Hay and E. Elizabeth Johnson, 30–67. Minneapolis, MN: Fortress Press, 1995.

————. *Surprised by Hope: Rethinking Heaven, the Resurrection, and the Mission of the Church.* New York: HarperOne, 2008.

————. *What Saint Paul Really Said: Was Paul of Tarsus the Real Founder of Christianity?* Grand Rapids: Eerdmans, 1997.

BIBLIOGRAPHY

Zetterholm, Karen Hedner. "The Question of Assumptions: Torah Observance in the First-Century." In *Paul within Judaism: Restoring the First-Century Context of the Apostle*, edited by Mark D. Nanos and Magnus Zetterholm, 79–104. Minneapolis: Fortress, 2015.

Zoccali, Christopher. "'And So All Israel Will Be Saved': Competing Interpretations of Romans 11:26 in Pauline Scholarship." *JSNT* 30 (2008) 289–318.

———. "Children of Abraham, the Restoration of Israel, and the Eschatological Pilgrimage of the Nations: What Does It Mean for 'In Christ' Identity?" In *T. & T. Clark Handbook to Social Identity in the New Testament*, edited by J. Brian Tucker and Coleman A. Baker, 253–71. London: Bloomsbury, 2014.

———. "Rejoice, O Gentiles, with His People": Paul's Intra-Jewish Rhetoric in Philippians 3.1–9." *CTR* 9.1 (2012) 17–31 (Author's revised version, ATLA database).

———. "What's the Problem with the Law? Jews, Gentiles, and Covenant Identity in Galatians 3:10–12." *Neot* 49.2 (2015) 377–415.

———. *Whom God Has Called: The Relationship of Church and Israel in Pauline Interpretation, 1920 to the Present*. Eugene, OR: Pickwick, 2010.

Modern Authors Index

Ancient Documents Index

‹⊕›

APOCRYPHA